SECOND CACHE BULL PEN CHRONICLES

More I-Witnessed Brouhaha of a Stony Mountain Game Warden

STEPHEN H. PORTER

BACKGROUND

Historically, bison skulls, bones and horn sheaths were regularly discovered throughout North Park, hence the Native Americans calling it the 'Bull Pen'. Cousin Tim and I discovered this ancient bison skull buried in a sod covered, floating bog in Damfino Park. Pulling on its visible horn protruding from the grass, we were amazed at the size of the emerging skull. This beast lived and died near the location pictured on the front book cover. Peculiarly, Wildlife Officer Sir Don Gore discovered several bison skulls by poking a steel rod through a similar bog, hitting bone, and digging them out. Both skulls are used as clipart throughout the Second Cache. Damfino Park, from my overly biased perspective, was a better place when bison roamed its meadows.

DEDICATION

To my son, Marc Alan, and my daughter, Anne Marie. You are the sunshine on my shoulders, the moonglow on my face, the warmth in my heart.

Marc and Sue, Anne and Cris, you have extended our family legacy with five magnificent grandchildren, Lane, Kylie, Ciera, Conner, and Sage, making your mother and I's life complete. We are blessed!

WARNING SHOT

"Every journey into the past is complicated by delusions, false memories, false namings of real events."
Adrienne Rich

It has been said there are not truths, only stories. What follows are my stories, written to entertain, educate, and baffle the reader. If, perchance, they torture your soul, consider them the misery of a haunting conscience.

"To him who is in fear, everything rustles". Sophocles

And remember, even though I retired long ago, I am always looking – once a warden always a prick!

October 2, 1978 – TOP SHOOTER OF THE DAY

CONTENTS

AND THE WARDEN SAID,

"I BET YOU WONDER HOW I KNEW!"

BACK TO THE BEGINNING

The summer of '57 found me, a lad approaching nine years, thriving in the suburbs of a moderately sized northwestern Ohio town. Neighbors, raising bountiful broods, generated the twentieth century baby boomers. Mother, completing a street combing census, announced seventy-eight rogue juveniles were wandering our neighborhood. Constantly outdoors, nasty weather or not, we ran wild, thriving in the adventurous joy only kids our age can experience. Our backyard bordered a railroad, a rising buttress bordered by brambling thickets separating my civilized world from the unexplored 'wild country'. Boundless views of farmhouses, woodlots, weedy fencerows, croplands, and creek bottoms relentlessly tempted my pioneering fortitude. The rails provided rapid access to an abandoned factory, a huge livestock sales complex, and the house of an elderly farmer and his wife. My 'home range', unbeknownst to me, was setting the stage for the rest of my life.

STRIKING FLINT

And there I was, the end of one November week, school mundane and weekends sacred, witnessing a spectacle engraved into my mind forever. It came without warning early one frosty Saturday morning while I impatiently waited outside for my slow rising comrades. Spying two men zigzagging through waste high weeds soon to be developed into more houses, I hid in a brushy fence corner like the Indian I imagined myself to be. Carrying long-barreled guns, I knew they were hunters from father's embellished tales of hunting with my uncles. Aware the field held pheasants, quail, and an abundance of rabbits, I wildly sensed something amazing was about to happen. Suddenly, a cackling rooster pheasant blasted from the rough sending me into a series of uncontrollable jerks, first at the sight and sound of the flushing bird, and twice at the resonating blasts of two shotguns. On full sensory alert, I watched a cloud of feathers float from the wilting bird pummeling to the ground. *Holy crap!*

One hunter quickly retrieved the wing flapping bird and, without hesitation, wrung off its head! Hooting and hollering, his buddy shunted the pheasant into his vest, and they hunted on. Inquisitively creeping to where the bird landed, imagine the shocking sight of the beheaded bird's beak involuntarily convulsing, its life-bright golden eye piercing mine, and bloody windpipe worming from its neck. Kneeling for a closer look, I stared in awe as the morning sun reflected a shimmering kaleidoscope of brilliantly blended indigo and purplish hues boldly contrasting with the red waddled eye, and white ringed neck ring and eyebrows. This larger than death drama, too much to fathom alone and, even worse, who would believe it. Watching the hunters meld into the weeds, licenses pinned on their backs, the long tail feathers of the headless bird pointing upwards from one's vest, a spine-tingling shiver roused my spirit as I pledged, 'One day, no matter what, I was going to be a pheasant hunter!'

Of course, I could not wait to share my incredible adventure. Haughtily gathering my friends, I watched them rudely roll their eyes as I elaborated my story. Proudly escorting the disbelievers into the field, would you believe the 'winged dragon's' head had mysteriously disappeared! *OH, THE HUMILIATION!* Relentlessly harassed for months, it took me years to understand the mystique of the vanishing head was a gift from NATURE, HER way of enhancing my lifetime list of unsolved riddles to continually ponder. There was something more that eventful morning, an unfamiliar voice tweaking my inherent desire to hunt, yet whispering thoughts of remorse for a pheasant no longer stalking 'my' weed patch. This was my ever-evolving conscience, characterized during my college literature classes as Arvins, God of the Hunt, influencing my outdoor behavior to this day.

A CALL TO ARMS

As boys do, our gang outfitted ourselves with slingshots, a progressing succession of weaponry constructed of peeled forking tree branch frames, a leather pouch, waxed string, and powered by rubber sections of old tire tubes. Social status earned by style and accuracy, each newly manufactured rock flipper looked and shot better than the last. Old models were bartered until every neighborhood boy was armed and potentially dangerous. With an endless supply of marble-sized 'coke' found along the railroad, we were held responsible for every broken window, shattered glass, or wounded cat in the neighborhood!

Initially, everything considered 'game', we flipped rocks at anything, living or non-living, offering a challenging target, including wayfaring hobos traveling in the train's open box cars. Such mischievous behavior abruptly ended after bouncing several projectiles off the windshield of a small motorized 'railcar' transporting railroad workers. Visualize our despair when it screeched to a halt and two 'Herculean' coverall-clad giants gave us the chase of our lifetime. Adrenalin and youth on our side, we scrambled through the brushy tangle like fleas in dog hair, easily outmaneuvering the heavily booted men. However, this proved more excitement than we could handle. After all, "We could have been killed!" In an extraordinary moment of youthful wisdom, we unanimously voted limiting our quarry to inanimate objects and undomesticated life forms, our first set of self-imposed behavioral rules! The railroad 'incident' was exaggerated among friends (never adults) for years, delivering me a shivering smile to this day.

Of course, my slingshot escapades did not end there. Trouble, in my view, was the devil tempting my youthful innocence. Father, however, perceived my calamities as the self-inflicted strife of a mischievous boy. Whatever it was, I was often mired in strife up to my eyeballs and not enjoying the view. And so it was, one warm summer morning, Satan tricked me into taking an overwhelmingly irresistible and unbelievably accurate shot at my sister Cindy strolling her baby buggy down the sidewalk. Taking cover behind a fire hydrant, I sensed trouble before impact, viewing the projectile arc precisely towards her buttocks. It was a soft shot, absent of malice, surely not causing harm, but the strict laws of sisterdom forbade missing any opportunity to take down her older brother. My tantalizing shot disintegrated into terrifying distress as she ran into the house crying a rendition of taking a mortal wound in the hind quarters. Disavowing the very covenants negotiated with my comrades, a flurry of decisions raced through my mind... hiding, running away, joining the circus... However, knowing my fate was sealed from previous mishaps, I elected to turn myself in and plead for mercy. Mother, judicious from my past ploys, made it clear my shot caused a flaming welt. *I was doomed!* Ignoring my confession, she sentenced me to the solitaire confinement of my bedroom until father returned from work. Facing an inevitable butt cracking paddling, a fair and just punishment, mother wisely stalled my 'stay of execution' knowing six hours sweating out my penalty was far more painful than the whooping itself. The stinging of father's hand gone in a flash, the 'end' result was permanent; hand-crafted old school punishment worked, I never again pointed or fired a weapon at anyone. Never!

Most weapon education coming from experience rather than my parents, I miraculously eluded major mishaps. One extraordinary event, however, transpired after handing my slingshot to a younger cousin, a town girl with an attitude. Watching in total disbelief as she, in one fluid motion, closed her wrong eye, aimlessly stretched the rock laden pouch <u>away</u> from her face and fired! Suffering a self-inflicted blow between the eyes, she could have shot her eye out! Eye's watering and an ugly forehead bruise, she cursed me for her stupidity! Contemplating facing my uncle, father, or both, I fibbed she ran into a shed door and, surprisingly, she backed my lie and we incredibly dodged trouble.

Courageously ranging further into the outback, I told countless suppertime tales prompting skeptical glares from parents and sisters. Like a moth to flame, instinct lured me to unfamiliar woodlots or a mile further down the creek. Cardiac busting quail and pheasant flushes, fleeting glimpses of fox and flashes of unidentified fur or feather enhanced the wild's spellbinding unknowns. I prized studying a weird walking stick or tailed tadpoles in a frog's egg mass as Nature rewarding every venture. And OH, THE BIRDS! Their abundance, diversity, and songs invigorate me to this day. Intriguingly, I also discovered the outback not only supported an abundance of life but also a preponderance of death! Mangled, dismembered forms of fur, feather, and bone narrated stories of wild chaos, calling for investigation and interpretation. Haunted, mystified, captivated, mesmerized, whatever I was, Nature's hypnotic spell was something I could not live without.

A 'Bear' fiberglass long bow Christmas gift sent me afield, flinging cords of wooden arrows, broken and lost shafts keeping me in constant bankruptcy. Inevitably, a misfortunate ricochet sent an errant arrow directly into the neighbor ladies D-cup drying on her clothesline. My reluctance to retrieve the distended projectile provided an evidence trail leading to a weapon confiscation, allowing time to save for the next expensive quiver of arrows.

Before my 12th birthday we moved into the country, a lifetime dream of my English father and Pennsylvania Dutch (Mennonite) mother, placing me in boyhood paradise. Increasing my arsenal with a Daisy Scout BB gun, I literally shot out fighting armies of strategically placed toy soldiers in bark and root ravines of a backyard maple. Replacing the Scout with a pump action Model 25 and, with its peep sights and more power, I sharpened my shooting skills by hunting abundant countryside 'game'; bumblebees, wasps, flies, frogs and my all-time favorite, the raspy sounding flying grasshoppers! These spring-loaded flying fortresses, abundant in the weeds behind the barn, provided ample opportunities for flushing, stalking, and assassinating them with lethal head and thorax shots. Whacking a flying grasshopper nearly impossible, I miraculously experienced the Holy Grail of BB gun hunting, putting a few down in mid-air! Wing shooting darting bats pursuing unseen bugs across the farmyard airways, sporadically hearing the snap of a hit, I managed wounding only one. Examining the loathsome, sonar equipped, pointed eared, pug nosed, fine furred, fleshy winged, sharp-fanged beast, made it crystal clear why so many people abhor bats.

My first 'take,' a barn pigeon plunked from the rafters of my uncle's barn, peculiarly initiated bittersweet feelings of success, peppered with an unforeseen hint of sorrow. Haunted by similar dilemmas: the regret of an eye shot dove drilled off the railroad tracks; a sparrow launched into space by my arrow, the agony of sliding it from its neck and watching it fly away; the anger felt discovering a mound of frogs shot and left to rot at a favored fishing hole; the frustration of watching boyhood friends shoot small, songbirds whenever afield; Arvins again whispered, refining my code of field behavior.

IGNITION

Nearing 14, I purchased a used .22 bolt action clip fed Mossberg target rifle. Scoped with a Weaver 6 power, I became deadly accurate at distances exceeding all expectations. Farmers contacted me, some providing ammunition, to kill infinite numbers of pests – starlings, pigeons, English sparrows, rats, raccoons, and ground hogs – raiding their grain bins and croplands. Nothing striking more harm to the varmint world than a boy armed with an unlimited supply of .22 cartridges, I found my place as the 'go to hunter' for pest control.

Naturally, advancing to firearms led to additional life lessons; father's heated scolding after hearing mother's grotesque tale of a starling sniped high off the TV antenna, the bloody mass falling into her clothes basket. What I considered an outstanding headshot, father reduced to an irresponsible act of an unthinking delinquent. When asked if I gave any thought to where my skyward shots eventually landed, I must admit, up to that day, I had not.

Beginning a lifetime of firearm barter, and the haunting wonder why I sold any of them, I traded the target rifle for a new, Marlin Golden 39A lever action rifle. Scoped with the same Weaver 6 power, and a beautifully walnut grained stock, it too proved a splendidly prized weapon. Father countered by purchasing a matched pair of 16 and 20-gauge bolt action Mossberg shotguns. Heavy, unbalanced and fitting no earthly being, they proved a poor choice for a lad new to shotguns, causing wing-shooting deficiencies lingering with me to this day. But, with the theory 'if there's lead in the air there's danger', I bagged my first rabbit on a drizzly Ohio morning stalking a fence row with father. An aimless shot at a disappearing flash of fur, visible only to me, led to father's reprimand for carelessly firing at 'nothing' (besides scaring the bejesus out of him). Imagine our surprise when I hoisted the rabbit's lifeless corpse from the fencerow bramble. Rewarded with an evening feasting of wild rabbit and father's impressive tale of my remarkable shot, I puffed up like a spring tic.

During the 60s, Northwestern Ohio game species were scare, victims of clean farming and corresponding diminished habitats. But the relative abundance of squirrels, groundhogs, raccoons, pigeons, and unprotected birds provided ample tinder to fuel my blazing hunting passion. I now understand it was this sparseness of game that taught me essential lessons of hunting lore. Continually afield, firearm in hand, snow and the insidious Ohio mud revealed the covert signs of beasts rarely seen. Hunting in fresh snow, tracking a ghosting pheasant or an elusive covey of quail, honed my senses and hunting skills. Repeatedly humbled by missing a 'sure' shot at a pheasant or choking on an exploding covey of quail stimulated me to return and try again. Outdoor magazines my bible, the authors my disciples, I became the proverbial obsessive-compulsive outdoor lunatic. Nighttime family drives found me staring with the headlights searching for reflective eyes of a raccoon, possum, fox, or feral cat. Daytime drives found me scanning fence-lines, woodlot edges, and roadsides for a pheasant or crop eating ground hog. Crossing only one deer track my entire boyhood, I trailed it for miles until nightfall sent me home, haunted by a stag unseen.

Hunting, habitually alone yet never lonely, I withheld my adventures knowing, but not fully understanding, most friends had little interest in them. Never considering myself barbaric or inhumane, I was aware some did (sisters included). Believing, as suggested by my parents, I would outgrow my desire to stalk the wilds, my inherently fueled passion intensified. Despite my hectic high school years working summers, playing sports, raising runt pigs, a garden, training a pony (Misty, a mulish, unrideable beast bearing a grudge for having him gelded), and wooing Betsy, I spent ample time afield. Graduating from high school in 1966, attending a year of college in a nearby town, I needed a change in scenery. Father, a World War II veteran who enlisted with the Royal Air Force at 17 as a tail gunner defending England from aggressive German invasions, mentored his worldly wisdom with two recommendations redirecting the course of my life. One, insisting Betsy was the girl for me and two, I must follow my heart seeking a path not enslaving me to a factory job like he endured. His advice pushed me west to pursue a degree in Wildlife Biology. Twenty days prior to my 20th birthday, Betsy and I married (*Hell, I hunted groundhogs on the morning of my wedding day!*), packed her Dodge Dart with a few possessions, and headed to Logan, Utah where she worked while I completed my degree. A fortuitous summer job with the Forest Service opened doors for additional summer employment in Wyoming and Utah, a year with the U.S. Fish and Wildlife Service in North Carolina, all providing the experience necessary for permanent employment with the Colorado Division of Wildlife. Our free roaming spirits settling in the Bull Pen, Betsy and I found the place where we belonged.

This I know, spying on two pheasant hunters that eventful November morning, I was meant to feel the strong, inherent, forces linking me with Nature. Grasping little of Luck and nothing of Fate, those mystifyingly divine sisters befriended me and, with the grace of God, I was gifted a lifetime of timely events and golden opportunities guiding my obsessions, decisions, and perseverance, chasing dreams yet dreamt, leading to what came to be - OUR DESTINY!

"If one advances confidently in the direction of his dreams, and endeavors to live the life which he has imagined, he will meet with a success unexpected in common hours. He will put some things behind, will pass an invisible boundary; new, universal, and more liberal laws will begin to establish themselves around and within him; or the old laws be expanded, and interpreted in his favor in a more liberal sense, and he will live with the license of a higher order of beings"
Henry David Thoreau

PARADISE FOUND

From out of the East a stranger came A law book in his hand......
Liberty Valance song by Gene Pitney.
Written by Burt Bacharach and Hal David

In 1973 I requested and was granted one of two open North Central Colorado districts as a Wildlife Conservation Officer with the then Colorado Game, Fish and Parks. During my field training in 1972 I spent a week working North Park with WCO John Ellenberger and was overwhelmed by the stark beauty of this vast mountain park. Instinctively, I sensed this was the place vital for pursuing my life's vision quest. A remotely wild high elevation valley forming the headwaters of the North Platte River, labeled 'New Park' by early explorers and trappers, accurately endured as a name for my family's new home. Settled by white men relatively late due to the arrogant protectionism of the Native Americans (Ute, Arapaho and Cheyenne) battling intensely for dominion over these sacred, wildlife rich hunting grounds, I learned the Mountain Utes called this mountain rimmed valley surrounding the abundant bison population, the Bull Pen.

Buffalo skulls, horn sheaths and bones can still be found across the sagen valley and in the high mountain meadows. North Park, infamous for its long, harsh winters and temperamental springs has filtered out heavy settlement to this day; the time train not stopped but slowed enough to discourage rapid modern-day progress. An isolated empire for outdoor enthusiasts, supporting a local populace of beavertail tough Frontier spirited people, offered this warden the alluring scenario of seclusion, diverse wildlife populations and wide-open landscapes in a Stoney Mountain paradise.

Imagine Betsy and I, Buckeye State natives in our early twenties, moving into a western culture we knew nothing about. My familiarity with western agriculture, logging, mining, oil and gas was zilch. Well-equipped, thoroughly trained, a ticket book and six-gun in hand, I was guided by the advice of our Law Enforcement Chief to "use my own good judgement" when enforcing wildlife law yet charged to get along with a community well known for its independently stubborn populace. A job description outlining a 24/7 schedule divided equally between law enforcement, wildlife management and public relations, my strong work ethic immediately made me a very busy man. Even more, picture moving into a mountain valley with as many bars and liquor stores as churches, no stoplights, ranches putting up hay and feeding livestock with horses, packs of dogs running at large; a community enduring limited days relatively free of measurable wind chill, incessant ice bulleting blizzards, snow and freezing temperatures common any month of the year (a 33-day growing season), and tenacious winds welcome only when scattering thick clouds of ruthless mosquitoes. Then envision 1600 square miles, 65% public land, a sky portraying ridiculous amounts of night stars, vast areas of designated Wilderness, large tracts of diversified landscapes teeming with wildlife, stunning scenery, picturesque Indian Summers (weather God's willing), fish laden mountain streams and lakes; a place tendering the magical tranquility so many seek but will never have. I enthusiastically and Betsy suspiciously entered the Bull Pen with great expectations of creating a good home for our two-year-old son Marc, and six-month-old daughter Anne.

Finding the local people mostly friendly yet noticeably mistrustful, we sank our roots by joining a church, participating in school activities, playing softball, becoming involved in 4H, the Boy and Girl Scouts, bowling and joining the local Game and Fish Club. My law enforcement demeanor was instantly tested, scrutinized, judged, and critiqued by the local hunting and fishing public. Given most residents are associated in some manner with outdoor sports, I ultimately reached out and touched the majority, rapidly becoming familiar with those playing outside of the rules of the hunting and fishing games. Soon, certain local rowdies caught breaking wildlife laws began crying foul, expecting special privileges above and beyond those from the 'outside'. However, most were justly judged by a community aware of those warranting apprehension. In any small mountain society where gossip and news scatters like stampeding buffalo, the majority good rides herd over the minority bad and occasional ugly. Ultimately my *modus operandi* was accepted (by most) as consistently fair and just. People began regarding me as a sincere crusader for the wild beasts and an ambassador for the good people cherishing their wildlife resources.

The 'Pens' natural resource and ranching fueled economics supports a wide assortment of highly opinionated, change resistant, hardworking people cherishing their chosen, simpler lifestyle. Carving out a living in the high elevations wilds generates wide ranging perspectives regarding natural resource management, especially on the public lands. Understand, most consider themselves experts on managing timber, mining, wildlife, oil and gas, public roads, endangered species ... proffering an open-minded warden buffet of highly variable, often conflicting insights. Their cold forged mettle nurtures a mountain logic I not only began to understand, but also appreciate, widening my viewpoints when making resource management decisions. Paying close attention to select seasoned elders, including one astute retired wise man, Russel Crowder, I considered my second father, and Sir Don Gore, my aged warden mentor who trapped beaver in the Bull Pen before I was born, tendered me their time-tested commonsensical wisdom earned as long standing, respected members of the Bull Pen. Learning to listen and sort out the perpetually dynamic viewpoints and assessments of the local mass made me a better man and a better warden.

Blessed, my family lived and breathed North Park's fresh mountain air for over two decades. While never achieving the proverbial Golden Fleece status as 'locals', we were accepted by most as valued members of this closely-knit society. The Bull Pen proffered our family a strong sense of purpose and place. Excluding a few I choose to disremember, we will forever regard the community as cherished acquaintances, unique as fingerprints, forming everlasting friendships based on rock-solid trust, a trait I hold sacred to this day. Understand, while it was the wild remoteness of this sparsely populated community initially attracting me to the Bull Pen, it was its people who kept me and my family there. The Bull Pen seasoned our lives with the salt and pepper of a culture living within the raw sugar and spice of its wild. A great place for a warden to raise a family; indeed, a good place to take!

"Think where man's glory most begins and ends,
And say my glory was I had such friends."
William Butler Yeats

TRAINING DAYS

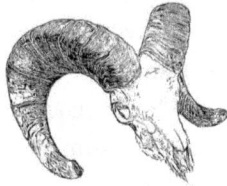

C olorado rookie wildlife officers, 'trainees', must pass a year of intensive classroom and field training providing essential skills for their upcoming district assignments. In 1971 approximately 1600 applicants applied for twenty plus jobs, and those lucky enough, me included, to make the cut were labeled the cream of the crop. Graciously accepting our employment, most realized in addition to dedication and perseverance, fate played a pivotal role in our selection. My training proffered field experiences bordering from the nonsensically ridiculous to the logically intense. One assignment while working with a highly animated wildlife officer, presented a multitude of adventures:

BART WILDHARE

My assignment with Wildlife Conservation Officer Bart Wildhare began with a tour of the northern end of the San Luis Valley on a Friday, the day before the big game season opener. Enthralled by the spectacular mountain landscapes teeming with wildlife, our journey ended with a highway stop to view a mix of antelope, bighorn sheep, deer, and elk scattered across Trickle Mountain, a scene rarely observed from one location anywhere. Interestingly, a hawk circled, and I exclaimed, "A Red-Tail!" Bart's memorable reply, "You only need to know two species of hawks, the Greater and the L.B. Js!" Rising to the bait, I inquired, "L.B.J.s?" Bart followed, "Little Brown Jobs, the 'Lessors'! *Seriously?* Stopping at the local restaurant for supper, Bart introduced me to his supervisor, Wilt Shoefit, a man steadfastly committed to advertising his administrative title.

Understand, trainees routinely telegraph their experiences throughout their ranks, and I was forewarned Bart exercised several techniques for indoctrinating newbies. One, after driving through a maze of mountain roads, often after dark, Bart would request his trainees to find their way back to Saguache. Another ploy was testing surveillance skills by pointing out something he <u>may</u> have observed and questioning the trainee if he/she noticed whatever it was.

I in the driver's seat, we patrolled late into the night visiting hunting camps and chatting with hunters. Pulling up to a large motor home, lights out and obviously everyone asleep, Bart insisted waking them as they were always eager to chat with him. Rousing them, it was embarrassingly evident they were not happy campers. Moving on, Bart asked me to pull into a camp I warned we had visited earlier. Chuck-ling, Bart realized his mistake only after opening the wall tent's flap door. The hunters asking us in for a drink, Bart fabled we were searching for a certain group of hunters and asked if they had observed their vehicle. Humbled, Bart never requested me to find our way back to Saguache! Bart dropped me off at my hotel after midnight and said he would pick me up at 5a.m.! No restaurants open, I crunched down a Snickers bar and hopped into bed. On schedule the following morning, Bart indicated there was no time for breakfast as we needed to search for an open jeep with hunters illegally spotlighting game the previous night. Starving, I pounded down another Snicker's bar, jumped into the driver's seat and headed towards the mountains. Crossing paths with Wilt, he introduced himself as a supervisor a second time, catching even Bart off guard! Driving on, we topped a ridge and spied an open jeep, possibly the one we were looking for, stopped in the middle of the gravel road with two hunters standing in the back looking through rifle scopes at several elk milling fifty yards away in the sagebrush.

Easing back so only the top of our vehicle was exposed, we watched in awe as Wilt flew by, parked his truck behind the jeep, disrupting the entire hunting scenario. Joining the cluster, Wilt ordered me to check firearms while Bart checked licenses. Settling for three fully loaded firearms in their vehicle (illegal) charges, Bart warned the hunters shooting from the road or from their jeep was also illegal. Moving on, scratching additional tics, we discovered a hunter searching for his wounded deer. While Bart checked the man's license, I located and tracked the blood trail through heavy aspen, found the dead buck and field dressed it. Impressing Bart and the hunter, I helped drag out the buck while Bart patiently waited at our vehicle.

Once again dropped off after the restaurants closed, I ate snacks from my daypack and flopped into bed. Up before 5 a.m., I pounded down my last Snickers bar and we once again headed into the high county. Hunters everywhere, we came across a man and boy field dressing a small buck on a sagebrush hillside. Glassing the duo for several minutes, it was clear father had no idea what he was doing, providing great entertainment watching him slice through visceral connective tissue while the boy stumbled backwards pulling out a string of intestines. Approaching, I instructed a lesson in Field Dressing 101, while they gazed in awe at the mass of internal organs removed from the buck's body cavity. Afterwards, Bart expressed great pleasure with my work. I was on fire! We were kept busy checking hunters and scratching tics throughout the day. Just before dark, Bart suddenly commanded me to flash our red and blues and pull over a pickup traveling ahead of us. Warning they were malicious law violators, Bart ordered me to park a short distance behind their vehicle, declaring he would cover me while I made contact! *WHAT?* Not knowing what to expect, I cautiously approached the vehicle and discovered four hunters as frightened as I was alarmed! The driver, nervously asking what was wrong, I tensely said we were making a routine stop to check for loaded firearms, licenses, and any game they may be transporting. All firearms unloaded, no game in the pickup bed, I walked the licenses to Bart for his inspection before returning them to the frazzled hunters. Back at our pickup, Bart alleged they were not the poachers he thought and praised my professional behavior during the contact. Calming my obvious distress, Bart treated me to a steak dinner at an elaborate resort community bar and restaurant. Covered in blood and gore, smelling of buck deer, I ravenously wolfed down the colossal meal despite my appearance. Exhausted, I began to unwind and relax. Bart, never short of surprises, asked if I would like to be entertained by one of the fancy 'ladies' sitting at the bar affirming, for a phenomenal fee, I would not be disappointed. *Yup, he was serious!* Replying as much as I hated disappointing the girls, I needed to return to my hotel and sleep. Speeding down the highway, Bart queried if I noticed the brass rifle cartridges lying along the edge of the road. Replying I had not and offering to turn around, Bart said that would not be necessary.

Again, picked up at five a.m., Bart indicated we were headed to a remote area thriving with deer to fill his buck tag. Great news, as I needed a break from our exhausting routine. Winding through a section of remote back country, Bart suddenly yelled, "STOP THERE'S A BUCK." Sure enough, there stood a small four-point fifty yards above the two-track. Thrilled, I watched Bart carefully pull his rifle from its case, quietly open the door, tiptoe to the rear, and light a cigarette! *Seriously?* Maintaining a Clint Eastwood calm, using the vehicle as cover, Bart walked to the front of the truck, scoped the buck over the hood with his rifle, returned to the back, crushed the cigarette with his boot, knelt, and KABLAM! Watching the deer bound over the ridge, I exclaimed, "You missed!" Chuckling, Bart laughed, "Not at that range. We'll give it time to die before tracking it." *OK!* Bart smoked another cigarette before trekking the steep ridge. Gasping for air, Bart fell behind while I followed the buck's fresh, bloodless tracks. Cresting the ridge, would you believe I found the skeletal remains of a nice four-point buck. Topping the hill, Bart breathlessly inquired, "Did you find it?" I replied, "Yes, but man it's a skinny son of a bitch!" Spying the bony buck's sun-bleached rack, Bart chastised my humor with a wide-mouthed grin. A skiff of old snow blanketing the north facing slope, we tracked the buck a quarter mile through thick aspen, soon realizing it escaped unharmed. Hunting until noon with no luck, we met Shoefit for lunch at Villa Grove and, wait for it, he conceitedly introduced himself as Bart's supervisor!

Meeting Bart the next morning at his residence to review my merit rating, he soberly handed me the document. Delighted with the high marks and complimentary notations, I was surprised when his final comments graded my overall performance unsatisfactory because, "my legs were too short to reach the pedals on his pickup." *WHAT?* His grin and belly laugh easing my chagrin, he handed me the authentic evaluation praising my good work!

While many colleagues felt differently, I thoroughly enjoyed working with Bart. The assortment of experiences, his dynamic personality, and his peculiar tactics provided me a cross section of valuable training experiences.

Once established in my Bull Pen district, I too was assigned trainees, finding most anxious to learn and prove themselves worthy. Deeming mentoring newbies a tremendous responsibility, I maintained a close eye while providing loose reins during their field contacts, experiencing scenarios ranging from critical blunders to comical adventures. Some treasured nuggets of warden gold:

-Watching two Lake John boat fishermen motoring near the shoreline towards us, one's voice, clearly amplified by the morning chill, "It's the f...ing game wardens!" Taking command, my female trainee waved them in, courteously checked their licenses, and politely proclaimed, "Sir, I am not a f...ing game warden!" Both fishermen staring in gaping awe, I deemed her worthy.

-A very airsick trainee flying with me during our winter big game counts, the helicopter pilot and I writhed as the recruit malodorously retched his entire stomach contents out the back seat door's plexiglass window! To our dismay, the putrid stomach blowback smeared the trainees face as well as the inside and outside of the chopper's door!

-Late on a cooling midsummer night, the Big Eye mounted on my driver's side window, two women trainees hidden below in sagebrush, we spied on a late-night boatman at North Delaney Butte Lake regulated as 'fly and lure' only. The women whispering giggles and swatting mosquitoes, the fisherman's lantern light revealed he was illegally fishing with multiple rods and handlines baited with worms and salmon eggs. We waited patiently for the fisherman to handle and bait his poles. Detecting the familiar behavior of a man preparing to take a leak, I warned the trainees to pay close attention as he was about to handle one of his rods. Intently focusing their binoculars, watching the fisherman relieve himself, the women began laughing uncontrollably, causing the alarmed fisherman to jerk it in while intently scanning the dark shoreline.

-Working a busy highway wildlife check station a trainee, clipboard in hand, walked around the front end of a jeep with the large antlers of a bull elk tied over its hood, and asked the driver, "Have you had any luck?"

-Liver Worst. Driving into an abandoned camp reported to have killed an illegal elk, a newly recruited wildlife officer quickly exited and began nosing around like a lab puppy. Zigzagging through the campsite before I had time to exit, I watched him pick up a blue plastic bag and holler he found a liver. Sticking his face into the bag, his facial contortions initially tattled the liver was spoiled, but the reality was he had nosed into a disposable toilet bag!

-On a brilliant late summer afternoon, Wildlife Officer John Wagner, a new recruit, and I pitched a picture perfect timberline camp in a Never Summer Wilderness meadow. The next day the opening of bighorn sheep season, our plan was to mentor the trainee through her first experience riding horseback over rugged terrain to check hunters. John, an experienced horseman, and I not so much, we helped pitch her tent before enjoying an evening meal around a blazing campfire. Predictably, the Never Summers holding true to their name, a massive late night winter storm buried our camp in 18 inches of snow. The trainee, not having the benefit of our warming wood stove, softly voiced if she could join us. Welcoming her into our warm and dry abode, we all comfortably slept through the night's blizzarding wrath. The storm ending the next morning, after brushing the snow off our tents, shoveling out the campsite, tending to the horses, drying out our gear, and eating lunch, we saddled up and began riding the snowcapped high country. Bucking deep snow drifts through a mountain pass, we found the windblown main trail contoured a very steep, shale covered sidehill. The trainee sheepishly (no pun intended) asked if she could dismount and walk her horse. Wagner replied, "Of course!" At the end of her assignment, expecting a negative written evaluation due to her inexperience, we surprised her with high scores citing the immense personal fortitude she displayed facing difficult tasks under adverse conditions.

-Returning to our truck after checking an elk camp displaying dead grey jays, squirrels, and chipmunks hanging from tree branches, I asked the trainee what we should do to address the dangling beasts. His reply, "What beasts?"

Trainees created memorable adventures throughout my career. Hell, at the very least, they listened in sheer amazement to my stories! One of my favorites:

HOODLUM WINKED - Where there's meat, there' wolves!

There we were, my trainee and I pulling off on a county road to check several hunters standing around a pickup on Coyote Creek. Detecting irregular body language – milling, murmuring and one turning his back – familiar signs of warden shock, I instructed the trainee to initiate the contact while I stood back to observe. Scanning the area, I noted boot traffic in the fresh snow entering the aspen and a bloody handprint on the rear fender of their pickup.

As the trainee returned with licenses in hand, I noticed one smirking hunter share a wink-wink moment with his comrades. *Something was amiss!* Asking the trainee if she observed anything out of the ordinary, she cautiously replied she had not. Humbled when I pointed out the bloody handprint, I asked her to recontact the hunters and investigate the pickup's bed. Discovering a doe deer, she waved me over, shattering the hunters' false sense of reprieve. Following the boot tracks to the edge of the aspen, we found a blood-soaked drag mark prompting the groups' leader, Richard Bagscum, to begin a series of contradicting lies. Aware shooting female deer on the Bull Pen side of the continental divide was illegal, Bagscum fabled he killed the doe the day before west of Steamboat Springs. Inserting my meat thermometer deep into the doe's hindquarter, reading 98 degrees, combined with the doe's unglazed eyes, I informed Bagscum the deer was alive less than an hour ago. Believing our idiocy was greater than his, he wove another yarn of jumping several deer, firing at a good-sized buck, and mistakenly killing the doe. Easily reading the snow-white pages of an open book, we traced Scumbag's boot prints to a fresh gut pile. A single set of hoof prints clearly indicated the lone doe fell in her tracks when shot. Arrogantly spouting new lies, I rudely turned off Bagscum's spigot by forcefully requesting him to shut up.

"Never miss a good chance to shut up." Will Rogers

Sensing things were about to go ringside, it was time to ring Bagscum's bell. Leading him to deer tracks 30 yards from the doe's gut pile, I pointed out they were made by a doe with two fawns, not a buck. DING! Requesting his driver's license, while Bagscum dug through his wallet, the trainee detected another doe tag issued to Scumbag's absent son. DING! Truth be told, making one in a row, Bagscum admitted he would have filled his son's tag if given the chance. DONG! After confiscating the deer and scratching a fat tic, I reviewed the incident with the trainee. I began describing how the hunters' initial behavior betrayed their misdeeds, and followed how she continued missing the obvious by focusing on their hunting licenses and not her surroundings. Lastly, I eased her mind explaining these were common, crucial errors made by most recruits.

"I am not a teacher, but an awakener."
Robert Frost

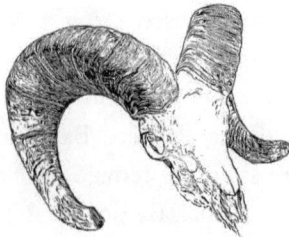

BEAR WITNESS

The Fool on the Hill

I met the Minnesota hunters in the early 70's at their rented cabin in Cowdrey. A hardy lot of mixed ages, I found them friendly and eager for current information concerning deer and elk populations. They were quite familiar with the Independence Mountain area having hunted there for over a decade. Checking their licenses in the field, I soon discovered they were seasoned experts at playing the party hunting game - each individual hunter purchasing a single license for a different species – one licensed for bull elk, another with a cow elk tag, one licensed for a buck deer, one with a small game license (coyotes, fox, blue grouse etc.) and one licensed for bear, allowing each hunter to (illegally) shoot all game encountered until the deer and elk licenses were filled. At that time this was legal despite Colorado's longstanding law prohibiting killing another's game. An enforcement nightmare, this clan of veteran poachers proffered a challenging game I was anxious to play. The laws eventually changed requiring a hunter to be licensed for either deer or elk before purchasing a small game or bear license.

In Minnesota it is legal to party hunt, harvesting game for others is deeply woven into their hunting culture. My annual lectures concerning the criminalities of party hunting in Colorado and the logic behind shooting their own game fell on deaf ears; smilingly daring me to catch them. Even when I detected an obvious violation, their coordinated stories were bullet proof; armored falsehoods I could not penetrate. Their schemes were based on economics (non-resident licenses are very expensive) and pounds of harvested meat, knowing the odds of getting caught were slim to none. Truth is they were! Like most Minnesotans, they were exceptional hunters, returning home with their deer and elk tags filled. Cold inclement weather did not deter these northern nimrods from hunting the worst weather the Colorado high country offered.

So, there I was, one cloudless, icehouse still November morning patrolling Independence Mountain during the combined deer and elk season. Parking just below the mountain's crest, I scanned the heavily timbered draws spotting a lone hunter standing point on a sage knob overlooking a large aspen stand. Several vehicles parked on the bare ridges at the end of the draws suggested a strategically planned drive was in place. Mounting the 'Big Eye', I focused on the hunter and recognized Lanzy Groove, the older member of the Minnesota hunting clan. Lanzy was also glassing me and noticeably uncomfortable. Driving down I parked next to his vehicle and walked uphill to say hello. With my signature smile, I asked for his license making small talk while he dug through his coveralls and several layers of heavy undergarments. Handing me a bear license I asked if he was hunting deer or elk, aware he was not licensed for either. Lanzy replied this year it was his turn to hunt bear. *Interesting!*

In his fifties and obese, he was standing guard while his younger, more physically fit buddies disturbed the timber below. Asking if they were pushing game towards him, he hesitatingly stated they were all hunting on their own. Knowing their game plan, I tickled his mind affirming spring bear hunters baited several large bears in the draws below and maybe one will run past him. The odds of seeing a bear were quite low as most were denned for the winter.

On good ground, my catch-dog drive would not allow me to leave. The wide-angle view and proximity to the Minnesota gang offered high potential for chasing shots and swiftly rooting out an illegal hunter before his compadres arrived. *The games afoot!* For Lanzy, things were not so good. He was beside himself because I was beside him. Welcome as a fox in a henhouse, I continued chatting with the jittery chap.

Perceiving movement, as sure as sharp on porcupine quill, a gang of elk materialized slinking single file through the aspen below; cows, calves and one heavily antlered bull. Lanzy instinctively grabbed his rifle, dropped to one knee and scoped each animal. Glancing up at me as if asking for permission to shoot, I whispered, "Don't do it, Lanzy!" The elk, no more than fifty yards distance, momentarily milled and, in a blink, were gone. Grinning at his chagrin, I proclaimed, "Damn, no bears but that was sure a nice bull!" Speechless, he offered only a cold, deep stare. I rudely lingered, waiting for the arrival of his fellow hunters needing a ride to their vehicles. One by one I checked their licenses finding two with unfilled elk licenses, one carrying a cow elk tag and the other a bull license. Of course, one flaunted his small game license and another his unfilled deer license. My presence clearly unwelcome, one insinuating warden harassment, I stuck my verbal knife to its hilt and twisted, declaring, "No bears, but Lanzy and I sure enjoyed watching the large bull and his harem you chased into the aspen below!"

No doubt Lanzy would have poached the bull before attempting to shoot a cow. But today their party was crashed by a warden playing his end game. Of course, this event did not curtail their party hunting and I, never able to catch them, incessantly made my presence known by contacting them in camp, tracking them down when hunting the mountain, and widely spreading word I was closely watching them. *Once a warden, always a prick!*

Sometimes you eat the bear, and sometimes the bear eats you!

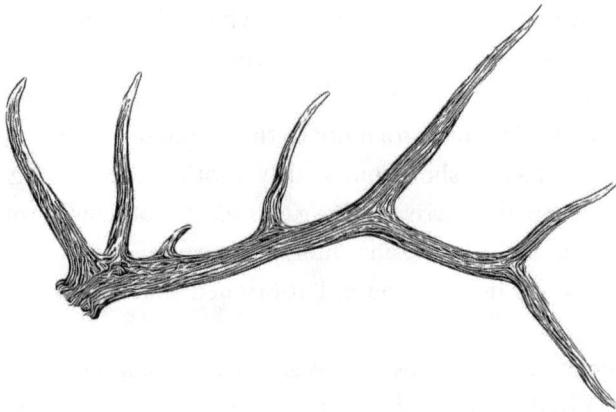

CONSTITUTIONAL AMENDMENTS

Field Flux

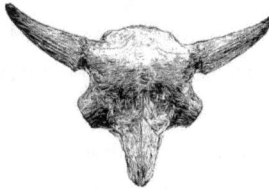

Nature calls in a myriad of ways, ranging far beyond the resonances of wild beasts. Correspondingly, answering those calls come in an equally diversified of ways and means.

Effective wardensmanship often requires burning the night candle at both ends, resulting in off routine or missed meals, noxious junk food and consequential disruptions of daily bodily functions. I frequently raced the sun to rouse the hunting and fishing public. Wolfing down a large bowl of something-flakes flushed with a glass of Tang, my hurried departures left no time for my morning 'movement'. Inevitably, the urge rarely occurred within range of the few outhouses available on public lands;

Thus bringing closure to the age old question, "Does a warden shit in the woods?

I imagined my sphincter was somehow linked to my vehicle's steering wheel transmitting pulsating stimuli provoking an evacuation of the previous day's food intake. These peristaltic urges increased in direct proportion with the distance driven from Sage Hen. Trial and error over years spent afield, I mastered the skills necessary for open-air bowel movements. My high metabolic rate generated a narrow window for successful elimination, compelling the development of rapid defensive strategies for off-road toiletry expertise. Site selection critical, many locations became traditional earth closets; bridge 'abutments', culverts, timber, tall sage, deep draws and rock piles. Forested areas required expertise in selecting the proper diameter and height of smooth-barked, stob-free downfall in relatively flat comfy zones. Hillsides required secure uphill vegetation within grasping distance to prevent messy backward falls. Tree branches for hanging coats and gun belts were preferred but not essential. Proficient choice of dump zones sanctioned comfortable positioning of one's posterior allowing safe 'shooting' trajectories away from boots, shirt-tails, suspenders etc. For those males taking notes, a critical squatting technique involves pushing 'Winston' backwards at the perfect angle for pin-point streaming <u>between</u> your boots. Of course, large amounts of readily available toilet paper and 'baby wipes' stashed in your vehicle are essential trappings. I tactfully passed on these dynamic corporeal maneuvers to my sons and grandsons as a part of my legacy.

It should come as no surprise wardens occasionally find themselves in uncomfortable situations once assuming the crapping copse crouch. An inborn trait found throughout the animal world, I was instinctively aware one must veil himself and remain on high alert during field craps to avoid discovery by man or beast. But, as you will see, not all situations where this warden was caught with his pants down were humiliating, some even rewarding.

FIRST AMENDMENT

Seasoned game wardens are practiced specialists in answering the public's many and varied questions; expertise improved by constant bombardment of everything from sensible inquiries to those bordering on the galactically ridiculous. "How far from the state line can I legally kill a deer on my Colorado license", or "When do deer turn into elk" serve as two representative examples. Some questions came at less opportune times, catching even a veteran off his game.

November 1974. One revolting development occurred during a predawn drive up the backside of Independence Mountain to investigate an illegally killed elk during the deer season. My intent was to secure the crime scene prior to the return of the alleged perpetrators. Switchbacking the steep two-track in six inches of fresh snow my morning Wheaties shifted, necessitating an impulsive roadside stop and instantaneous departure from my vehicle. My window of opportunity in severe jeopardy, I grabbed a tactically placed bag of butt wipes from the door's side pocket and rushed into the lodgepole. Removing my down coat on the run, I proficiently located a horizontal, barkless, stob-free log of proper height and diameter leaning against a standing, mature pine displaying desirable shoulder high pegs. Systematically hanging my coat and gun-belt, dropping my drawers and draping my hind quarters over the deadfall, I took a deep breath and settled into business. All systems ago, my hope for a quick release was foully interrupted by the sound of a vehicle grinding its way up the road. *Houston, we have a problem!* In haste to maintain the integrity of my tightywhitie's, I inadvertently failed to close the truck's door, an open-air invitation to anyone driving by. I scowled upon hearing the vehicle come to a brake-squeaking stop, the metallic grind of a door opening and the sound of snow crunching footsteps heading my way. In the crouched paralysis of expelling the previous evening's casserole, I suffered the agony of witnessing a corpulent man outlandishly blazed in reams of hunter orange invading the privacy of my public land privy.

Without hesitation, this uninhibited deviant gazed down at my violated position and asked, "How ya doin'?"

How am I doing? For God's sake, I am taking a crap!

Map in hand, the nimrod said, "I am hunting big buck deer, and would you point out where timberline begins?"

Between face grimacing contractions, I grunted (literally!), "If you would return to your vehicle, I will talk to you in a few minutes."

The oblivious and obviously irked nimrod stomped away without another word. Finishing my end of the paperwork, I returned to my vehicle and sarcastically commended the man for his excellent tracking abilities; words flying well over the uncouth man's head. Marking the hunters map and answering his mostly ridiculous questions (the low elevation Independence Mountain had no timberline), I gave the man a good head start before continuing to the reported crime scene. Incidentally, I found the cow elk spoiled beyond salvage but thanks to tips from the hunting good, the culprit, described by his friends as the "Ugly Midget," was tracked down in Denver. After a grueling hour-long interrogation, the young hairball druggy answered my question with ridiculous statements. His best, "I am really good at jumping on a trampoline." The tic was scratched and after arrested on a warrant, the diminutive, mangy scrote and his vulgar accomplice were found guilty in Jackson County Court, sentenced to an exceptionally high fine or jail!

SHIT HAPPENS!

Warden to poacher (awakened at his home at 2am): *"We found an untagged cow elk hanging at your mountain cabin."*

Poacher to warden: *"Oh, that's my father's elk"*

Warden to poacher: *"Does your father know he killed an elk?"*

Poacher to warden: *"No, we were going to tell him in the morning."*

ROAD SNARES

"In the midst of chaos, there is also opportunity."
Sun-tzu

C **haos!** An accurate description of the worthy mayhem often encountered on law enforcement check stations routinely set up by wildlife officers varying from remote dirt tracks to Interstate Highways to surprise an abundance of individuals transporting wildlife. An effective tool for capturing game thieves, these choke points set on the busy State Highways exiting the Bull Pen often required temporarily shutting down when all available officers were tied up scratching tics. New recruits rapidly acquire a mixed bag of on-the-ground training interacting with the good, bad, and ugly behavior of outdoor recreationists. Illegal fish and game were found in women's purses, camper bedding, five-gallon gas cans, hidden coolers, glove compartments, and even secret, built-in compartments under vehicle chassis. We once discovered hundreds of trout in a camper's black-water tank (cleaned and sanitized strictly for hiding fish), thanks to a tip from a member of the fishing good. Illegally tagged big game, lack of or faulty licenses, illegal drugs, outstanding warrants, protected species, and game taken out of season were regularly encountered and eagerly attended by sheriff's personnel, federal agents, and state patrolmen to address illicit activity within their enforcement purview.

DOC'S HOLIDAY

And there I was, one warm summer afternoon on a Willow Creek Pass check station, all nine Wildlife Highwaymen scratchin' tics. Supervisor Don Benson, waving a fish monger's license, shouted, "Is there any officer not writing a ticket?" The parking area full, Benson instructed the point man to wave on all but the most promising customers. Batches of illegal trout were being counted, bagged, tagged, and iced. Two small kids in a camper, under their mother's direction, were discovered shoving illegal trout into a pillowcase. The state patrolman was citing a man driving with a suspended driver's license. It was an outstanding enforcement madhouse! Guiding a ticketed poacher's vehicle onto the highway, I spotted a trainee engaged in a verbal confrontation with a foul-mouthed fisherman hollering we should have better things to do than disturb the peace of a harmless public. Invading the loud mouths comfort zone, I sternly countered, "You have it all wrong, these check stations are strongly supported by the fishing and hunting good." Claiming to be a doctor, screaming in my face, his vile words stunned me with the nauseating thought, *this man's breath could bark an oak tree!*

Eh, what's up doc?

The good doctor, proclaiming an IQ exceeding all of us combined, viciously ripped the hind ends of everyone present. Claiming to be a gastroenterologist, I dubbed him a colon binding proctologist whose inflamed personality matched the hemorrhoidal flare ups of his patients. His fishing license identified Dr. Benjamin Dover and, as luck would have it, Wildlife Officer Sir Don Gore smirkingly announced the doctor was transporting well over his limit of trout. Violating all ethical parameters of the Hippocratic Oath, the medical hypocrite continued slinging mouthfuls of vocal crap, catching the undivided attention of everyone present.

"Time to shoot, when you have to shoot, shoot. Don't talk".
Tico in the Good, the Bad, and the Ugly

Without hesitation, I instructed the trainee to begin scratching a tic, triggering Dr. Ben Dover to declare he had a patient dying on the operating table this very moment and would hold us responsible if he died. *Seriously!* Sir Don, a normally quiet yet seasoned warden, instantly coiled, his glaring eyes snaking into the doctor's and, shaking his index finger, strikingly rattled, "Now you listen here, we'll turn you loose after writing your ticket, and when you leave I suggest you find a phone, call the hospital and let them know your patient is going to die!" *Warden gold!*

DANGLING CONVERSATIONS– short take

And there I was, point man on Willow Creek Pass, flagging down a young man driving an old, beat up station wagon. Explaining we were checking fishermen and hunters, I spied a fishing pole propped against the passenger side front seat revealing a water-soaked worm dangling from its hook, and a wet wicker creel lying on the back seat. My well-rehearsed dialogue:

Warden: "Have you been fishing today."
HookWorm: "Nope!"
Warden: "Did you fish yesterday?"
HookWorm: "Nope!"
Warden "Are there any fish in the creel?"
HookWorm: "Nope!"
Warden: "Do you mind if I take a look?"
HookWorm: "Nope!"

Opening the creel, I uncovered over a dozen freshly caught 8-10-inch brook trout wrapped in wet meadow grass.

Warden: "You said there were no fish in the creel."
HookWorm: "Those ain't fish, they're brookies!"

Warden: "Do you have a fishing license?"
HookWorm: "Nope! Is there any chance you could sell me one?"
Warden: "Nope!"

I instructed HookWorm to pull into the parking area and scratched a tic for no license and illegally possessing fourteen trout. HookWorm asked if he paid the fine (over $200) on the spot could he keep the trout, becoming quite irritated when I explained he could not because a license was required to transport them. However, I gave him the option of backtracking to Rosebud, purchasing a fishing license and after returning and paying the fine, I would allow him to keep the trout. Retaining his driver's license, that is exactly what HookWorm did! His final words, "This will be the last time I'll ever fish without a license." Calculating the trout cost HookWorm nearly $80 dollars per pound, I replied, "A wise decision, indeed,"

"Honesty: The best of all lost arts." -Mark Twain

CAMP WENCH

Contacting married men with their wives or 'girlfriends' riding shotgun during big game seasons tendered warnings these women may be present for reasons other than bestowing a warm bed. Often carrying 'extra' licenses to cover illegal game and fish, further scrutiny was required to determine who actually harvested wild game discovered during our contacts. Experienced warden dogs develop an extra sense for sniffing out irregularities regarding legal versus illegally taken wildlife.

And there we were, eight wildlife officers and two trainees running a game check station on Willow Creek Pass, enjoying a lull after a remarkably busy day. Tired and weary from weeks of burning the candle at both ends, we were running on empty and agreed calling it a day when a cab over camper pulling an open trailer transporting two elk carcasses was guided into the parking area. Hastily exiting the vehicle, the driver rudely invaded my comfort zone, shoved two hunting licenses in my face and commanded we do our job and let them be on their way. Crisply dressed in Levis, a heavy leather belt flaunting a plate sized silver belt buckle, a western shirt and a black Stetson, the sturdy, broad shouldered, lantern jawed man carried the stature of a bull rider.

Sensing trouble, I stepped back and cordially explained checking the elk should not take long. A review of the licenses identified the man as one Buck Grifter, who indicated the cow license belonged to his wife, Liza. Buck explained the 5X5 antlers in front of the trailer belonged to his bull and both elk had been harvested on the same day near their camp in the North Sand Hills. Inspection of both headless elk carcasses revealed neither had the supplementary evidence of sex organs attached (testicles/penis for the bull, udder/mammary for the cow) required by law.

I must admit, however, 'evidence of sex' was quite evident on the eye-catching, well-trimmed lady exiting the camper door. Thick, flaming red, curled, shoulder length hair, crystal blue eyes, this woman was inappropriately dressed (for hunting season) wearing fancy heels, tight leather pants, and a tight fitting, loosely knit, mohair sweater. Sashaying across the parking area, her voluptuous scent permeating the air *(Hoo-Hah!)*, she flaunted her assets well. Grabbing Buck's hand, she curtly probed, "Is there a problem?" *Yup!* Bejeweled in turquoise, this home wrecking she-wolf sported a feminine attractiveness laden with testosterone. Literally the whole shebang, bearing an audacious air of dominance capturing the attention of all present, Buck announced this was his wife, Liza.

But I wander. Paying close attention to the cow license physically describing Liza as a black-haired, brown eyed, 110-pound female. Standing before me was a red-haired, blue eyed, woman easily weighing 160 pounds, later identified as Ima Camphor. Requesting a driver's license, Ima replied she was not driving. Asking for the date of birth printed on the cow license, she stumbled and turned to Buck for help. Refusing to answer my inquiries regarding harvesting the cow, it was obvious she had not hunted a day in her life. Cheekily inquiring if they were married, Buck tersely responded I was asking questions that were none of my business. The license clearly not belonging to the woman standing before me, tic's pending for evidence of sex violations, I was on good ground and explained we would be issuing citations for a multitude of charges.

When you stand well, stand still!

Buck and his faithful camp wench reacted with extreme anger, Buck howling for an attorney while Ima caterwauled I was on a witch hunt. *Yup!* Quickly dousing their fiery threats, I informed if they did not truthfully answer my next questions, I would resolve their dilemma by calling the phone number printed on Liza's license (the same number on Buck's license) and inquire: "Is this Mrs. Buck Grifter? Have you harvested an elk in Colorado? Was it a bull or a cow? And the ***coup de grâce***, Was there a red-haired woman in camp!"

Hell hath no fury like a woman scorned!

Trapped, Buck's rage transformed into panic. Not wanting the presence of his mistress divulged to a (dis)trustful wife, he wilted, declaring the phone call was not necessary, his real wife Liza was naive to his transgressions. Confessing he killed both elk, we confiscated the cow and scratched out a hefty tic before allowing the defeated Buck to drive away with his faithful gun moll riding shotgun. Oh, to hear the lies contrived on their long drive home! In this case it was not the warden, but beauty that killed the beast!

"The best laid schemes o' mice an' men. Gang aft a-gley".
To a Mouse... Scottish poet Robert Burns in 1786.

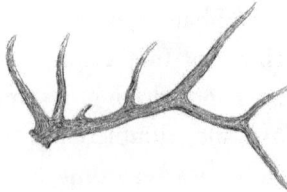

A MOOSE BUTCHER, A BAKER, MEETS HIS WARDEN MAKER

"Three things cannot be long hidden: the sun, the moon, and the truth."
Buddhist Derivations

September 1, 1990. The radio call from the Sheriff's Office was peculiar from the start. A vigilant archery elk hunter, Michael C. Olson, called the SO from Rosebud stating he knew the location of an illegally killed bull moose that had been cut up with a chainsaw, and abandoned. *SERIOUSLY?* Wildlife Officer Kirk Snyder and I met with Olson within the hour, who dutifully escorted us to a crudely divided, but not field dressed bull moose carcass located near a recently deserted campsite. While Kirk and I salvaged the meat and collected evidence, including a bloody camouflage broken arrow, Olson provided a detailed description of the vehicle belonging to two archery hunters he believed were involved in the incident; a van with Missouri plates with a distinctive mural of running wild horses on its sides, pulling a trailer hauling two ATVs.

Continuing, Olson stated today he hiked past this campsite well before daybreak where two ATVs with Missouri plates were parked next to two tents. Hiking the Hyannis Trail to the top of Arapaho Ridge, he began scanning a large timberline basin above the Missouri camp. Shortly after sunrise the mountain calm was rudely shattered by an ATV revving its engine and spinning its wheels, followed shortly by the persistent buzzing of a chainsaw. These hunt disrupting noises triggered him to relocate well away from the campsite. Returning later that afternoon, he found the camp abandoned and heavily scarred with ATV tracks, some leading to the sectioned moose carcass in the nearby pines.

Driving back Olson showed where the van and trailer were parked. Another hunter in a nearby camp confirmed watching the two Missouri hunters leave in the afternoon.

Make a new plan Stan

The poachers in the wind, Kirk and I returned to the Sheriff's Office and sent out a BOLO (Be On the Look Out) to all surrounding law enforcement agencies describing the vehicle with a request to hold it and any individuals associated with it. Patience not our virtue, Kirk and I spent considerable time cleaning up and donating the meat before spending the evening and the next day searching the south end of the Bull Pen for the game thieves. And would you believe, at approximately 5pm the following day, the Routt County Sheriff's Office informed us a Steamboat Springs Deputy spotted 'our' van at a gas station having a tire repaired and were holding two individuals at the Sheriff's Office. *Hoka Hey!*

Hastily driving to Steamboat, Kirk and I met with Wildlife Officer Jim Haskins at the Sheriff's Office and verified the van was the one we were looking for. Looking through its back window we observed a quiver attached to a bow holding arrows matching the one retrieved near the moose carcass! Preparing to meet the poachers', a deputy sheriff approached wishing us luck in cracking the case as the perpetrators adamantly claimed they did not kill a moose. He was convinced the son was telling the truth, while father displayed signs of deceit. Kirk winked at the smirking deputy and said, "wait 'l they get a load of us."

Our warden pluck roused, we entered the courthouse and were immediately hounded by a distraught young man wanting to know why we suspected them of killing a moose. Allowing him time to vent, we said listening to his father would probably clarify our suspicions. Prepared for the worst, we walked into the bad guy room finding father pallid as a fresh butterball turkey. Knowing the simplest solution to a problem is normally the right one, I cut to the quick and held up the broken arrow found at the kill site. While Kirk introduced him to Miranda by informing him of his constitutional rights, I checked his nonresident archery elk license identifying one Gaffe Bowman. Kirk rapid fired that Gaffe's cooperation would prevent the confiscation of all equipment used in the illegal killing of a bull moose. Then, out of the blue clear sky, Gaffe raised his hands and confessed! Not carrying his burden well, Gaffe unloaded a detailed account of yesterday morning's events:

Yesterday, before sunrise my son left camp on his ATV while I hunted on foot from camp. Blowing my cow elk call, an animal responded from a heavy willow draw and began ambling my way. At twenty yards it stopped and I, detecting antlers and believing it was a bull elk, picked a spot behind its shoulders and fired an arrow through the thick willows. The animal instantly bolted, crashed out of the willows and incredibly, collapsed and died in our campsite. Realizing the animal was a moose, I panicked and attempted to drag the carcass away from camp with my ATV. Too heavy, I sectioned the carcass with my chainsaw and pulled them into the trees with my ATV. Not wanting my son to discover my mistake, I packed up camp, met him down the road and explained we were headed to Steamboat Springs to another good hunting spot.

While shedding his guilt like autumn antler velvet provided Gaffe great relief, the anguish displayed on his son's face was heart-rending indeed! Stunned, realizing his father's mistakes were covered by lies and deceit, the innocent son said not a word.

> *"When the truth is found to be lies*
> *And all the joy within you dies"*...
> Jefferson Airplane

As the tic was scratched Gaffe, a baker by trade, expressed although the fine proffered a major hit to his savings account, he fully understood the logic behind the charges.

I explained modern day hunting requires accountability. Not always black and white, mistakes sometimes place hunters into gray areas demanding judicious decisions. We are here because a concerned member of the hunting good took time out of his hunt to ensure justice for the moose by turning you in. The moral integrity of this man allowed us to salvage the meat of a very messy moose carcass and track you down. Honesty from the moment the moose died would have resulted in significantly less personal and financial torment than the current circumstances.

Gaffe's greatest mistake was deceitfulness; his greatest challenge would be explaining it to his son.

That my friend is the lying truth.

"A person often meets his destiny on the road he took to avoid it."
Jean de La Fontaine, Fables

BACK SLAPPED

A Beaver Tale

After milking down six biscuits of shredded wheat with an orange juice chaser, I stepped out my back door just as the rising sun began gold plating the Bull Pen. Checking my garden, I found my vegetables safe and sound, including the incredibly pampered zucchini. It was August, the moon of the ripening berries, and a strong ridge of high pressure forewarned the inevitable late summer frosts, notorious for slaying high elevation gardens. Last spring, I valiantly battled and ultimately surrendered to a late May arctic blast executing my seedlings and the potted tomatoes on my covered front porch! A growing season averaging thirty-three frost free days offers the ultimate challenge to a persevering green thumb; Bull Pen summers are often described as three weeks of bad snowmobiling! Nurturing my garden to maturity was a challenging priority.

Once my satin black lab Smokey wolfed down a gargantuan bowl of Purina, he nervously began fidgeting and whining the dread of being left behind. As I opened the gate, he sped straight to and expertly climbed into the back of the truck. Yesterday's phone call from the Cache La Poudre fish hatchery advised Teal and Tiago Lakes had been heavily stocked with catchable ten-inch rainbows; stockers I dubbed 'windup trout' because freshly planted hatchery salmonids initially whirl in lively circles, gulping anything resembling hatchery pellets. Today, Smokey and I were heading west.

Wayfaring the outback over Ridge Road while listening to Chris LeDoux, I pondered the fate of today's angling miscreants currently unaware of an incoming warden. Thwacking non-compliant scofflaws at freshly planted lakes was relatively easy for any persevering wildlife officer. Smokey, standing proudly alert in the pickup bed, nosed the wind for bounteous scents in ear flapping earnest. Well-papered, handsome, and extremely smart, he exemplified the one first-class canine afforded most dog owners during their lifetime. Now a mature, well behaved (most of the time) retrieving Labrador bull, his early training was relatively easy, other than breaking his horrid habit of thieving (sometimes consuming) fish from creels or stringers; hard-hearted disciplining sessions (in full view of those losing their fish) before finally accepting fish were not on his mandatory list of retrieves.

Noting the last remnants of glacial snow hugging the northern edges of the wilderness' cresting crevices, I realized the entire range would soon be whitewashed by imminent late summer/early fall storms. Crossing onto National Forest approaching Tiago Lake, I hid the truck in a willow thicket and filled my daypack with a spotting scope, lunch, ticket book, sunscreen and the mandatory bottle of Cutter's bug dope. Two weeks prior required several coats of repellent to avoid sacrificing myself to the tiny blood-thirsty woodland drill bits. Hopefully, the high elevation mountain frosts ended that problem. Strapping on binoculars and pulling down my baseball cap, I ghosted through the timber towards the lake, Smokey shadowing close behind. Stalking the west side shore, I posted the lab and began a game of hide and snag. Three fishermen on the opposite side, waded as far out as the lake's black mud allowed, were casting bubbles and flies to the edge of the lilies on my side; a fruitful ploy for catching trout. Two were landing fish that very moment. Rejoining Smokey, we crept into a favored haunt above an ancient but active beaver lodge; a perfectly veiled lair for stalking warden prey. Smokey assumed his position, instinctively spinning in the tall, cool grass before lying down, knowing his obedience prevented a return to the pickup. Removing my pack, I fastened the Big Eye to a tripod and placed a pen and notepad next to me. Only 9am, my stomach was already growling, I spread lunch out on a nearby stump. It would be devoured within fifteen minutes. *Why do I call it lunch?* The fishing trio were rapidly catching and keeping every trout caught, customary for those hooking cookie cutter rainbows. Boastfully announcing every fish saved made my piscatorial math elementary.

Then, silent as a submarine, a beaver surfaced in the middle of the lake. Smokey spotted 'Bucky' immediately and before I could whisper "No", he launched into the lake with a cannon ball splash, chugged towards the beaver like a steaming locomotive. Bucky dove in a tail slapping dive before the fishermen perceived his presence. Spotting the dog, one remarked, "Look at the beaver!" Another answered it was a black lab and, believe it or not, proclaimed knowing the game warden had owned one. *BUSTED??* Smokey spent a fruitless five minutes searching for Bucky while I, not wanting to expose myself, let him enjoy the water. When he returned, I gave the remorseful dog my best finger pointing 'Bad Dog' glare. Shaking off the water, he cowered back into the tall grass.

Discussing where the dog came from, the fishermen continued angling their way towards wardenville. One walked around to my side and began casting twenty yards from my location. The warm sun roused a colossal caddis fly hatch and the entire lake was soon dimpled with rings of rising trout. Thirty minutes passed and the lone fisherman, jealous of his compadres' continued success, complained he could not even get a strike. Their voices resonated across the timber rimmed lake with the clarity of a well-engineered amphitheater. One passed gas, the reverberating wader flatulence causing all three to howl with laughter. *Warden field entertainment.* Frustrated, the loner continued bemoaning his bad luck. One compadre, later identified as Filch O'Dare, stated he had reached his limit of eight and would delightedly catch his hapless friends final four. In the same breath he aired a plan of returning to camp, hiding the fish and catching a second limit. *Hoka Hey!* Daily bag and possession limits were the same for trout meaning any one person could keep eight trout in one day and could catch no more until all or a portion of their possession limit was consumed. *What is wrong with catching your own fish?* Watching the fishing pair continue landing fish, my concern the fishermen sensed a warden's presence evaporated with the morning's dew.

Amazingly, Bucky, or his facsimile, surfaced from the depths two rod lengths from Filch. In a blink the fur-bearing beast raucously slapped his tail and disappeared, shattering the lake's solitude. Filch, caught completely off guard, all but soiled his waders. Waste deep in water, feet firmly gripped by the lake's black goo, he began falling backwards. Arms spinning like a windmill, rod launching skyward, he ditched into the lake like a two propped seaplane. Disappearing into the boggy depths, his fishing hat floating above his boiling wake, time seemingly took a short break before Filch resurfaced spitting water and gasping for air. Dripping with humiliation, he saw the rod's tip floating in front of him and happily retrieved the entire rod and reel. Recuperating, he began snickering away his embarrassment and soon all were once again buckled in uncontrollable laughter. Indeed, a precious warden event. As the tsunami waves reached the beaver lodge Smokey, now at full alert, appeared to be smiling, his loosely hanging upper lips pulled up and back revealing his back molars. *Quite a sight, huh Smoke?*

Filch continued verifying today's entertainment was far from over. He soon began counting his fish – OUT LOUD! Boisterously tallying twelve, his partner followed suit declaring his limit of eight. As they began walking towards the campground, I fast-tracked the lake shore in plain sight of the lone fisherman, now staring in resounding silence. Spotting me, the fishing duos' facial expressions displayed a head on encounter with a fish cop was not in their game plan. Frozen in their tracks, both began uttering undecipherable verbal exclamations. Entertained by their oral incompetence, I made contact and tried breaking the ice by smilingly congratulating Filch for his spectacular beaver dowsing. The third fisherman, Les Baggs, joined the party and while all three stared at the familiar dog by my side, I requested their fishing licenses and escorted them to their camp. Filch readily admitted possessing an over bounty of trout, deceitfully claiming eight belonged to him and four were caught by his buddy Les. Cautioning I had been watching them for over an hour, I warned it was not in their best interest to fail my field test; silly little secrets would not cover silly

BACK SLAPPED • 43

little lies. I scolded stashing fish in camp was a bad idea and if I had continued watching they would all undoubtedly be in trouble. Filch, comprehending I had eavesdropped his ruse for catching a second limit, wisely confessed catching four trout over his limit. I scratched out his tic for keeping four trout over the limit, explaining limits allowed the fishing multitudes equal opportunities to harvest their own limits. Filch, spreading his saturated clothes on a sun heated boulder, apologized for his misdeeds. The third fisherman, Coy Dabbler, a limit of eight in his creel, maintained an awkward quietness throughout the contact. I reminded Les he could still catch and keep four more trout and by eating some or all tonight, they could fill their limits the following day. Since they were using flies, I suggested pinching their barbs and carefully releasing fish the rest of this day. My warden wrath complete, Filch smiled and said, "Nice Lab"! I returned his smile and headed towards Teal Lake, a ten-minute stroll to yet another hidey-hole and, of course, a new adventure. Who says fishing is not a spectator sport?

And that's the way the stick floats!

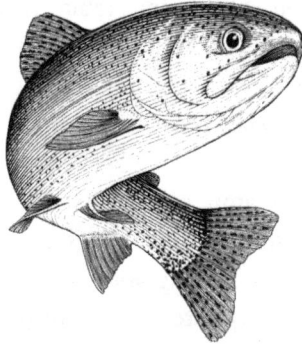

A DIK, A DEAD DOE, AND A DECOY

September 1987. Archery season. There we were! Wildlife Officer Kirk Snyder and I rendezvousing at the Arapaho National Wildlife headquarters to eat lunch after resolving two wildlife issues. Snyder's, a report of someone shooting elk becoming a landowner shooting porcupines, and mine, a fisherman reporting a strange acting moose turning out to be an arrogant, rutting bull.

Lunching outside on their picnic table, two nearby gunshots triggered us to jump into my truck and head east. In less than a mile we spied two men carrying rifles searching the sagebrush 100 yards above a parked jeep. Seeing us, they returned to the jeep, and we drove down to greet them. Kirk asked what they were shooting at and one, Shank Longbow, answered they apparently missed a coyote. Noting archery equipment and blood-soaked game bags in the rear of the jeep I requested hunting licenses, finding both were hunting archery deer and antelope. Cleverly, Kirk requested Shank to join his search for blood, providing me opportunity to question his comrade, Dik Loudarrow. Inspecting the bloody game bags, I discovered two hind quarters and a bag of boned out meat with Dik's archery deer tag attached. Inquiring why the shoulders and rib cage were missing, Dik replied they did not pack out the rib cage as his arrow passed through and ruined both shoulders. Pointing out the quivers attached to their bows were filled with arrows, I asked to see the arrow that killed the deer. Dik replied he left it at the kill site. Requesting the location of the gut pile, Dik, quaking like summer aspen leaves, answered he shot the deer early in the morning along Highway 14 east of Cameron Pass. His mouse in a snake pit demeanor told me to take this dog for a hunt. Returning to the jeep, Kirk revealed they found nothing but running antelope tracks. With a wink, I indicated the meat lacked the rib cage and shoulders and announced a trip to the kill site was necessary. Parking their jeep at the Refuge and storing the meat in a cooler, we headed towards Cameron Pass. Dik riding shotgun in my vehicle and Shank riding with Kirk allowed us to interrogate them individually and compare their stories.

My arrowing words causing Dik to quiver, he quickly teared and confessed to shooting the deer with his rifle. For crying out loud, I would rather suffer an aschew than listen to this wailing poacher. Passing Gould, Kirk radioed Shank was also bawling about their rifling misdeeds. At the kill site, the massive shoulder trauma verified the deer was shot with a rifle. After snapping pictures, we returned the weeping wimps to the Refuge and scratched the despondent Dik a hefty tic for his misdeeds and a written warning to the humbled Shank. Kirk raised their eyebrows warning additional charges were forthcoming if we discovered a dead or wounded antelope east of the Refuge.

Begging us to keep their misdeeds under wraps, Kirk smiled and said we'd do our best. Both members of a prominent Fort Collins archery club regulated by strict legal and moral covenants, they wanted no one hearing about their misdeeds. However, someone leaked their case, and a newspaper article covering their illicit behavior was pinned to the club's wall putting their membership in jeopardy. Who was that masked man! The gratification of taking out two game thieving land pirates rewarded not only us, but also the lawful hunting majority. ARGH!

Fast forward a year later during the October rifle big game season. Riding shotgun with me was Paul Day, a front range TV reporter gathering information for a televised story involving the use of decoys to capture miscreants illegally shooting from their vehicles or road right of ways and/or using artificial light to take wild game after dark. Paul, well-respected and woods savvy, was always welcome to ride with us. Leaving early, our adventures began when Colorado Parks Officer Jay Wenum, intercepted several vehicles near North Michigan Lake (Colorado State Forest) transporting freshly harvested elk. Riding with the adult hunters was a jubilant lad harvesting his first elk. Checking licenses and congratulating the boy, Wenum drove on discovering the bloody aftermath of their hunt clearly scribed in the snow covered Bockman Meadows; shell casings littering the road, scattered gut piles, disappearing blood trails, all signs of an elk massacre. Backtracking, Wenum recontacted the hunters and radioed for assistance. Officer Snyder, Paul and I joined Wenum's party, our interviews quickly led to those culpable, including the poor lad naively entangled in the adults' wrongdoings. Paul, camera rolling, began interviewing Kirk questioning how wildlife officers handle young hunters involved in wildlife crimes. Stone-faced as Rushmore's Lincoln, Kirk replied, "We castrate them, preventing their contributions to the poaching gene pool!" **CUT!**

Lucky for the jesting Kirk, this priceless piece of film amazingly vanished, forever lost in the archives of media boondoggles. Oh, to have the recorded rendition of Kirk's fabled logic for juvenile justice available at his retirement party! Paul glared in disbelief until Kirk' expressionless face broke into a possum grin! Cut from rare cloth, Kirk's clever wit and sharp tongue were often misconstrued and/or rightly taken as maliciously rude. He was one you must know well to understand. Even in death, Kirk remains my 'Kemo Sabe'. Writing the wrongs of the irresponsible adults, and schooling (not citing) the boy on the logic behind wildlife law, we sent the hangdogs down the road.

DEAD DEER STANDING – Build it and they will come

After a hearty supper at the Cookhouse in Gould, it was time to set up our decoy, Herbie. Wildlife officers, like hunters, possess toys to increase their enjoyment, effectiveness, and success. Placing a full body deer or elk mount or a pheasant during the small game seasons along frequently traveled roadways tenders an efficient tactic to enforce commonly violated, difficult to detect, illegalities. It is not entrapment because wildlife officers are utilizing legal methods to capture those performing illegal acts.

These life-like decoys, with reflective eyes, some equipped with remotely controlled movable heads, trigger interesting human reactions:

- The unobservant driving by.
- Slowing down or stopping to observe, maybe snapping a picture.
- Walking out, touching, and even pushing it over.
- Interesting discussions concerning whether it is alive or fake.
- Comrades goading a 'hunter' to shoot before the animal gets away.

My interest in decoys began when watching a video taken by Arizona wildlife officers of an archery hunter jumping from a moving vehicle and shooting a painted plywood rendition of a mule deer buck. The twang of his bow and the vibrating thump of the arrow hitting wood was further enhanced by the eagerness of the hunter to illegally shoot from the road and his humiliation once captured. Decoys are warden candy, breaking up daily routines while affording exciting opportunities for catching violators.

And there we were, Kirk, Paul, and I sitting in night's stilling black on an Owl Mountain timbered hillside above a well-traveled county road. Our vehicles hidden, two officers concealed in their vehicle a quarter mile above, all we needed was hunters. Midseason, many hunters were returning home contentedly transporting their game, while others, dejectedly desperate, returned empty handed. Herbie, our full body 4-point mule deer mannequin, was strategically placed on a curve where vehicle headlights would light him up. Boldly standing in tall sagebrush, he was ready for business despite having been shot and patched many times from previous shootouts.

Initially experiencing light traffic with no one interested in our decoy, Paul tuned in his satellite radio, and we listened to the world series. Suddenly, the rumbling of a fast-moving vehicle caught our attention just before its headlights lit up the decoy. A cab over camper roared around the bend, the driver slammed on the brakes and canted the headlights towards Herbie. Jumping out with pistol in hand, aiming at the decoy over the pickup hood, a man shouts to a woman (later identified as his wife carrying an unfilled deer tag) driving another vehicle stopped behind his camper. "Do you want it? (Louder) DO YOU WANT IT?" She yells, "YES" and, after firing a barrage of shots, he senses trouble and screams, "ITS A DECOY, LET'S GO!" Speeding away, they are quickly intercepted by the awaiting officers. Driving up, Kirk and I immediately recognize the shamefaced shooter as the infamous Dik Loudarrow. Dik, in a version of gallows humor, laughingly joked about being in the wrong place at the wrong time. Cackling he knew all the time it was a decoy, he continued lying until his words betrayed him. Realizing we were not amused, he, once again, began crying! *Damn!* Pathetically sniveling in front of God, his wife, and a pack of wildlife officers, I wondered if his balls missed him.

Scratching Dik a tic for using artificial light and shooting from a public road, he joined our elite club of two-peating poachers. Kirk advised a suspension of his license privileges was inevitable. Disgraced, Dik acknowledged he deserved whatever punishment we dealt. Finally, a word of truth, making one in a row!

Press hard Dik, remember there are five copies.

Paul Day, of course, assembled a great story expounding the effectiveness of decoys in catching illicit hunters.

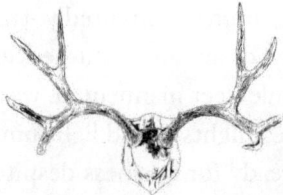

GRANDPA'S MANTRA

August 1988. And there I was! A grand August Friday evening working the night shift at Delaney Butte Lakes. Such marvelous weather, so tightfistedly guarded by the Bull Pasture's weather Gods, is often the norm as the aging summer metamorphoses into a juvenile fall; mosquito-free, warming days and cooling nights, no measurable wind chill and good fishing, highlight this most pleasurable time of year. The 'natives' earn this weatherly treasure after seemingly endless winters and relentless springs; spring weather testing their personal fortitude with hints of melting warmth promptly backhanded by icy fingers of relentless winds, wet snows and bulleting hail. Colorado's high mountain parks are truly Zeus' playground where he, with his weather friends, takes great pleasure toying with the ravages of inclement weather.

As evening serenely dimmed into night, a coyote howled echoing its concealed presence off the mountain's cliffs, tailed by the telegraphing, distant yowls and yips of another, then another, then another....... A bald-faced moon peaking over the Medicine Bow Range, I surveyed the campfires and lanterns flickering like so many candles off the shimmering South Delaney Butte Lake. Dusk was orchestrated by the sounds of camp conversations blending with the lyrical serenades of the areas birdlife. Feeling the nights cool stealing in, I sniffed blends of wood smoke, lantern fuel and boat exhaust fouling the fresh mountain air. A nighthawk roared its wing buzzing presence over the lake prompting a child to ask, "What was that?" I chuckled when the kid's father answered, "probably the jake-brake of an eighteen-wheeler." For me, being 'out here in the field' was my place to be; in the words of the Mountain Men, "it was a good job to take."

My truck, disguised in the camp of an old friend, I began tonight's game afoot, silently peregrinating through familiar sage to a bench above the lake's northwest corner. These heavily fished shallows provide an alkaline, algal soup of invertebrates and minnows, luring larger trout from their deeper daytime haunts. Newly implemented restrictions on bag and possession limits and corresponding declines in fishing pressure allowed the lake to increase the size and number of rainbow and cutthroat trout. Predictably, as word of the good fishing leaked, the crowds returned bringing with them those skels yearning to wreak mutiny on the lake's bounty.

Stalking night fishermen, a favored ploy, often allowed the stars of good fishing, fish poachers, and a warden to align. I shared my pen with many angling culprits veiled in the night's cover; tics needing scratched, patience's reward of revealing those who often go unde-tected. I quivered hearing the shrill cries of a jack rabbit squealing its fate in the ominous darkness east of the lake; the sad sounding wails heard only by the alert few who stopped to listen in wonder. I earlier observed Bubo, the great-horned owl, hugging the trunk of a cotton-wood pretending to ignore the pesky crows incessantly harassing his presence. I now imagined the very same soft-feathered marauder silently soaring through the hare's sagen lair, its life driving death zen striking the unsuspecting jack in its vise gripping, knife-point talons. Tonight, I would hunt covertly with the coyote and the owl, making a living upwind and silent, stalking my quarry of miscreant piscators defying the laws allowing the lake to sustain an abundance of trout.

As I platted the lights of the night fishermen, Bubo hooted, seem-ingly asking, Who! Who! Who!, would fall prey tonight to the warden's watchful eye? Posting myself above and between two camps set thirty yards apart, I used their blazing lanterns and campfires to watchdog fishermen, focusing my binoculars first on three men in a tent camp busily preparing their tackle. The second camp had a cab-over camper sitting close to a medium-sized motorboat anchored on the shoreline. Two women, sitting in lawn chairs around a campfire, were joined by an elderly man stalking from the willows carrying an empty fish stringer and wiping his hands with a towel. Assuming he just cleaned and iced some fish, I watched him bait, cast, and tend four fishing poles. The women were enjoying the evening chatting in the firelight, showing little interest in handling 'their' poles. The old man, handling four identical Eagle Claw Trail Master rods with matching Mitchell 300 reels, displayed all qualities of a 'party' fisherman, using the women's presence as an excuse to fish with extra poles and to catch their trout. Studying the old codger in the strobing campfire light, I noted his large hunch-backed frame, bronzed arms and face and short steel wool beard. His unkempt wavy grey hair protruded from a John Deere baseball cap. Combined with a gruff voice relentlessly woofing out obscenities, he emulated a man having the disposition of a silver-tip grizzly bear. I gazed in awe as he, neck to neck with a bottle of Jim Beam, swigged several large gulps. Pickled but not well preserved, wearing his age poorly, the old man's eyes flickered red with the fire, like those of a loon. Add his buzzard beak raspberry nose, pot belly and waddling walk he was the 'redneck' version of Saint Nick himself.

Soon, the three men in the first camp were busy catching, sorting, releasing, cleaning and icing down the 'keepers' in individual plastic bags. Slowly reeling in barbless bead-head flies, suspended below a casting bubble they successfully lip hooked their trout allowing soft and safe releases of the smaller ones. In less than an hour they each had caught and kept their limit of two pink fleshed fourteen to sixteen-inch trout, and quit fishing. No need to worry about these sportsmen contentedly sipping scotch around a blazing fire. I, thirsting for the peaty taste of good malt, admired these true sportsmen whose responsible behavior, if followed by all, would allow this fishery to prosper.

Obviously, the old man was in need of warden charge. Using practiced night skulking moves, I cut the distance in half and sat down in the tall sage just out of their lantern light. Close enough to hear the whispering gossip of the two women I learned they were a mother/daughter duo spending the weekend with 'grandpa'. The youngest, in her early twenties, was noticeably enjoying the drunken antics of her grandfather almost as much as he was enjoying playing center stage. Her mother, however, obviously found little amusement in her father's inebriation. Relaxed in my back-row seat, I readily enjoyed this real-life comedic tragedy, in spite of knowing its most predictable ending.

The softly refined women boldly contrasted with the coarse vulgarity of the old man. Tolerating him for what he was and was not, they worryingly gazed as his drunken endeavors increased proportionally with his spirited consumption. Not nearly as forgiving as the women, I judged the old man having a whiskey proof IQ; a thug with secrets hidden in the disease he wore on his breath. His liquor induced brevity a thin shell covering his insecurities, evidenced by his incessant stares into the darkness around him. *Did he feel a warden's presence?* I understood that to the paranoid, stillness is suspect. Warden mettle requires professionally disguising my dislike of this disgusting elderly scumwad, something I would later find very hard to do.

I watched the old man hook, land and keep trout from all four poles. After setting the hook, Gramps allowed the women to land three trout, but caught all others on his own. Sorting out the larger trout and releasing the smaller, deep hooked or not, the old man used his rod tip to nudge them until they swam away or drifted out of sight, even if they were 'belly up'. Starkly focused, I was unexpectedly startled by the blinding glare of a flashlight as a man and woman walking a lap mutt passed by. Backing out of their light and pressing my fingers to my lips, I smilingly waved them on. Both obediently smiled and, without a word walked by, their little 'watchdog' totally unaware of my presence.

The old man, later identified as Fishbert Bluffmile, entertained me for over two hours. My gambit to follow him into willows was delayed as Fishbert continued filling the group's entire limit. To my delight, granddaughter began quizzing her grandfather about fishing laws. Her voice previously the blithe song of a spring towhee changed to the serious timbre of a prattling crow as she sought the old man's counsel on discerning right from wrong. With the inquisitiveness of a pollen searching bumble bee, her sincere and logical questions put me on full alert, yearning to hear Fishbert's response to her sharp-witted questions penetrating his inebriated mind.

She blurted, "Do you worry about getting caught? Was there not a reason for the laws and are not they enforced? What would he do if a warden showed up?" Her dark eyes sparkling in the campfire light revealed an innocent face earnestly waiting for meaningful answers. Fishbert's Montana Sky ego, about to burst out of his Grand Canyon mouth, swelled like a puffball at the chance to justify his misdeeds to a captivated audience; two known and one yet to be identified. A volley of hollow-pointed rationalizations shot from his mouth, chanted in a razor-sharp mantra honed over decades of violating wildlife law. His intoxication momentarily masked, the melodious justifications of this dabbling dupe were devised not only to benefit the attentive women but also to bask in his own glory. He presented himself as the immortal fish poacher having lived forever and a day; a seasoned hero of the waters; a wise man in full control of his errant ways. He bragged about a lifetime of breaking laws without ever being caught, daring anyone to try. Guzzling another swill of Jim Beam, distilling any guilt arising from his underutilized conscience, the final words of this arrant coward were warden gold:

"Look around, do you see any law? Wardens are much too lazy to work at night. Besides, there is nothing wrong for making up for times when fishing was bad. Such violations are not taken seriously by anyone except Gestapo driven, ticket happy assholes fulfilling meaningless quotas by preying on innocent sportsmen. If a warden appears, do not worry, I am quite familiar with 'warden schemes' and can easily con my way out of any wrongdoing."

It was time for the song of the proverbial obese woman. The old bull was about to meet his matador. Tonight's Corrida would be decided by the sword. But as if on cue, Fishbert's granddaughter posed her final question. "What would it cost if they did get caught? Rather than exposing my cape, I verbally maneuvered into Fishbert's sloshed mind before the drunk could barf out an answer. In a booming, perfectly clear voice I declared, "$25 for the first illegal trout and $10 each for all others."

This is the moment when warden heaven and poacher hell meet. My words hit the group like a stun bomb. The night went from 'live' to slow motion as the three turned to witness a uniformed man prowl in from the darkness. Considering their chalky, wide-eyed, mouth gaping faces flickering in the firelight, I must have appeared as the devil himself. The crescent moon smiles worn all evening were now eclipsed by a warden shadow. If time did not stop, it was certain that Grandfather's clock surely missed a few ticks as the speechless, wavering old man, wearing his guilt like apple butter on a bull's ass, was deeply suspended in a state of mind I routinely referred to as 'warden shock.'

Expecting the whiskey to do Fishbert's talking, I was surprised by his silence. Explaining I had observed him catch and keep six of the nine trout on the stringer made it crystal clear I had been watching them for a very long time. Next, I methodically began answering the granddaughter's questions by clarifying Fishbert's responses:

"Quotas!" Wardens have no quotas. We are allowed to write as many tickets as we want. *(oh, how I liked this one!)*. As for innocent fishermen, wardens prey only on the guilty by lowering themselves to their own bottom feeding level. Catching real poachers is the best use of my time and tonight he had captured a genuine fish thief, stealing from the lake as well as from those obeying the laws.

Pissing on Fishbert's post, I broke him down with practiced eloquence, binding the drunkard's liquor looped mind into a frayed knot. My leaden, well-patterned words sent piercing wounds through Fishbert's skillet head, brutally folding the old man into a speechless mass. The old man's unibrow formed a dark line shadow over glaring eyes and grimacing face, indicated he was soured by eating his own words. When I asked about their other trout Fishbert, lying as the errant always do, gruffly stated there were no other trout. Entering the willows, I quickly located a tarp covered cooler holding six large trout, cleaned and iced. Fishbert arrogantly denied the cooler was his. I asked the women if the cooler belonged to them and the speechless lassies only shrugged their shoulders. Having countlessly hunted this dog and satisfied with my current hand, I played warden 'joker' by confiscating the cooler explaining anyone wanting to claim it should contact the sheriff's office. Fishbert, realizing he was going to lose a very nice

Coleman cooler containing his days catch, reeled but was much too bigheaded to claim it. Returning to the stringer I counted nine trout and asked which trout were caught last. Fishbert said he did not remember and watched in awe as I confiscated the four largest trout.

Chipping at the old man's obsidian ego, I reminded him these hefty trout were a product of the lake's current bag limits. I scolded Fishbert for returning deeply hooked fish back into the lake and told him he was lucky there were no wounded or dead trout in sight. Winking at the women, I explained it was the license dollars of men and women that pay wardens to catch violators and it was my job to clean up trash. Tonight, I was playing garbage man.

Scratching out the tic, I recited the old warden tune the citation would hopefully encourage Fishbert to change his venal behavior. *Yeah, right!* However, I knew breaking Fishbert down under the attentive eyes and ears of his offspring was by far the greatest punishment of all. All three gazed in frozen silence as I disappeared into the night carrying the cooler. The sting of my sword, on this night anyway, was greater than the thrust of the old bull's horn.

Suum Cuique – to each his due.

IF THE BOOT FITS...

I call it "Desperation Season", the time when hunters possessing unfilled licenses face the anguish of returning home with no wild meat. For the hunting good, it is a time to take advantage of fewer hunters and utilize their skills to track and harvest game. For the hunting bad, it is a time to take higher risks violating wildlife law. For wardens, it is a time to pay meticulous attention to the slightest details.

October 19, 1985. Saturday. And there we were. Wildlife Officer Keith Kahler and I patrolling Owl Mountain during the early morning hours of the last weekend of elk season. Four inches of fresh snow covered the Mountain, refreshing the hunting spirits of the remaining diehard hunters and an open book for wardens to read, interpret, and apprehend! *Seize the day, Warden!*

Discovering an abandoned Ford pickup parked along the main County Road bordering a section of State School land, we examined fresh boot tracks indicating several individuals had entered a second vehicle. Recording the plate number, I informed Kahler we were on good ground, sensing the empty vehicle implied hunters were stalking a large block of mixed public and private lands supporting a bountiful elk population; a meaty recipe for roasting bad guys, our patience was essential. Using a key provided by the landowner, I drove through a locked gate and parked in timber overlooking a large section of the Mountain. Kahler, in a manner of minutes, fell asleep. Around 11:30 a.m. his lengthy nap was disturbed by a volley of rifle shots on the Mountain above our location. Urging him to grab his binoculars and scan the area, we briefly spotted two men wearing hunter orange just before they disappeared into heavy aspen. Driving towards the shots, we found the Ford pickup had been moved to a narrow road entering the State School Section and observed two sets of boot prints entering the timber. Persistently searching for hunter activity, we eventually discovered a hunter, Snarly Knothead, propped against a tree where the Ford pickup had been parked. Snarly, rifle leaning against a tree, stated he was not hunting but waiting for his hunting party to return. Checking his cow (antlerless) elk license, I asked if they had killed any elk and he dismissively did not respond. *Clue #1.* As I waited for his answer, Snarly changed the subject by pointing out the Ford pickup transporting two hunters headed our way. Parking behind my vehicle, the driver, Otlaw Duper, quickly approached Snarly and proclaimed, "You know Waldo has a bull down?", an apparent signal to synchronize their stories as to who killed the elk. *Clue #2.* Snarly, clearly knowing the location of the dead elk, unhesitatingly asked if I could obtain permission to enter the private property to access the bull. I replied the responsibility was theirs, not mine. Recording their elk licenses, I found both Otlaw and his passenger Queazy Scruples were also licensed for cow (antlerless) elk. Queazy wordlessly remained in the vehicle. *Where's Waldo?*

Noticing me inspecting blood on his clothing, Otlaw volunteered he had been with Waldo when the bull was killed. After field dressing it, Otlaw said his brother hiked back over the Mountain to his blue van and returned to Otlaw's home where he currently was staying because he had to work the following day. Knowing the difficulty of trekking the long distance over rugged, hard to navigate terrain, I winked at Kahler and suggested it was unusual for a hunter to shoot an elk and leave. Snarly proclaimed Waldo was 'different', not really a hunter, one you must know to understand. *Clue #3. Something's amiss!*

Receiving a radio call from a colleague who witnessed a hunter shooting from the county road (illegal) and killing a cow elk on private property, he reported the landowner arrived and wanted to file charges against the trespasser. The incident occurring less than a mile away (we actually heard the shots), I told Otlaw this was their chance to obtain permission to retrieve Waldo's bull and they should follow Kahler and I to meet the landowner. At the scene, the agitated landowner demanded I write a citation to the trespasser and confiscate the cow. Scratching the tic, my conversation with the trespasser revealed he was associated with Otlaw and, upon observing him walking down the mountain late this morning, gave him a ride to his Ford pickup, learning Otlaw had killed a bull elk. However, after a private conversation with Otlaw, the trespasser changed his story and told me it was Waldo who killed the bull. *Clue #4.* Amazingly, a hunter I knew well drove up on his ATV and said he had spoken with these three individuals driving a section of private land in the Ford pickup early this morning. *Where's Waldo Clue #5.* After loading the illegal elk into my truck, the landowner, perceiving I was trailing scent, gave me permission to escort the Otlaw gang to the dead bull through his private land. *Release the hounds!*

Winding up the slippery road to the Forest Boundary fence line we parked our vehicles and set out on foot. Queazy, developing a case of the Warden Flu, remained in their pickup while Otlaw led the search. Persistently firing loaded inquiries, I was pleasantly amused listening to Snarly and Otlaw vociferously coordinate their perceptibly fabricated stories: all four, after parking the Ford pickup on the county road before daylight, were ferried to the other side of the Mountain in Waldo's blue van and began hunting towards the abandoned pickup; Waldo killed a bull, hiked back over the Mountain to his blue van and returned to his newly purchased home, address unknown, 'somewhere' in Littleton, CO. *Now their story really gets interesting!* Otlaw, indicated Waldo could not be contacted because he did not have a job or a phone. Reminding Otlaw he previously stated Waldo was living with him and needed to return to work, his blank expression revealed the poacher he was. Darkness approaching and obviously on a wild goose chase, I declared Kahler and I would take over leading the search even if locating the bull took the four of us all night.

Taking advantage of the fresh snow, I beelined to the Forest boundary fence and easily located Otlaw's boot tracks trekking the private side, eventually crossing onto public land not 30 yards from our pickups! Following Otlaw's zigzagging tracks up the Mountain, they led us to the dead bull. *Elementary!* The bull was wearing brother Waldo's signed, dated, and punched tag on its antlers. Pointing out only one set of boot tracks led to the bull, were around the bull, and returned to the private fence (where they did not have permission to hunt), I asked, "Where's Waldo's tracks?" *Wait for it!* Otlaw countered by articulating he and his brother had previously purchased the same brand and size of boots before the hunt. *Seriously!* No boot tracks heading back over the Mountain, my next preposterous query was literally, "How on earth did Waldo return to his vehicle by not making any tracks?" Otlaw, without a blink, answered they approached the dead bull walking in the same tracks and Waldo returned to his van doing the same. Indicating the absurdity of Waldo walking backwards in the one set of tracks, I curtly repeated Waldo could have saved a great deal of time and energy walking the short distance downhill to the Ford pickup! Otlaw, skipping silly and going straight to stupid, replied he was taking offense to my questions. Enjoying the moment, I held my aces to enjoy watching Otlaw continue playing his worthless cards. Requiring all four of us to drag out the bull over heavy aspen downfall, we loaded it into their pickup. Otlaw expressed he needed to gas up and phone his wife at the KOA campground before returning to camp because she expected him home today. Forgetting he previously divulged he was hunting through the weekend, I drew another ace. Following their vehicle down the Mountain I radioed the Sheriff's Office in Sage Hen and asked Deputy Rick Rizor to phone Otlaw's residence, ask for Waldo and question him about killing an elk. Deputy Rizor was extremely skilled at interviewing tight lipped hunters. I also radioed Parks Officer Mike Hopper and asked him to investigate the Silver Creek camp prior to our arrival. Deputy Rizor radioed back no one answered the phone. Officer Hopper radioed no one was present at the Silver Creek camp but discovered a cow elk hanging from a tree, the attached carcass tag signed by Lethe Nescient and marked as being killed Friday, the previous day. Requesting Deputy Rizor to phone

Lethe, he later radioed back stating Nescient nervously uttered he was unsure if he had killed an elk but quickly changed his story to killing an elk midweek before returning home. Lethe was unable to answer the Deputy's questions concerning the details of when, where, and how it was killed. Stopping at the KOA campground while Otlaw gassed up, I approached Snarly and Otlaw and expressed if they had anything to say, now was the time! Otlaw's grimacing demeanor indicated he wanted to speak, but Snarly rudely declared they would talk at their camp. Catching both off-guard, I mentioned the cow elk hanging in their camp. Startled, Otlaw conceded Lethe killed a cow elk the previous day and returned home. When asked, Queazy replied he knew nothing about Lethe's elk hanging in camp, having arrived after dark Friday night, and leaving before daylight this morning to hunt. *Yeah, right!*

Arriving at their camp after 8 p.m., Otlaw again appeared to have something to say but Snarly interfered, declaring he needed to talk to a lawyer. I replied that may be a good idea because Kahler and I were not buying what they were selling. I continued firing questions and asked who moved the Ford pickup that morning. Surprisingly, Snarly admitted he and Queazy had hunted from the pickup all morning and moved it several times. Entangled in mistruths and contradictions, Snarly lost his temper and belligerently exclaimed, "every cop I know is a son of a bitch." Asserting the necessity of interviewing Queazy, now inside the camper and still not feeling well, further infuriated Snarly who declared we could not enter his trailer without a warrant. Making it clear I was questioning Queazy even if it took waiting for a warrant, Snarly grudgingly gave permission and violently slammed the door behind me as I entered the camper alone. Queazy, suffering the gut-wrenching wrath of the current events, fretfully verified hunting the morning with Snarly and moving the Ford pickup to hunt different areas. I asked if Waldo was present Friday evening or Saturday morning, Queazy confirmed he was not.

Sharing Queazy's statements with the other two, Snarly brusquely repeated he needed a lawyer and advised Otlaw to do the same. Informing we would return early the next morning, Kahler and I left and phoned a Wildlife Officer in Broomfield, CO from the KOA campground advising we needed officers to track down and interview John P. Lethe at his residence and, if possible, locate Waldo ASAP. *No sleep tonight!* Arranging a phone call to my home at 3:30 a.m., Kahler and I returned to Otlaw's camp to assess any changes in their demeanor and surprisingly found the Ford pickup missing and all three hunters gone. Contacting hunters at several camps adjacent to Otlaw's, we learned no one had observed a blue van associated with Otlaw's camp the entire week.

Kahler and I returning to Sage Hen to skin and quarter the trespasser's illegal elk. On cue at 3:30 a.m., I received a call from Wildlife Officer Jay Sarason stating he had contacted Lethe by phone and although not confessing to anything, Lethe admitted not being in camp all week due to his mother's illness. At 6:30 a.m. Sunday morning Kahler and I returned to Otlaw's camp, finding the Ford pickup back and all three hunters now present. I explained we were issuing citations and confiscating the bull and the cow elk. Once again requesting their licenses, I carefully watched Otlaw thumb through his wallet and noticed the top half of an antlerless elk license belonging to John P. Lethe. Handing it to Kahler, he immediately compared signatures on the Lethe's license to the tag on the cow elk and indicated they did not match. Nonetheless, Otlaw and Snarly insisted Lethe killed the cow. Explaining our evidence clearly indicated otherwise, we had no choice but to seize both animals. Kahler and I assumed Otlaw or Snarly would admit killing the cow since both were legally carrying cow licenses, which could have resulted in a lesser 'failure to tag' citation and the possibility of maintaining possession of the cow. Stubborn pride has sunk many hunter warships, a common defensive mechanism for veiling one's misguided misdeeds. Reminding Otlaw of our indisputable evidence proving he killed Waldo's bull, he still would not budge.

As the wide-eyed Kahler lowered the elk into the bed of my pickup, Snarly blew a gasket and bluff charged me twice. With fists clenched he dubbed me "a 'cocky son of a bitchin' banty rooster", belittling my stature by declaring "the smaller they are the more of a son of a bitch they are." Stepping back in a defensive stance, right hand covering my enforcement baton, apparently thwarted both attacks as if an invisible wall separated us! Belligerently threatening me with a lawsuit warning I would lose my job for entering his camper without a warrant, Otlaw politely requested Snarly to settle down and apologized for his friend's behavior. Both demanding court appearances, I clarified appearing before a neutral judge to review their issues and our evidence was mandatory. After transporting the two elk to Sage Hen, Kahler and I returned to the kill site, traced Otlaw's boot prints on a note card, and followed out his tracks from the bull to where he entered the trespassers truck. We also collected a spent 30-06 shell casing approximately 25 yards from the gut pile, matching the caliber of Otlaw's rifle.

Days later, Officer Sarason personally interviewed Waldo, who demanded his brother's presence. Otlaw readily filled in the blanks whenever Waldo faltered answering Sarason's detailed questions. Interestingly, one of the few questions Waldo did answer, was maintaining he shot the bull using his brother's 30-06 rifle, an obvious ploy to distort our evidence the bull was killed by his brother. Later, Sarason's personal interview with Lethe substantiated his absence the day 'his' cow elk was killed by formally admitting he had not been in camp the entire week due to his mother's illness. Sarason issued Lethe a citation for illegally transferring his license. Sarason tactfully completed his side of the investigation by taking all legal documents, licenses and tags signed by the hunters to a handwriting expert with Boulder Police Department, eventually verifying Otlaw had signed Waldo's tag and Lethe had not signed the tag affixed to the cow elk hanging in camp.

Long story short, after hiring and no doubt entertaining their lawyers, all parties entered guilty pleas in Jackson County Court and were heavily fined based on the preponderance of evidence presented: Otlaw guilty of killing Waldo's bull; Waldo guilty of transferring his license to his brother; Lethe guilty of transferring his license to Otlaw; and Snarly for the illegal cow elk in his camp. Taking their guilty pleas into account, no charges for hunting private property without permission were filed.

In this case, Colorado's law requiring one hunter utilizing his license to harvest game was broken. Hunter behavior, normally veiled in wild landscapes, is based on an honor system dictated by a hunter's moral compass. Hunting laws requiring hunters to harvest their own game are written to maintain the integrity of recreational sport hunting in the spirit of equal harvest opportunity for all hunters bound by the ethical principles of fair chase and legal pursuit of free ranging, wild game. Wildlife regulations manage harvest at pre-determined levels of success, meaning not all hunters will kill game, ensuring a percentage of the population survives into the future. Otlaw, by killing his brother's elk, stole away opportunity for another hunter to legally hunt and possibly harvest that bull, and/or the ability for that bull to live and continue sustaining the elk population. Otlaw and/or Snarly, utilizing Lethe's license to tag a cow elk, continued hunting with full intent of illegally killing a second cow as well as a bull utilizing Waldo's license. These men characterize the hunting bad wardens work tirelessly to apprehend for the benefit of the hunting good and the beasts they legally and ethically pursue. Caught and convicted of cheating in the wild hunting game, these four poaching collaborators fought the law, AND THE LAW WON!

"Life's tough...... It's even tougher if you're stupid." -John Wayne

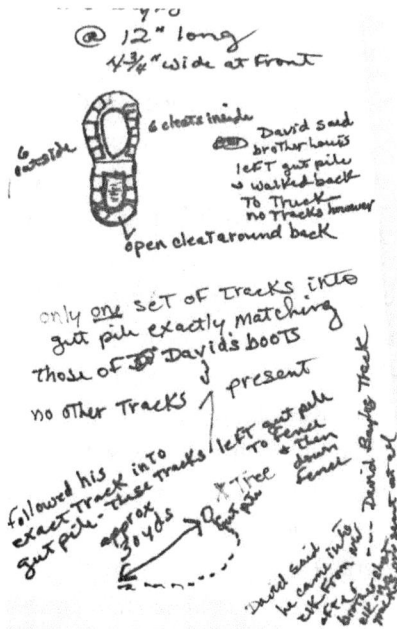

THE PLANE TRUTH

Most do not realize the essential role aircraft play in wildlife management. Pilots are the unsung heroes of wildlife conservation worldwide. Colorado's Wildlife Division employs a battery of talented fixed wing pilots critical to the management, conservation, research, and law enforcement sections of the agency. State and Federal wildlife agencies also contract extensively with the private aircraft sector for wildlife reconnaissance and census.

Colorado's former northeast regional pilot, Wayne Russel, represented the very best. An easy-going wind warrior, his thorough geographical knowledge of the entire state, hawk eyes, and extraordinary skills for maneuvering his Cessna 185 through the thin mountain air crafted a highly professional, reliable member of the state's wildlife team. Russel expertly rode the wind with a smoothness sanctioning those with the weakest of stomachs to fly comfortably. I did not fully appreciate Russel's tender competence until upchucking breakfast into a barf bag on my initial ride with a different pilot; a gut-wrenching experience where I queasily desired nothing else but planting my feet back on dry land.

I accrued considerable flight time with Russel on bighorn sheep and antelope surveys as well as reconnaissance flights searching for lost wilderness hikers, law enforcement missions and familiarizing myself with the Bull Pen; essential time to thoroughly explore my district on the ground and assemble the land puzzle from the air. For safety reasons, Russel prohibited passengers when aerial planting fish, avoiding extra weight while cautiously threading his plane through the rugged, steep canyon basins and cirques cradling the high mountain lakes. Russel laughingly related a story of a fisherman wading the shallows of a wilderness lake who, as Russel plunged into the cirque, swiftly back pedaled towards shore finally falling in mouth gaping awe while showered with a load of fingerling cutthroat trout. Reading the stocking reports, I discovered Russel released fish into many nameless, relatively unknown waters providing recreational opportunities for those willing to wander off the main trails.

One late September, Russel and Wildlife Officer Jim Jackson picked me up at the Sage Hen airport for an early morning flight over the Never Summer Range to census bighorn sheep. We were gifted crystal-clear skies and air still as a midnight church. It was muzzle-loader season and the high country was carpeted with a diversified panorama of strikingly bold fall colors. Gliding over a wide drainage of thick willows and alders bordering Rocky Mountain National Park, Russel spied a herd of elk guarded by a large six-point bull nervously hounded by several menacing raghorns. The bulls remained oblivious to the plane, but the cows began threading their way downward, pulling the bulls with them. Skipping into the next drainage, Jackson spotted a lone hunter, muzzleloader rifle in hand, walking atop the ridge and not wearing the daylight fluorescent orange hat and vest of required by state law. Russel banked widely momentarily losing site of the hunter but when he came back into view, would you believe he donned an orange cap and vest blazing in the morning sun. Making another circle, Russel glided over the wide-eyed chap as Jackson grabbed the microphone and declared a booming **"THANK YOU"** over the outside speakers. A memorable story indeed, for hunter, pilot and the wardens. I pondered if the hunter was aware of the elk herd one canyon south of his location. The same morning, we spotted a herd of bighorn sheep on a steep, rocky outcrop near Baker Pass. Russel circled, significantly reducing the plane's speed, barely clearing the ridgetop, allowing the plane to literally float downward into the basin. Experiencing the holy grail of roller coaster rides, I watched Jackson's eyes flutter like the wings of a butterfly. The sheep hastily fanned downwards into the steep basin and Russel asked if we had counted and classified them. *Yeah, right*! I requested another pass, but Jackson quickly interjected in a sphincter clenching voice, "Let's move on!"

I routinely requested Russel to locate hunting camps in remote areas prior to the big game seasons. Poachers use the quieter days before season to illegally kill game before the invasion of the hunting mass. Malicious first-degree poachers as well as opportunistic second-degree miscreants play this illicit game and, all too often, escape unreported or undetected. However, as my grapevine grew so did accounts of illicit pre-season misbehavior from the majority hunting good.

Early October 1982. It was the day before elk season, the eve of burning the candle at both ends when days are measured long before sunrises and long after sunsets. For devoted wardens the seemingly endless hunting seasons provide a challenging yet rewarding time of the year. On a whim I selected an area in a remote section of the west range to ride with my compadre, Wildlife Officer Howard Spear, one of the agency's essential horseman and only mule skinner. *(Howard's mule's name was Slim)*. Poaching problems revolving around party hunting and illegal license transfers were routinely reported in this area. Many hunters were granted quick access to the remote public lands by friends owning adjacent private land holdings. Other hunters and commercial outfitters accessed the back country from established trailheads, setting up traditional camps deep in the forested wilderness. Comfortably distanced from wildlife law, some developed a deceitful sense of security. Backwoods contacts before and during the season vigorously rattled the grapevine as word of a warden presence quickly bulleted through the hunting ranks. Patrolling on horseback dressed as hunters, was an effective and enjoyable means of working the backcountry, but we also rode in full uniform 'flying the colors' advertising our presence. I, anything but a cowboy, preferred cross-country trekking the back country as a loner on day trips or 2-3-night jaunts. However, I also enjoyed riding the backcountry with my compadres and their sturdy mountain steeds, each mount displaying unique personalities, and most (not all) seemingly enjoying the ride as much as the wardens.

So there we were, Spear and I riding as hunters through heavy timber in the crisp morning air domed by an unclouded translucent crystal blue sky. Steadily warmed by the radiating sun, we could not have marshalled a better mid-October Indian Summer day. The ability to cover miles with little physical effort absorbing the wilderness ambience in the name of essential warden work made it a very good job to take. Today's ploy entailed riding the south end of the Grizzly-Helena trail staying just below the snow line, west to Aqua Fria Lake paralleling Beaver Creek and returning to our vehicle via Butler Creek. Early snows made the starkly white high mountain tops contrast with the merging gun barrel blued timber below. Today the forest was remarkably quiet, only a whisper of a west wind; a serenity soon to be shattered by an invasion of armed nimrods. Detecting little sign of man or beast, other than a line of days-old horse tracks, it seemed we were being rewarded with nothing more than a quiet, atypical soul cleansing mountain ride. Or were we?

Late afternoon found us lazily relaxing, Old Sol melting us into a leafy crisp aspen patch. Like refusing to rise from an o'dark-thirty winter bed, we purposely ignored returning to our truck and trailer hidden below until voices over horse hooves rudely disturbed our placating spell. Two mounted hunters appeared with another on foot, hanging onto a horse's tail towing him up the mountain. Stopping to rest, one introduced himself as Headly Bone **Junior**, disclosing they were headed to their upper camp. He asked us to be on the lookout for his billfold lost somewhere on the trail below. Spear replied we were scouting for tomorrow's hunt (*we really were*) and would keep our eyes open. Thirty minutes later, the shrill bugle of a forlorn bull proclaiming the sadness of a waning rut, permeated the late afternoon forest quiet. Mesmerized by the persistent, trumpeting calls, our allure was shattered by six rapid rifle shots declaring the probable demise of the bull and a hard day's night for Spear and I. Mounting up we tracked towards the shots, staging at the junction of the Aqua Fria road. Senses on full alert, another man on horseback appeared stating he was returning to his hunting camp located several miles below. Identifying ourselves as wildlife officers investigating a poaching incident, I inquired if he was a member of a hunting party camped nearby. Checking the man's license identified one Headly Bone **Senior**, firmly denying any knowledge of such camp despite Spear specifying we had spoken with his son hours earlier. *The game is afoot!*, We trailed the discernably shaken man a half mile down the road before circling back to where we heard the shots. Darkness fell and I radioed our Sage Hen compadres for assistance and food, knowing they could easily maneuver a 4-wheel drive vehicle into our remote location. Pilot Russel was contacted and confirmed knowing our position and would arrive shortly after daylight. Several hours later Wildlife Officers Johnny Hobbs, Larry Budde, trainee Alan Czencush and wildlife administrator Harlan Riffel arrived with supplies. Not wanting to alarm the potential poachers we waived the comfort of a campfire. After pounding down a preponderance of junk food, Hobbs opened a can of mini tamales and we ravenously began devouring them. Finding the outer wrapping difficult to masticate, Hobbs assured they were perfectly edible corn shucks (discovering later each to be individually wrapped in wax paper). *DAMN!* Settling in for the night, Spear and I used saddles as pillows and stenchy saddle blankets as bedding while the others prepared to spend the night in the trucks. Once relatively comfortable (I fell sound asleep within minutes) I was rudely awakened when yet another man on horseback materialized, and, without a word, rode through our camp, flashlight in hand, the horse's hooves barely missing a very nervous Spear.

Sorely awakening well before daylight, I vigorously stretched my main frame hoping the stirrup indentations in my backside were not permanent. Soon, the familiar drone of the agency's single engine Cessna blissfully attracted our attention. Russel, making wide circles above us, easily located the camp and the dead bull, gut pile blazing ruby-red against a snowy background. Flushing the miscreants like a sharp-shin hawk on sparrow, he radioed, directing me towards the camp's smoldering campfire by flying directly over it while the others located the elk and began collecting evidence. Spear discovered a bullet placed on a nearby log, its lands and grooves shining liquid red declaring the identification of at least one poacher's rifle. Good wardensmanship necessitated implementing an airborne and ground battue to drive the poaching prey from cover. Russel radioed one hunter was headed towards camp and I soon watched the hunter cautiously circle twice before entering. Unpleasantly surprised, the hunter denied knowledge of an illegal elk. I picked off two more singles, who also played stupid while displaying the behavioral traits of guilt-ridden minds.

> *Truth be known, they had:*
> *"No more chance than a grasshopper in a hen house."*
> Festus Hagen Gunsmoke

Huddling up, the three began recovering traces of wisdom when we confiscated their firearms and packed up their camp; the seriousness of the situation sinking in as Russel made several wing tipping circles, his way of saying, 'Cheerio'.

Ironically, Officer Budde crossed paths with Bone Senior later that morning learning the faithful father, last night's midnight rider, futilely spent the night attempting to locate their high camp. Although his endeavor to 'Paul Revere' the warden's presence failed, he continued firing blatant lies to Budde's loaded questions, sticking to the story his son would never poach an elk. *Yeah, right!*

Spear and I rode horseback with Bone Junior and his accomplice Rowdy to their lower camp. As we vociferously discussed strategies for inventorying and storing their camp and boarding their horses until the case was settled, they began expressing their willingness to cooperate. Both were good men; young, overanxious opportunists whose moral compasses were shattered by a tenacious bull singing its way to their meat pole. Tics were scratched to each in the lower camp as Bone Jr.'s wayward father looked on. Once again, the wardens had set and run the traps, and the catch was good.

Bone Junior's final words were, "What did we hurt? We had expensive nonresident licenses and killed the bull within hours of opening day." Scowling, I answered, "Let's ask the hunters in the camp a mile above yours or the hunters walking in before daylight this morning.

Their chances to legally harvest the bull were stolen away. You are poachers, not hunters, cheating the sports critical element of fair chase promoting equal opportunity for all to harvest the bull, or not."

That evening, a progressively intoxicated Wildlife Officer, Talkin' Tom Lynch earned his namesake while incinerating fresh elk liver covered in onions at our Sage Hen office. Ritually drinking (mostly) good whiskey, we were entertained by Tom's endless yarns. However, the more he drank the more he yakked and, as Maker's made its Mark, the less we listened. Predictably, a call came in outlining an illegal incident involving several dead elk needing immediate attention.

Saddle up wardens

Poacher to warden: *"Why are you asking me such stupid questions?"*

Warden to poacher: *"I am just trying to level the playing field."*

LUNCH PREYERS

"On no subject are our ideas more warped and pitiable than on death. ... Let children walk with nature, let them see the beautiful blendings and communions of death and life, their joyous inseparable unity, as taught in woods and meadows, plains and mountains and streams of our blessed star, and they will learn that death is stingless indeed, and as beautiful as life, and that the grave has no victory, for it never fights."
John Muir

AN AIR STRIKE

When all was quiet and time permitted, I made a high priority of lingering in a secluded place to revel the vast landscape views proffered by the Bull Pen's mountain ranges. Lunch often provided me a bit of precious lone time to soak in life's wild; the in-betweens – my dining room with a view enjoying the plants and animals, and, my favorite, the wild birds. Death, always present in some form, played a critical role in my overall appreciation of the overwhelming power of life's instinctive drive to survive and thrive in the natural world.

And there I was, sitting in my truck enjoying lunch in a remote off-road campsite overlooking the upper North Fork Valley. Not a soul or vehicle at the Grizzly/Helena trailhead, I contemplated a wilderness jaunt into Blue and Twin Lakes. Detecting a shadow floating across a distant brushy slope, I grabbed my binoculars and traced a golden eagle effortlessly riding the mountain thermals. Following the shadow while munching a PB&J, I detected movement as it passed over a rocky outcropping. Mounting the 'Big Eye' on the side window I focused on a young yellow-bellied rock chuck on top of the outcrop soaking up the late morning sun. Soon the entire outcropping came alive with a family of marmots, several feeding in the grassy sage below. Zooming in on the basking pup I immediately witnessed it becoming air struck by the clamping claws of the eagle. *DAMN!* The golden 'war eagle", wings raised high in balancing flaps, paralyzed the struggling pup with its vise gripping razor-sharp talons. Forcefully yanking out one eye and then the other with its hooked beak, roots and all, the eagle paused momentarily until the young whistle pig expired, Launching off the rock with the weighty load in its claws, the eagle struggled with powerful wing beating strokes maintaining just enough elevation to clear the sagebrush draw before awkwardly crashing into the sidehill. In less than an hour the previously contented young marmot had been reduced to a head and feet attached to a sinewy backbone, and a scattered mess of bloody fur.

WAGH!

A GROUND STRIKE

And there I was, savoring a lunch of sardines in hot sauce, saltines, a Mountain Dew and a candy bar dessert during a lull in fishing activity on the North Delaney Butte Lake. My truck veiled in the lake's north-west corner along a high ditch bank, I enjoyed today's in-betweens, observing a Great Blue Heron stabbing small minnows along the lake shore below. Hearing the high-pitched whistles of Richardson's

Ground Squirrels, my attention was drawn to the ditch bank where a flurry of stampeding rodents rushed to their dens just ahead of their key enemy, a lowriding badger. Now it is well known badgers, a carnivorous predator fearing nothing, dine on these flea infested rodents at will. Add to its menu a plethora of prairie dogs, mice, voles, birds, eggs in bird nests, rabbits, grubs, insects, marmots etc. this weasel on steroids rarely suffers from hunger.

Watching the beast canter the ditch bank, paying no attention to the terrified ground squirrels, I figured the normally nocturnal beast was returning to a den site to attend its young. Suddenly, it stopped, pointed its nose skyward testing the air, and effortlessly augured its way into a squirrel den. Dirt flying in all directions, it rapidly disappeared into the enlarged hole. In a blink, it reappeared hard mouthing and devouring a small squirrel kit. Diving back into the nursery, it brought up another, then another, and another, reducing them into mangled, bite sized cutlets. Apparently stuffed, it disappeared into the sage while I pondered the entire spine-chilling event, lasting less than five minutes.

Some consider such observations savage. My avocation as an outdoorsman and wildlife officer provided opportunities to witness countless life and death scenarios involving everything between dragon flies capturing mosquitoes to coyotes killing fawn deer. I once witnessed a coyote, feasting on the afterbirth of a recently born angus calf, surrounded and fatally trampled by a group of mother cows. Death, Nature's heartless mechanism for sustaining life, must be witnessed before one can begin understanding its striking significance to the living.

"Death will come, always out of season."
Big Elk Omaho Chief

Local moron to warden: *"There are too many government regulations."*

Warden: *"I hear that a lot, but what exactly do you mean?"*

Local moron: *"Things will not get better until blood is shed. You know, like what happened during the Industrial Revolution!"*

LEFTY

The Bull Pen waterfowl season is quite popular because of the abundant populations and diversified species inhabiting large areas of public lakes and streams. Although relatively short because of early high elevational freeze up, the first weeks of the season attract many eager to train and work their dogs in relatively mild fall hunting conditions.

And there I was, the Big Eye focused on a hunter sitting in an island blind in a long, shallow wetland paralleling the east side of Lake John. The hunter, on good ground, was actively shooting ducks passing over his blind or landing in his decoys. Puzzled by the awkward handling of his wildly swinging shotgun, I was correspondingly dumbfounded by his accuracy, wilting most every duck he shot at. Midmorning, I was not surprised when the successful hunter loaded his decoys and brace of harvested waterfowl into his boat and began motoring towards me. Hidden in brush, I waited until he was near shore before making myself known. Audaciously, the hunter hit the bank hard enough to cause his chocolate lab to awkwardly hurl onto the bank. As I secured the boat's bow onto the bank, I noticed the hunter was missing his right arm, conflicting with his otherwise stunning rustic appearance. His wind-weathered wrinkled face blending through griz-zled grey whiskers epitomized the age-old hunter he was. A sprig of drake mallard curly arse feathers decorating his leather cap comple-mented his waxed canvas tan hunting coat and heavy green wool shirt. A lanyard draped over his neck displaying timeworn duck and goose calls, was decorated with collections of aluminum identification bands taken from the legs of ducks and geese harvested over countless years. Add the banged up yet irreplaceable humpback Browning Model 12 16 gauge shotgun draped over his weather checked LaCrosse hip boots and painted chipped Herter's decoys covered with a half dozen harvested ducks, composed a picture perfect image suitable for the front cover of a 1950's Field and Stream magazine. A blast from the past, I wished I had my camera. Hunting waterfowl tightly bound in the DNA of the lab and his master; both were in their happy place.

Exchanging greetings, the hunter started handing me his shotgun, BARREL POINTING DIRECTILY INTO MY MIDSECTION! Jumping to the side while pushing the barrel away with the edge of my hand, I immediately snarled out a badger biting ass ripping! Watching the hunter's head drop and his shoulders slump, it was evident I had wilted his ego like a decoyed goose absorbing a full load of Number 3 Steel Shot. My wrath whisking away his hunting spirit, a sense of remorse began gripping my conscience. Sitting before me was an elderly hunter whose blazing passion for waterfowl hunting was doused by my verbal barrage demeaning his carelessness. The black lab, sensing trouble, sat with a head cocking stare searching my eyes for acceptance. Talking shop to ease his pain, I praised his ability to iden-tify and harvest lower point ducks extending the number of birds allowed in his limit. Checking his license and stamps and limit of ducks, he was legal on all accounts. And yes, his legally plugged shotgun was fully loaded with three shells. The hunter, notably embar-rassed, responsibly accepted my reprimand.

My overly inquisitive thoughts running wild, I could not help asking how he had lost his arm. Taking a deep breath, he sighed a sound like a rusty oarlock and replied, "A hunting accident in a duck blind a long time ago!" I was wordlessly flabbergasted! He followed by expressing, "Although you may not find this funny, my friends call me Lefty!"

"A man's got to know his limitations."
Dirty Harry

Warden to Poacher: *"Would you please stick with the facts?"*

Poacher to Warden: *"This is my hunting story. There are no facts."*

CACHE REFUNDS

October 1978. And there we were, District Wildlife Manager Howard Spear and I patrolling Lone Pine Creek on a sun-drenched late October afternoon. Pre-season snowfall boosted early elk harvest but hunting pressure and fair weather pushed us into the ruggedly inaccessible high country or the lower private land sanctuaries. This highly predictable scenario when elk seemingly evaporate, persists as one of many mysteries haunting all but the highly seasoned hunters. Inclement weather not in the forecast, harvest would come only to those having the personal fortitude to track them down.

Leapfrogging the numerous camps along the Forest access road we intercepted five young Iowa hunters headed into Sage Hen for groceries. Asking for any tips where they may find elk I, recognizing their youthful grit, suggested hiking high into Red Canyon, a steeply jagged piece of timbered draws known to hold late season elk until forced out by heavy snows. As young men do, they smirkingly inquired what bars the Sage Hen women frequented. Not playing favorites, I suggested spending time in both the Elkhorn and the Stockmen's Bars, doubling their odds on scoring with the local wenches. Besides, both saloons were within crawling distance of each other. After proudly producing their pricey Non-Resident elk licenses we wished them luck and continued up the canyon.

Discovering the Hawkeye gang's empty camp next to a large beaver pond meadow and never by-passing an opportunity to search for miscreant spoor, we immediately struck scent; a wash pan sitting atop a log brimming with over 70 brook trout heads. *Release the hounds!* An additional 39 cleaned brook trout were stashed in a plastic bag under another log. Lone Pine Creek was well known for its trout laden beaver ponds scattered through the wide bottoms of the otherwise narrow stream canyon. The small, pink-fleshed char provide mouthwatering table fare, seventy (70!) fish heads declaring the flavorsome bounty the beaver ponds' tendered the young men. Their camp offered a spectacular view of fingers of aspen and spruce penetrating up the scarping hardscrabble towards the sky-scraping crags provide a breathtaking serenity treasured by so many. Knowing the testosterone driven 'Hawkeyes' intent to sample the local culture would hold them in Sage Hen until the bar's last call, I contacted another officer to locate them at Corkle's Market to see if they had fishing licenses (they did not) and send them back to camp.

The boys returned within the hour, their long donkey faces expressing full comprehension of their predicament. Ashamed but surprisingly honest, they readily confessed that not purchasing fishing licenses was a risk taken to save money. Friends and family hunting here in years past advised them the great fishing did not require a fishing license because they had never been contacted by a warden. *Oops!*

Predictably, the gang expressed shrewd interest in the economics of their misdeeds, opening the door for my greatly rehearsed lesson of Fish Poaching 101. Detailing the fine for not having fishing licenses was $50 per man ($250) plus the penalties for illegal fish calculated at $35 per man for the first and $10 for each additional trout ($1115). Piscatory math totaled a whopping $1365! I explained the cost for purchasing five day fishing licenses would have been less than $100 for all five, money used for fish management and law enforcement. The extremely generous limit of eighteen brook trout per license afforded ample campsite feasts plus the opportunity to legally transport their limits back to Iowa.

The pie-eyed, droopy jawed nimrods, now crapping down both legs, shared the pain of counting their coffers. Suddenly a grey jay, commonly called a camp robber, pluckily landed on the wash pan and stole a fish head. Flying upwards into the thick branches of a nearby spruce the bird instinctively cached the contraband. Assessing the situation, one quick witted Hawkeye proclaimed, "There goes ten bucks! How about giving the jays more time for reducing our fine?" Everyone laughed except the one making the statement. He was dead serious. Officer Spear chuckled this was not the bird's first fine reducing theft. As the jay chortled his good fortune, we assessed a cut-rate fiscal transaction based on the five's combined net worth, only charging each for not having licenses. The boys willingly paid the fines and were issued receipts for full payment of their misdeeds. Stung but not smitten, all promised to purchase the appropriate licenses in the future and graciously thanked the us for their considerate professionalism. These were good young men, their honesty and integrity rare gems in a warden's world. Recognizing youth as hunting's greatest resource, I mapped out a shortcut into Red Canyon asking in return for a promise to report any wildlife crimes they may witness. And the very next year, after harvesting two bulls, the boys reported witnessing a poaching incident involving a well- known camp of men and mules in a very remote part of Red Canyon, resulting in making hay on a major wildlife crime.

Hoka Hey!

SLED DOGS

Legally hunting coyotes provides worthy sport hunting opportunities, a means for reducing livestock predation, and the economic benefits of selling their pelts. During times of high fur values, even ranch women driving kids to school, packed a rifle. Inevitably, the percentage of illicit coyote killing increased proportionately with fur prices. Chasing, shooting from, running over, smothering, and/or bludgeoning coyotes while riding snowmobiles became routine amusement for a small group of coyote killers, economic gain erasing their legal or moral compass. Captured violators often pled the big bad wolf defense; what is the problem with using any means to kill a predator that preys on wildlife and livestock? My answer was simple; it is against the law; killing wildlife using motorized vehicles is considered inhumane by the majority hunting public and, of course, the mainstream of those who do not hunt. Believe me, as a witness to this behavior, it is not a spectator sport and inflicts tremendous negative impact to the image of sport hunting. This I know, there will always be coyotes, hunted or not, playing an integral predatory role in the complex food chain in the Bull Pen's wild.

While it is true coyotes, mountain lions, and bears routinely kill livestock, landowners and their employees are legally permitted to protect their personal property by almost any means possible (including federally permitted aerial gunning). Unfortunately, the 'protection of private property' law is often utilized as an excuse to chase down and kill coyotes using snowmobiles, often without regarding private land trespass or crossing onto public lands.

During the winter months, we received multiple landowner complaints reporting trespassing snowmobilers chasing coyotes, breaking down fences, scattering cattle, and recklessly shooting from their machines. Bull Pen citizens, hunters and nonhunters alike, strongly vocalized their intolerance of hunting from snowmobiles. The number of complaints, greatly exceeding the sum of miscreants captured, tallied a familiar list of usual suspects and their vehicles to search out while on patrol. Many of those apprehended were two or even threepeat offenders, having shared our pens on a variety of wildlife violations, proffering a warden cat and mouse game of chasing, catching, tic scratching, turning them loose to catch another day!

Concealed on ridges scanning the valley with the Big Eye, binoculars and listening for noisy machines, we not only made some good cases, but also high-quality contacts warning motorized coyote slayers the wardens were watching:

Witnessing one repeat offender chasing coyotes with his brother, members of the Earp gang, I met him attempting to load his snowmobile into the back of his truck. The guilt laden man, crapping razor blades knowing a ticket was imminent, crashed his machine through the vehicles rear window!

Another noteworthy incident involved snaring Meat, the Chex gang's paternal leader and repeat offender, for chasing, shooting from, and killing a coyote from his snowmobile. Interviewing Meat at the Sheriff's Office, his wife questioned why we constantly picked on her husband and sons. My attempt to explain because they devoted so much time afield violating wildlife law increased their odds of warden capture, was interpreted as they were easy to catch, and did not go over well with either Meat or Mother Chex. She, normally an angelic lady, rewarded me with an aschew imprinted in my mind to this day! Members of the Chex gang were later apprehended chasing a coyote when I was flying our winter big game helicopter census, adding to their ever-increasing file of wildlife misdemeanors.

MOTHER OUTLAW

January 2, 1982. There I was, patrolling the Bull Pen's west side for coyote hunting activity, when I received a call from the Sheriff's Office regarding snowmobilers chasing coyotes west of Sheep Ridge. The incident, reported by the good senator's wife, Jerrilyn, a vigilant, reliable witness intolerant of wildlife violations who witnessed a trespassing snowmobiler chasing and running over a coyote on their ranch property.

Paralleling the North Fork River, I spotted some individuals loading snowmobiles onto trailers and pulled off the road. Discovering they were members of a family branded and deeply rooted in the cultural history of the Bull Pen, I also recognized my badge carrying friend and colleague Gusty Fomentor, a charismatic, witty, fun seeking joker, married into this local family. Uncharacteristically, Gusty remained silent while his wife and in-laws played busy loading their machines. *Somethings amiss!*

Gusty, an employee of the Arapaho National Wildlife Refuge and a well-respected member of our wildlife enforcement corps, carried both state and federal credentials. Actively engaged in our enforcement efforts, Gusty's presence disallowed my suspicion they were involved in the reported illicit activity. A dedicated coyote hunter/caller like myself, I knew Gusty was legally and morally against utilizing snowmobiles for chasing down any wildlife.

Asking if they witnessed anyone chasing coyotes with snowmobiles, all remained abnormally quiet. Gusty's face bearing a gut punched grimace, his eyes voiced a lingo familiar to anyone experienced in law enforcement, good wardensmanship kicked in and I elected to back off. Making clear I was calling it a day to watch college football, I winked at Gusty and headed towards Sage Hen, anticipating a phone call.

Arriving home, the call came before I had time to change out of my uniform. Gusty's mother-in-law, Ginger, on the line, caught me off guard as I listened to her boldly confess to killing a coyote with her snowmobile. Rendezvousing with the family at their home, Ginger deviously apologized for placing Gusty and I into such an awkward position knowing our dedication to enforcing wildlife law. Guiltlessly affirming her misdeed, she brazenly proclaimed she would do it all over again, her hatred of coyotes arising from the costly predation inflicted during their family's sheep ranching days. Shedding her guilt eased the tension, especially Gusty's, while I lectured trespassing while chasing, and killing a coyote posing no threat to personal property was not only illegal, but also considered inhumane by the hunting good, Gusty and I included!

Peculiarly, this case was initiated by a principled woman honorably defending the rights of a coyote by turning in a law-breaking woman believing killing vermin by any means is a justifiable, God given right; the only good coyote is a dead coyote. This I know, as both a hunter and a witness to such misbehavior, the law and morality my compass, I, too, steadfastly defend the coyote!

Press hard Ginger, there are five copies!

ONE DEER SHORT

September 1975. Muzzleloader Season. Independence Mountain, located on the northern end of the Bull Pen, is a hodge-podge of sage, aspen, pine, perennial streams, and meadows supporting abundant wildlife populations. Accessible by a maze of gravel, dirt, and two track roads, it is a year-round recreational destination for camping, sightseeing, and touring in 4-wheel drive vehicles, ATVs and snowmobiles. Seasoned during the fall with blended batches of hunters, the mountain provides the essential ingredients for making warden stew.

There I was, cresting the mountain's summit and locating a deserted tent camp wrapped in a gold-plated aspen grove, I decided to patrol nearby and wait for the return its occupant(s). Hours later, rounding a curve on a narrow, rough two track enclosed in thick timber, I nearly collided head on with a fast-moving jeep transporting a deer on its hood. The driver and I staring in a time ticking Clint Eastwood style standoff, he made the first move by fumbling with something at his side. Quickly exiting I approached the open jeep, interrupting his attempt to tear the carcass tag from a deer license. Colorado law requires a hunter to sign, date, and remove the carcass tag immediately after harvesting a big game animal, and attach it to the carcass for transport or storage. Inspecting the license, issued to one Dudley DoWrong, nervous as a sheep on tic dip day, I found it valid for hunting deer in Game Management Units 6&7. Independence Mountain, his camp, and the deer on his jeep located in GMU 161, Dudley had some explaining to do. Returning to his camp I helped Dudley hang the deer from a meat pole while firing rounds of loaded inquiries regarding his hunt. Giving him rein, I listened as he twitchily devised a dialogue of killing the deer this morning above the North Platte River in the Teepee Creek drainage (GMU 6 where his license was valid) and dragging it nearly two miles to his vehicle. A rough start considering the buck's hide, hair undisturbed, showed no evidence of being pulled out of what I knew to be a very steep, rocky canyon. Not to mention he accomplished this task before noon (Teepee Creek was an hour's drive from his camp)! Advising I also hunted Teepee Creek, his guttural grimace tattled deceit. *Release the hounds!* Casting doubt, I requested Dudley to accompany me to the kill site and he, asserting the difficulty of relocating it, reluctantly offered to try. *Really!* Rattling his cage, I clarified he need only show me where he parked, allowing me to backtrack the drag mark a short distance, to validate his story.

Dudley riding shotgun while I drove down Independence Mountain's winding, gravel road, his silence and fidgety behavior confirmed we were on a fool's errand. In a few bone jarring miles, DoWrong's inner turmoil exploded into a resounding confession of killing his buck in the wrong unit. Rationalizing the mountain's abundant roads provided great opportunities for harvesting deer, Dudley transitioned from a proficient backwoods' hunter into a driven, dyed in the wool road hunter. Expressing the familiar liberation of one haunted by a guilty conscience, Dudley apologized for his malicious wrongdoing. Driving back to camp, DoWrong challenged my ability to prove his buck was killed in the wrong unit.

Understand, wildlife officers' catalogue well-rehearsed one liners for certain situations whenever they arise. Avoiding Dudley's discernable anxiety and unachievable hunting tale, I, without pause, answered, "I made a deer count this morning and came up one buck short." Wide-eyed and mouth gaping, Dudley gullibly answered, "Really?" Momentarily bewildered, Dudley slowly appreciated my tongue-in-cheek humor. Insisting I reveal what gave me the confidence to prove his guilt, I replied, "Knowledge and experience!" While DoWrong mulled my response, would you believe his hunting partner, Flint Frizzen, drove into camp. Discovering Flint's deer license was also valid for Game Management Unit 6, I commended him for not killing a deer. Noticeably confused, the frazzled Frizzen watched me scratch Dudley's tic, confiscate his illegal deer and clarify his deer hunt was over. Before leaving, I strongly suggested moving their camp to Unit 6.

Go long warden!

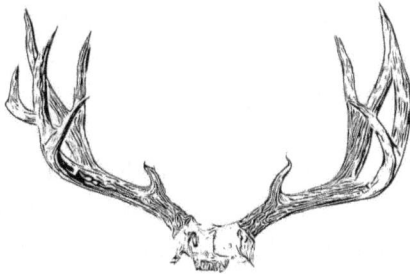

SECOND SHIFT

July 25, 1979. Mosquitoes! Clouds of drill biting pests swelled like winged dust as I pulled off the Forest Road into thick willows to hide my truck. The blood sucking spitfires had all but disappeared in the lowlands as ranchers dried their hay meadows for harvest but endured in ruthless hordes throughout the forest. *Oh, if they were only butterflies!* Before exiting my truck, I painted myself with a primer coat of "Cutter" cream followed by a full body aerosol spray of the same once outside of the vehicle. Daily coats of 'bug dope' caused me to wonder if DEET ran through my veins.

Today's plan was working Teal Lake, a five-acre kettle pond concealed in pine on National Forest Lands on the Bull Pen's west side. Teal and her lily pad cohort Tiago were peacefully sequestered below the gnarly granites of Rabbit Ears Peak. Heavily stocked with hatchery raised, eight to twelve-inch rainbow trout offers sure-fire attractions for those keeping more than their fair share; a place where I scratched many tics, including the Grande Coupe of 100 or more fish over the limit! I planned on spending the entire day, waiting on the lake's Second Shift where scoundrels catch their morning limits, returning in the afternoon to catch their second. Several calls regarding illegal activity at both lakes sending me here, I was particularly interested in one from an anonymous lady about an older man catching an over-abundance of trout using young kids and the licenses of others as cover. Her report detailed trout were cached in coolers and camper freezers scattered throughout the campground to con any curious wardens. Documenting campsite locations and vehicle license plate numbers, the informant accurately described a clan of poaching huckleberry's needing picked.

Sporting binoculars and a backpack, I rimmed the campground and easily located the reported campsites. Squirrels tattling my presence, their annoying chatter falling on the deaf ears of an unperceiving public. Retreating, I bushwhacked the north end of the lake, stopping momentarily along an aspen meadow to watch and to listen. Stealthily stepping through the lush vegetation, I felt the swooshing wing beats behind my head a fraction of a second before a Goshawk angrily shrieked, "yik, yik, yik." *Holy Shit!* Often bragging I fear nothing, I jerked wildly and all but crapped my drawers. Taking refuge behind a large quaker, the blue forest darter returned to its stick nest built high in the aspen crowns. Through binoculars I could see the fuzzy heads of two goshawk chicks protruding from the top of the nest as the fiery red eyes of the female lasered through mine. Any movement, even when I sneak-peeked around the tree, launched an instant aerial assault by the feathered missile, armed with beak and claw. I scolded myself for failing to heed the wild's subtle warnings as moments before the attack I heard to the prattle of teasing crows undoubtedly harassing the goshawk. *Yeah, and I made fun of clueless campers.* Regaining my composure, I slowly backed out and took another route into the lake.

Glassing the lake, sure as slime on fish, I spotted an old man surrounded by a herd of kids stampeding up and down the bank. Three women basking in lawn chairs watched Gramps and a middle-aged man counting trout on six separate stringers. Gramps unwittingly announced to this hidden warden the total count was 72, a precisely calculated limit for five licensed adults and eight kids. The kids began throwing rocks at a flock of gluttonous gulls retrieving the fish guts Gramps pitched into the lake. I watched the adults, each carrying a trout laden stringer and a lawn chair, head towards camp while the kids buzzed around like so many bees. Lady Luck permitted detecting the group' morning catch firsthand and now I would embrace her sister Patience, and tenaciously lie in wait for their expected reappearance. Time shared investments in waiting out fish mongers payed large dividends in their capture. Knowing the odds of the old man's return weighed heavily in my favor, linger I must.

Before settling into my pine clad lair, I sprayed on an additional coat of Cutter, paying close attention to my back, neck, pant cuffs, and the surrounding vegetation. *Oh, for a mosquito shedding breeze!* Sitting, I assessed my ambit, a perfectly camouflaged observatory of the lake's entire shoreline. Cradled in a large fir's steel tough, serpentine roots anchoring it like a living dead-man, there I was, a woods copse excitedly anticipating my next adventure. My grey uniform shirt melded into the mottled grey bark while a wall of low saplings shaded my face and blended nicely with my green jeans. Now I would sit and wait, knowing Nature would compress the hours with continual wonders, proffering the difference between killing time and living it!

Eating my sack lunch - a Mountain Dew, wheat crackers and cracker barrel cheese, a tin of smoked oysters and lots of water, I listened to sporadic thermals puffing woodwind duets through conifer boughs blending with the rhythm of leaf pattering aspen. A kinglet, wing flicking through the lower pine boughs near my feet, royally displayed his diminutive ruby crown. A wren rasped out its song weaving through and disappearing into the marsh grass. An unseen hermit thrush echoed a lyrical opus of spiraling notes, answered by the waning songs of others across the forest amphitheater. An ant dragging a large beetle in clamping jaws, strength beyond anyone's imagination, caught my eye. Then, at arm's length, a rusty-red dragonfly made a solid six-point landing on the terminal shoot of a pine sapling, its smashing jaws masticating a cranefly it snatched from mid-air. Biding time recording fishermen activity, I found no signs of illegal activity. It was a good day.

It was mid-afternoon when the lake's serenity was broken by the stomping feet and nattering babble of the young mavericks, trailed by the limping old man carrying a bundle of rods in one hand and a tackle box in the other. Pops soon arrived with the three women carrying lawn chairs. In no time, the men worked six baited rods propped on forked willow sticks stuck into the shoreline mud. The highly predictable second shift had arrived, anxious and ready to take it to the limit, one more time. The kids ranged in age from a diaper clad toddler to a boy and a girl pushing ten to twelve years old fishing with their own rods. One tyke began crying when Gramps scolded him for tangling his line into a soft-ball sized mass of entwined monofilament, a bird's nest of eagle proportions. While the men tightened lines and adjusted poles the eldest girl asked how many fish they could catch. Gramps, without hesitation again announced, "Seventy-two!" I gave Gramps an 'A' in math as eight unlicensed kids taking four trout each plus eight trout for the five licensed adults equaled, once again, a precise count of 72.

Not today, old man. Gramps was on his way to becoming a paying, carbon copy carrying member of my ever-increasing club of miscreant outdoorsmen. The two older kids were catching their own trout but the younger ones soon lost interest and disappeared into the forest. Pops returned to his lawn chair while Gramps picked up the slack and ran the gauntlet of constantly twitching rods. Gramps was in his zone, casting, reeling in, baiting, casting out, catching and stringing fish, a lot of fish. Normally enjoying my encounters with the elderly, most appreciating the opportunity to spend their well-earned retirement basking in the great outdoors. But the aged also possess a stereotype of frustrated, grumpy wretches violating wildlife laws as a rite of passage into the ranks of senior citizenry. Perhaps recognizing aging as 100% fatal, they faced mortality with a vengeance, pilfering everything possible to make up for lost times. Today, Gramps fit this mold perfectly, a man whose goals were to catch fish, conspire to fool the wardens and bitch. I could see he was highly proficient at all three. The fish would be too small, the licenses cost too much, and the wardens were crooked. A burning cigarette constantly dangling from pursed lips, his raspy voice yowled like gravel rolling in phlegm so characteristic of a chain smoker. His piercing eyes, heavy brow, square jaw, zigzagging nose, large hands and long arms protruding from a sleeveless shirt, I imagined him to be an aged boxer. He wore a greasy dark blue Marine Corps baseball cap with the words *"The Few, The Proud"* embroidered in gold on its brim, an accurate description of this obviously confident man. Pops called him RED, perhaps because of the rusty locks protruding from the rear of his baseball cap. Gramps cursed a flock of stiff-winged pelicans sailing into the lake, grumbling how these trout hungry pests stole fish away from the public. Pelicans indeed have an uncanny ability of arriving right behind the hatchery trucks, as if spotting them while soaring high above the lakes and streams.

Today, I would not permit the gang to reach their goal of 72 trout, allowing Gramps to 'ripen' a bit more before hand picking the huckleberry. I would be his last bite. Paying little attention to the others, after tallying the old codger's sixteenth trout, I stiffly crept out of my lair and stalked within twenty yards of the group. Making my presence known, I enjoyed the wrath worn on all their faces, as they absorbed the threat of an incoming warden. Recovering, Gramps swaggered my way to talk face to face. Prepared for the inevitable oratory of concocted alibis, orchestrated lies and ranting rationalizations that undoubtedly would stream from the old geezer's mouth, I was not disappointed. He promptly began weaving loosely stitched fabrications beginning with a man he observed catching bucket loads of trout, grumbling there were no wardens around to catch him. Familiar Gramps was deflecting my attention from him I returned fire, declaring I was investigating a detailed report involving an older man fishing with several adults and a gang of kids and keeping too many trout. Out of nowhere the younger kids appeared and sat down on the bank. The older boy asked if my gun was real and if I was a cop. One of the women told him to hush. The kids, somehow sensing trouble, silently stared at me in awe. I announced witnessing them keep exactly 72 trout this morning. To reinforce my statement, I scolded Gramps and Pops for throwing fish entrails into the lake and the kids for throwing rocks at the gulls. Stirred but not shaken, Gramps flatly denied it all while Pops began slinking towards their camp. I stopped him in his tracks by sternly requesting fishing licenses. With licenses and stringers in hand I escorted the gang to their campsite. Laying the fish on a picnic table, I warned the stringers held more trout than the legal limit of those I observed fishing. Checking coolers and ice boxes, finding only a half dozen freshly cleaned trout and no frozen trout at all, I questioned the whereabouts of the trout caught earlier this morning. Gramps, pondering who snitched them out, flagrantly cried foul denouncing my accusations as deceitful acts of entrapment. Shooting feathers out of the old buzzard's wing, I stated I needed to check the groups other campsites. Realizing he was slow drifting up the proverbial Shit Creek, Gramps began searching for a paddle. I tactfully offered him the steering oar of speaking the truth.

Honesty: The best of all the lost arts."
Mark Twain

Gramps unremorsefully revealed the additional fish had been taken to his camp at the Hidden Lakes Campground. At his camp, I found an additional fifty trout, half of them frozen, bringing the total fish count to one-hundred and twenty-four; fifty-two over the entire camps legal limit of seventy-two trout. That is if I graciously awarded every individual in camp, (diapered kids, toddlers, licensed adults), whether they caught their fish or not, their legal limits.

Gramps unruly conscience once again taking him into fowl waters, he explained it was his understanding they could catch and keep one bag limit per day and legally possess two daily bag limits of trout. I tightened my grip, harshly informing the spellbound audience as much as the delinquent Gramps. "Two limits? What are you talking about? You have caught four or five limits just today! The bag and possession limits are the same, just as they have been for decades." Gramps, now hand-tied, and whip-finished in front of his family, I rewarded his audacity by stating he would receive the ($545.00) ticket for all 52-illegal trout! His arrogance shredded like bark on an antler rubbed tree, Gramps sobbed a story of wanting to be remembered by his kin as a highly skilled fisherman. *"Death does not a hero make!"* Reminding him a poacher is not a great fisherman, I donned my pack, lifted the arduous stringers of trout, and headed towards my truck. On the way I passed a middle-aged woman sitting in a campsite who waved and mouthed a 'thank you'. I waved back and mouthed a 'you're welcome'.

"So let it be written, so let it be done!"
Ramses II

THE GOLD DUST BOYS

HOOKERS??? Gazing through the 'Big Eye', I focused on what simply could not be. Just when I thought I had seen it all, something happened so out of the ordinary, it had to be documented.

There I was, parked on a wide curve overlooking the Encampment River, zooming in on three individuals trekking the riverbank. An abnormally warm afternoon, I quickly devoured lunch, I initially believed the trio to be fisherman. Imagine my surprise when I realized I was scoping three scantily clothed, makeup wearing, fancy haired 'ladies' dressed in high heels, hot pants, black patterned hose, and translucent low-cut blouses exposing enough cleavage to rouse a dead priest! Now understand, this section of the Encampment River called Hog Park, was allegedly named for the whores serving the substantial number of tie hacks in the area cutting railroad ties in the early 1900's. Confined in a small cabin, the tie hacks derogatorily called these back-woods beauties, "Hogs".

Being a curious fellow, an integral component of good wardensman-ship, I drove into the Park, headed upriver past the historical, still functional Guard Station, and discovered an overwhelmingly decked out elk camp exceeding anything I have ever witnessed! Imagine top shelf cases of liquor and beer stacked head high against two luxurious motor homes, large wall tents, cords of neatly piled firewood, a gigantic flaming campfire, several generators, and strings of multi-colored electric globes surrounding the entire campsite. Slack-jawed, I was stunned when 'My Ladies' swaggered into camp. **Hello!** Welcoming me with smiles, mindful their voluptuous appearance commanded my undivided attention, one softly whispered she had never been contacted by a 'forest ranger'. *Well, I had never been this close to an upper-class camp whore, either!* All three lavishly decorated in silver and gold foofaraw, wafting sinfully exotic scents, this camp embodied the 'Unholy Grail' of elk hunting brothels!

Naively embarrassed, I attempted to speak without staring at the double breasted, long legged, Vegas grade prostitutes. *YEAH RIGHT!* Undoubtedly making a complete fool out of myself, I initiated an awkward departure when two extremely intoxicated men drove into camp. Walking to the driver's side window, I found them trading gulps from a whiskey bottle, happy as a pair of lab puppies. Requesting them to step out, I was given permission to inspect their rifles, no doubt both believing I wanted to admire their custom-made firearms. Minds and bodies loaded, so were their guns, a safety violation taken very seriously by Colorado law enforcement. Their non-resident licenses identified middle aged brothers, calling themselves the 'Gold Dust Boys." Ingot residing in Nevada and Ore from Las Vegas, both became alarmingly agitated when advised I would be issuing citations for their loaded firearms. Reminding them they were facing possible charges of driving and hunting under the influence of alcohol, they quickly calmed down. One, shuffling a wallet packed with large bills in my face asked what it would take to forego charging them. Having rode this horse before, I replied my job was worth nothing less than a million dollars! Both staring as if I was deranged, their drunken looks of bewilderment made me chuckle out loud.

As I scratched out the tics one asked if this was not the best f......g camp I had ever seen. Eyeballing the lady stirring a pot of chili like no other cook I envisioned, I had to agree. Paying their fines with large bills, it was apparent my presence and even the tics were as much a part of their hunt as were the condiments of hookers, booze and the sensual comfort provided by the elaborate motor homes. Harvesting elk obviously not high on their list, I provided advice on places they should hunt if they genuinely wanted an elk. After collecting the fines, I jumped into my pickup, noticing the 'Boys' were already eye humping their campmates. Honestly, I do not make these things up!

One could say this is a historical tale of rags to riches, shabby early 20th century whores replaced by high pedigreed Vegas prostitutes; Hog Park harlotry spanning over twelve decades. Others may view this event as an extension of the old proverb, "you cannot make a silk purse out of a sow's ear"; a hooker is a hooker, prostitution is prostitution, no matter who, when or where. Sexual commercialism is what it is. This I know, the Gold Dust Boy's elk camp assured Hog Park's legendary namesake fulfilled its age-old reputation.

Oh, those thrilling days of yesteryear!
Hi Yo, Silver! Away!

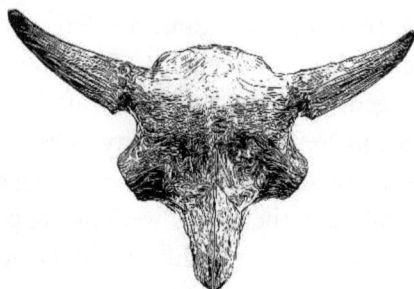

Warden to poacher: *"I am courting you."*

Poacher to warden: *"I beg your pardon!"*

Warden to poacher: *"You have no choice but to go to court, our judge really needs to hear your story."*

TRACKING BIGFOOT

After the initial reintroduction and subsequent population success of moose in the Bull Pen, my comrades and I unfortunately found ourselves spending considerable time investigating illegal moose kills. Probing spoiled and/or bony, melted down carcasses of illegally killed moose was a low point of an otherwise successful wildlife management program. Most illegal kills triggered by a hunter mistaking a moose for an elk were abandoned, offering little or no evidence leading us to the culprit(s). Mapping the kill site and leaving the carcass to be recycled by Nature, we faced the troubling frustration of an unsolved mystery. However, given the slightest clue, even a hunch, we often were able to weave the frayed ends of 'nothing' into strings we could pull and track down a few offenders.

Reviewing my file of moose shooters, I can honestly say all, whether turned in by themselves or others, or proficiently tracked down by wardens, were embarrassingly humiliated by losing their ability to identify their quarry. I never investigated an illegal kill where the shooter intentionally shot a moose. Continuing my interest in analyzing the psyche of illegal moose shooters, I add the following story to those scribed in the First Cache

November 1987. East Fork of Willow Creek. There I was, staring at what was undoubtedly the largest human boot print I ever encountered. Granted, my 8½s are considered small, placing my boot inside this behemoth Vibram imprint in frozen snow revealed 3 inches of free space at the toe and another 2 inches along the sides and back. *DAMN!* The crime scene was just as incredible - a large antlered, illegally shot bull moose abandoned in thinned timber next to a gravel Forest Service logging road. Boot prints around a large tree stump indicated where 'BigFoot' had been sitting. A partially consumed beer can, and the expended cartridge of a unique rifle casing (Norma 7.65 ARG) nearby tattled the tale of the bull's demise. The shell casing indicated BigFoot shot from the stump, killing the bull at close range (less than thirty yards) as it walked on the road towards him. Boot tracks revealed BigFoot and another individual drug the hefty carcass off the road into the timber and futilely attempted concealing it with brush. *Like hiding an elephant in city park!*

Wildlife Officers Kirk Snyder and Keith Kahler, receiving the early morning report of the dead bull from a concerned hunter, were first on the scene. When Officer Larry Budde and I joined them, Snyder disappointedly announced the 800 pound plus bull, killed the previous day, had spoiled, its meat unfit for human consumption. Taking photos and dragging the carcass out of sight of the road, we drove to a nearby camp and met Victor Hawkeye, the vigilant hunter who discovered the dead bull early this morning and contacted the Sheriff's office. With detailed accuracy, Hawkeye provided an approximate time the bull was killed (having driven through the area periodically the previous day), and a description of a vehicle he observed in the area - a milk chocolate 1979 Chevrolet 2-wheel drive pickup with an ATV in the back, a long, white CB radio antenna arched over and attached to the rear of the pickup. He also indicated the pickup, licensed in Iowa, was equipped with oversize mud grip tires. *WOW!*

Splitting up, we began contacting hunting camps and hunters without success. After dark, Officer Budde and I returned to Sage Hen to check motels and restaurants while Snyder and Kahler widened their search area. As luck would have it, we discovered a vehicle perfectly matching the informant's description parked at the Chedsey Motel. The snow-covered parking area also revealed BigFoot's boot prints. We snooped along the rooms and amazingly found a pair of Sasquatch sized boots in front two adjacent doors. Knocking on one, we silenced a roomful of Iowa hunters and, following a short round discussing rifle calibers, one awkwardly admitted his father had accidentally killed a bull moose on Willow Creek. *Hoka Hey!* Stating his father and mother were in the adjacent room, Budde knocked, and we were invited in by an elderly man. His wife, sitting on one bed busily knitting, the old gent sat down on the other. Nodding to his son, BigFoot stated he wanted to speak to us alone. As time took a break, warden logic told Budde and I to give him a moment. Pulling up his shirt with a hand the size of a pie plate, he traced a large scar on his belly with braut sized fingers and declared he was dying of cancer. *Oh boy!* Sitting before us was the withered shell of what was once a large, vibrant man. Beginning his woeful tale, his weathered, oaken face, punctuated with pain and embarrassment, and sad eyes probing through thickly knitted brows, spoke louder than his noble confession. Admitting having observed several moose on this hunting trip, BigFoot struggled explaining why he mistook the moose for a large antlered elk. With a deep breath, he meekly expressed he truly thought he was shooting a large bull elk and deserved whatever punishment his misdeeds demanded. As good women do, BigFoot's wife, seeking to end her husband's humiliation, asked the cost of and the procedure for paying the fines. While I scratched the tic, Budde spoke with BigFoot, explaining his mistake should not have ended after shooting the moose. Field dressing and notifying us immediately would have not only allowed us to salvage the meat, but also greatly reduced his charges, fine amounts, and eased his conscience. The look on BigFoot's face told all, killing the moose would haunt his mind forever.

Understand, this is not a tale of highly skilled wardens tracking down a bad man, an illegal poacher. Making the case was not rocket science, it had all but fallen into our laps. This is a story of an aged, proudly honorable man, nearing the end of his hunting trail, who made a tragic error in judgment. Age, poor health, and his drive for success blocked BigFoot's ability to perceive what was actually there and comprehend what he wanted to see.

Rendezvousing at our office later that evening, we asked ourselves whether BigFoot should continue hunting. All agreed he should never again hunt alone. In this case, however, Bigfoot's cancer would answer the question for him.

The full measure of a hunter cannot be judged by one single act. A hunter's heart, guided by his or her conscience, drums a lifetime ballad of conduct justly weighed by the lyrics of the entire song.

SHP

SMOKING GUN

O ctober 1989. There we were. My son Marc riding shotgun enjoying the opportunity to share a day working the chaotic elk season. Marc, a college freshman home for the weekend, we both were adjusting to his moving away from home (me more than him).

Heading north towards Camp Creek at first light, a call from the Sheriff's Office turned us south to investigate a report of an illegally licensed Tennessee hunter packing out a 4-point bull elk on private land near Spicer Peak. The informant, a good hunter having no tolerance for hunter misbehavior, regularly provided credible information leading to the capture of outdoor miscreants. Knowing Wildlife Officers Tim Davis and Steve Steinert were patrolling near Spicer Peak, I contacted them to keep their eyes open for a anyone transporting a bull elk. During previous hunting seasons I uncovered criminal mischief involving a Spicer Peak outfitter leasing private land. Looking forward to invading the fallacious security he believed the locked gates proffered, I accelerated south, racing past the well camouflaged State Patrolman, radioing a humble justification I was 'in pursuit'!

Leaving the highway and fast tracking the dirt roads below Spicer Peak, Officers Davis and Steinert radioed they intercepted the alleged violator, provided their location, and would hold him until I arrived.

Easily finding them, Davis handed me the hunter's Colorado resident elk license and Tennessee driver's license, both issued to one Sham Prater. Sham, sucking a mouthful of air through a cigarette, exhaled more smoke than a cold winter nights chimney. Marc, notably captivated, sat on my vehicle's tailgate to watch and listen. Greeting Sham with a smile, I pointed out his elk license indicated he had resided in Colorado for one year and asked if that was true. Stating it was, I asked why he had not registered in his vehicle in Colorado or acquired a Colorado driver's license, both required by law. Sham audaciously concocted a cock and bull (primarily bull) tale of not having time to do either, stating he provided the license agent with a year of rent receipts to prove his Colorado residency. Conceding knowing the law, he promised he would take care of his licensing illegalities when he returned home. As I persistently tossed verbal boulders regarding his residency (how long had he lived in the apartment written on his license, who was his landlord etc.) Sham's awkward responses sank him deeper into a deceitful quagmire.

Floundering, Sham unwisely requested we phone the number printed on his elk license and his girlfriend would verify his residency. The Sheriff's Office making the call, the poor girl, having no idea how to deflect the deputy's well-rehearsed questions, failed miserably. Sham's lifeline severed, I advised him to relax, smoke another cigarette, and give considerable thought before answering any more questions. Walking over to Marc, I asked if he believed Sham's story. He said he did and felt sorry for the troubled man. Asking Marc to count the number of cigarette butts surrounding Sham, I suggested he continue eavesdropping.

Resuming my interrogation, I found Sham still shaken but less stirred. Reviewing the number of charges and the cost associated with them, I made him an offer he could not refuse; his truths for my leniency. With a deep breath, Sham confessed faking the rent receipts to avoid the high cost of a non-resident elk license. He further admitted not changing his plates and driver's license because he was returning to Tennessee after finishing Colorado gunsmithing school. While I scratched the tic, Sham supplied a high-priced rifle scope as collateral until he secured funds to pay his hefty fine for the illegal elk.

Officers Davis and Steinert transported the bull to Sage Hen while Marc and I paid a visit to the outfitter, coincidentally also a Tennessee resident, who indicated he did not know Sham was hunting on an illegal Colorado license. *YEAH, RIGHT!*

A call sending us to Rabbit Ears Peak to investigate a hunter accidentally killing two elk, Marc expressed amazement of how the straight-faced Sham, staring directly into my eyes and, without a blink, brazenly lied. I explained lying to avoid turmoil was a natural human trait regularly encountered in law enforcement. The combination of Marc's interest in wildlife law enforcement and knowing he was headed back to college the next day, triggered the gut punching realization of the incalculable time I spent working alone while he was growing up. Our family time even more limited by his maturing drive to go his own way, as I did so many years ago, I reluctantly comprehended,

The cats in the cradle...

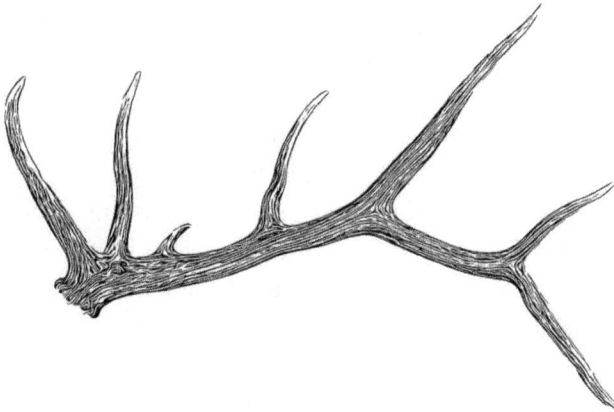

CARPET BAGGERS

July 3, 1983. There I was, veiled in sagebrush overlooking Seymour Lake focusing the Big Eye on three fishermen; two men and a boy with two trout laden stringers fastened on the bank in front of them. Totally engrossed spying through my spotting scope, I was caught off guard when local rancher Danny Meyring and his son Randy, riding horseback, trotted up to my pickup. Danny jokingly commenting on my sneaky harassment of innocent fishermen and Randy proudly palming an arrowhead spotted while riding. Both laughed when I explained arrowheads found on government land belonged to me. Watching them ride away, I contemplated what a great summer day to be a cowboy.

After the fishermen caught several more trout, they packed up and headed towards the parking area. Noting both stringers were put into a large passenger van, I radioed Wildlife Officer Sig Palm to make contact. Sig, finding only one stringer of freshly caught trout and enough old, iced down fish to complete their limits, totaling 20, radioed I must have been mistaken about a second stringer. Knowing no one better at rooting out illegal fish than Officer Palm, I advised I was positive there were two, one obviously skillfully hidden to deceive inquisitive wardens. Driving down to assist, I approached both men and clarified I observed two stringers of trout go into the van and would contact the local judge for a search warrant. One fisherman, Shagbark, smiling like a jackass eating cactus, howled back to search anywhere we wanted because they had nothing to hide. The mouth gaping, guilt ridden face of the suspiciously silent man and the boy's goggle eyes strengthened my vigor to push forward.

Working as a team, Palm and I extensively searched the vehicle and, finding nothing, I fretfully began looking under the vehicle. Spotting a large metal box welded onto the undercarriage, I asked Shagbark what it was. His toothy grin now a sneering scowl, he shruggingly claimed he had no idea. Turning up the heat, I re-entered the van and began yanking on the thick shag carpet, soon pulling up a disguised square attached to plywood revealing a cooler containing 16 iced, freshly caught trout on a stringer. *Hoka Hey!* Shagbark's cunning Icarian flight charred, Sig and I enjoyed watching the defeated man wilt, crash, and burn. Sig and I scratched tics to the first-degree poachers for 8 illegal trout each.

As the fish mongers drove away, I asked Sig how many times he thought they had fooled wardens. Sig replied, "Too many, just not today!"

An ass too big for his pants will be exposed in the end.

INDEPENDENT MOUNTAIN MEN

"Talk about a smelly mountain man, Mathew, that Pack Landers is the type of feller you gotta walk upwind of even if there ain't no breeze a blowin'."
Festus Haggan Gunsmoke

I f I'd been born 200 years earlier, I probably would have answered the call of the western wilds as a fur trapper. Tales, books, movies of the Mountain Men, those independent beaver trappers exploring and opening the western wilderness for settlement, have tickled my mind since boyhood. Learning the likes of Jim Bridger, Kit Carson and many others trapped the Bull Pen intensified my curiosities. Intriguingly, I crossed paths with a semblance of their protégés in late January 1977.

Beginning in early January, the grapevine began whining stories of two brothers dressed in buckskin who set up a winter camp on Independence Mountain. Winter snowfall, abnormally light, allowed vehicle passage on the mountain's roads. I kept my eyes peeled for sign of the two men. One afternoon, parked on a ridge overlooking Fisher Draw, I spotted smoke curling from an old, dilapidated homestead cabin. Focusing the Big Eye on two men and some horses. I found 'em!

Days later, patrolling over Red Hill, I spotted a man on horseback and pulled over to contact him. As he dismounted, a powerfully pungent stench literally stopped me in my tracks, and no it was not coming from the horse! Describing the fetid scent emitted by this malodorous, soiled-faced young man nearly impossible – a musky blend of wood smoke, fetid body odors from all crevices, perspiration-soaked, greasy buckskin, with a hint of sage – is the best I can do. Greeting me with a smile and a handshake, the reeking young man introduced himself as Lynus O'Brien. Maintaining my distance, I marveled at the detail of his brain-tanned buckskin leggings, breech cloth, shirt and hat, all expertly handcrafted except for his store-bought rubber soled, insulated Eddy Bauer boots.

My sense of smell continuing its deep nosedive, we chatted about the mild weather, trapping, and the authenticity of his brass adorned muzzleloader. Unbelievably, as we talked, would you believe a body louse crept out of Lynus' chest hair, switch backing a trail towards his chin. Speechless, my eyes locked on the translucent body beast, I watched the blood sucking creature slowly make a U-turn and return to the warmth of its compliant host. Lynus unflinchingly continued talking. *Damn!*

While contemplating the louse, a galloping horse thundered in from behind, the sturdy steed making a stiff legged halt several feet from where I stood. Awestruck, I witnessed another 'mountain man', in one fluid motion, dismount, hack a lugy into his hand, and reach for mine! And there I was, reactively accepting his handshake, disturbingly aware of the slimy ball of phlegm lubricating our palms. Smearing his greased hand on his buckskin shirt, he greeted me, "We've heard a lot about ya!", while I cavalierly wiped mine on my pants. Later reading this was a common greeting among the original fur trappers, I recommend it to no one.

Thus began our unique friendship, clouded in a haze of mutual distrust, that would flavor my ice cold, snow-powered winter and early spring. Keeping busy checking ice fishermen, coyote hunters, capturing late season poachers, checking snowmobilers, finalizing court cases, surveying game populations, the relative reduction of public use also allowed time to catch up on paperwork. As it turned out, tracking the brothers provided the icing on my cold season cake.

Routinely visiting their camp, I questioned their abilities to survive the Bull Pen's harsh winter in such an isolated, primitive dwelling. Affirming they possessed a good supply of legally taken Wyoming game meat, warm clothing and bedding, and the skills and equipment to live outdoors, they could fend for themselves. Carrying valid Colorado trapping license, they said money from selling beaver and coyote pelts would cover all required supplies. Independence Mountain, providing winter habitat for abundant populations of deer, elk, and antelope, was easy pickings for hungry poachers. Whenever leaving their camp, I tendered a cautionary warning that I routinely patrolled the area and to contact me if they ran across any illicit activity. *Yeah, right!*

The grapevine fermenting weal and woe tales of Tom and Lynus' adventures, I heard hired men working for the Bighorn Ranch had stolen Lynus and Tom's traps and a coyote. Lynus skillfully tracking them down and threatening to 'blow their brains out', the ranch hands wisely returned his traps and paid him $50 for the coyote.

Periodically, the roughly hewn brothers rode into Cowdrey and Sage Hen for supplies, turning the heads of the local populace. Nonchalantly warming their bones against the backdrop of the sundrenched town bank wall fueled restaurant and barroom gossip. After Tom and Lynus made the mistake of entering one of Sage Hen's drinking establishments, the town's bullying barflies initiated a barroom brawl. Although they held their own, Tom and Lynus wisely avoided future visits to the local saloons.

Tales of surviving the rigors of winter also surfaced. One involved the brothers caught in a late spring blizzard while illegally hunting beaver pond ducks on Rhea Creek. Unable to start a fire and facing a hypothermic death, they were rescued by a local rancher. On another occasion, I found Lynus drying out in the sundrenched window of the Cowdrey store, disclosing he had fallen through the ice while attempting to cross the North Platte River. Visits to their cabin, always enlightening, I once witnessed Lynus dry shaving his coarse beard with a Green River skinning knife - the sight and sounds of scrapin' hair off a tanned deer hide! On another visit, Lynus revealed how to polish the deer antler handle on his knife using the thick, grimy oil rubbed from the outside of his nose.

Hearing their meat supply was dwindling, I checked the county welfare freezers and discovered the large amount of illegal meat confiscated in 1976 had been dispersed to the local needy. Another report testifying they had killed, butchered, and were eating one of their horses, I knew poaching, if not already taking place, was inevitable.

During the spring snow melt, news arrived the brothers split up, Tom returning to Wyoming to increase their trapping opportunity and success to bolster their resources. Then, hearing Lynus was entertaining a woman companion, I inquisitively visited his camp and listened to him proudly describe her as the best-looking woman this side of the Mississippi River. *Maybe North Platte less than a mile away!* Granted she was not bad looking, her time with Lynus, of course, was short lived. For Lynus, the odds of keeping a woman any length of time never good, if it did happen, the goods would no doubt be quite odd. Receiving no reports Lynus was breaking wildlife law, it seemed he was faring well doing everything right. That is, until he was not.

In late March, the grapevine tattled Lynus needed meat. Corresponding with my sunrise strutting ground census of breeding sage grouse, I prioritized my morning hours to spy on him. Patience and perseverance, a warden asset, employing hours watching Lynus' daily routines, I found myself extremely fascinated by his work ethic; busily running traplines, skinning, fleshing, and drying coyote and beaver hides, constructing circular willow branch hoops to stretch wet beaver hides, gathering firewood etc. I once observed Lynus saddle his horse and, rifle in one hand, repeatedly charge his cabin at full gallop! Add his yoga style morning sunrise worship, I obtained a unique perspective of his extreme allegiance to a chosen lifestyle they idolized.

My increased surveillance and cabin visits providing no evidence of illegal activity, continuing reports spoke otherwise. The grapevine began rustling dismay at my inability to catch him. Learning Lynus purchased a 30-30 rifle due to his inability to kill anything with his muzzleloader, reliable information snitched he poached an antelope and cached the meat in a wooden box behind his cabin. Responding, biologist Steve

Steinert and I 'back doored' the timbered ridge into Fisher Draw and crossed a set of fresh boot tracks in melting snow matching Lynus' L.L. Beans, following the blood trail of a deer through thick pines. Finding the feathery, red foofaraw Lynus wore on his leggings snagged in the brushy undergrowth, the tracks left the wounded deer and turned back towards his cabin. Losing the boot tracks on the sagebrush hillside above his cabin, I informed Steinert I had enough circumstantial evidence to charge Lynus for hunting deer out of season. Immediately confronting Lynus with what I found, he unexpectedly praised my enforcement fortitude and humbly confessed to shooting and losing the wounded deer. Honorably accepting the citation, Lynus displayed the integrity of the honest man he was. At his request, I held the ticket to give him time to sell his hides and pay the fine. Aye, I scratched the tic, but remained apprehensive about the circumstantial weakness of my charge, and even more when Deputy District Attorney Art Apblanalp stated, despite Lynus' confession, my case was shaky at best.

Then, a reliable account of Lynus recently poaching three deer, making jerky, and caching the meat along the frozen bank of the North Platte River, intensified my desire to snag the poaching lad red-handed. And, on one warming spring morning, scoping Lynus riding horseback towards the river, my shining hope he was headed towards his cache quickly faded when he spotted my truck and headed my way at full gallop! Focusing the Big Eye as he closed the mile distance, I could feel the burning rage expressed on his face. Reining in his fast-charging horse at my pickup door, Lynus screamed a warning I had no right watching him. *Yeah, I did!* Falsely claiming I was classifying deer and not watching him, I scolded that his paranoia revealed he was doing something wrong. Glaring into each other's eyes, both taking a deep breath, I decided it was time to bury the hatchet. Sternly clarifying I would leave him alone and consider all illegal meat presently cached as his if he would cease killing wild game, adding I would vigorously investigate any new reports he was poaching. Lynus, credulously affirming he had enough meat to take him through the summer months, promised to stop poaching until it became necessary to acquire what he and his brother required to live. Removing his hand-made necklace of multi-colored Hudson Bay beads, Lynus presented it to me as his gift, declaring I was the only warden capable of catching him. The beads adorn my office to this day. Although standing on different sides of the legal fence, this was one of the rare times I found myself straddling it. Respecting the free-spirited brothers traveling a road less traveled, experiencing a sense of freedom and independence most cannot, I knew Tom and Lynus O'Brien were good men.

And, just like that, they were gone, ending the most interesting winter/spring season of my career. A local rancher and friend of the wayward pair transported them to Laramie, a drive he later described as the longest, foulest smelling trip he ever made. Knowing Lynus would not pay his fine and the probability of never seeing him again, I voided his ticket. Rumors Tom was working as a sheepherder in Wyoming and Lynus was living off the land around Glacier National Park. I will always wonder what became of both.

Interestingly, as good fathers do, I received a $50 check in September to pay Lynus' ticket. Their dad, a California pharmacist, attached a note thanking me for my kind treatment of Tom and Lynus. Never cashing the check, I filed it away as remembrance of treasured days long past.

BEAR PAUSE

B **EAR!** The word alone captures the attention of most. Bears have haunted humans throughout our evolutionary history, no doubt originating with the stark primal instinct, **FEAR!;** these aggressive beasts can stalk, chase, kill and consume us! However, the mysticism of Ursus extends far beyond their clear and present danger. Native American cultures regarded bears as spiritual symbols of strength and wisdom, possessing extraordinary medicinal powers integral to their religion and culture. Imagery of bears and bear claws in caves, on rock walls, teepees, jewelry, tattoos, totems, names of clans and individuals, legendary tales and tradition, embody the essential roles' bears played throughout Native American history. They still do!

Modern American society revels bears as icons of what is wild and free. Bears (and wolves) excite our inherent obsession for the wild. Road jams in National Parks are key examples. Our mystic charisma of black, brown and grizzly bears is reflected in our jewelry, artwork, lawn ornaments, clothing imprints, books and teddy bears. North American people are haunted by bears.

Growing up in Ohio, my enthrallment began reading adventurous bear tales scribed in outdoor books and magazines. Moving west into true bear country, my curiosities were significantly stimulated listening to bear tales of college friends and coworkers. This Buckeye State greenhorn, hungering for a bear sighting, was ultimately rewarded while riding horseback in the Greys River Range performing rangeland inventory for the Forest Service. Flanking a herd of domestic sheep, my horse spun and reared after scenting the wild beast, triggering it to cannonball into thick willows and bolt through a sheepherder's camp. Riding in, I found two Basque shepherds, 20-years old at best, unwilling to leave their tent. Not able to speak English, their wide-eyed facial expressions and hand gestures made it crystal clear they were deathly scared of the bear. Smiling and nodding my head, they eventually relaxed and offered a tin cup brimming with boiled, thicker than mud, coffee. After the initial shock of sifting grounds through my teeth, I found it boldly gratifying.

Managing nuisance bears as a Wildlife Officer, in addition to my hunting, fishing and hiking encounters with the beasts, proffered an entertaining mix of hair-raising and comical events throughout my career. Treasured memories I must tell:

Book Cliffs, Utah. Our range inventory crew encountered the reeking stench of regurgitated wild ground cherries and heaps of sludgy bear crap surrounding a 'ripe' road killed deer. A sow with two cubs, discerned by their tracks, expelled their fruit laden stomach contents to refill with the preferred protein of venison, including the blood rich antler velvet. Satiated, the bears complimented the toxic scene by marking it with copious amounts of excrement!

Battle Ridge. My father's reaction when I pointed out a shadowed rock expressing it resembled a bear, and our amazement when it materialized into a running beast disappearing into heavy sage.

Mexican Ridge. Muzzleloader season. The pleasure of watching a sow and two cubs amble into a kettle pond for a drink, followed by the splashing frolic of all three in and out of the muddy shallows.

Mexican Ridge. Muzzleloader season. A large brown bear sauntering our direction along a fence line entertaining our entranced hunting party shortly before Cousin Tim harvested a bull elk.

Bear's Ear. Archery elk season. Tottering a fallen log and leaning against an aspen trunk near an active elk wallow, I blew my bugle several times. Catching me completely off guard, a raghorn bull charged in, caught my scent, turned and rapidly disappeared. *DAMN!* If that was not enough, two bear cubs loping ahead of mother, appeared on the game trail I stalked only fifteen minutes before. DAMN, *DAMN!* The sow, nose to the ground, was clearly sniffing the musky elk urine sprayed over my shoes and clothing. The cubs, also tracking my scent, began blundering up the very log I was standing on! *DAMN, DAMN, DAMN!* Clearly aware of the eminent danger of mother bears protecting their young, I gruffly commanded, "Don't even think about it!" Freezing in their tracks, the sow woofed a warning to the naïve cubs, and both obediently retreated to her side. In what seemed an eternity, she cautiously turned away, one eye on mine, ears laid back, and carefully herded her cubs into the aspen undergrowth. *WHEW!* My life not flashing before me, as some report when facing death, the lightning bolt shooting through my core unquestionably disturbed my lower digestive track!

Mexican Ridge. Rifle elk season. My son's cow elk gut pile visited by a bear the day after harvest. Partially consumed, covered with grass and duff, the bear notarized its claw marks over Marc's name and date of kill carved on a nearby aspen. *PRICELESS!*

Mexican Ridge. Rifle elk season. Daybreak, a golden-brown bear eating the carcass of a cow elk I harvested the evening before. Alerted by the scolding chatter of crows and magpies in the trees, I slowly stalked in downwind. Predictably the bear sensed my presence, woofed and ran away. Knowing it was somewhere close, I found myself fervently surveying my surroundings heeding all forest sounds, imaginary or real. as I quartered and packed out the meat.

Independence Mountain. Archery hunting. Stalking adjacent to an aspen grove, a bigger than life bear suddenly stood before me in tall sage. Both frozen in time, calculating our next move, I frightfully studied its cocking head, poised front paws, sniffing nose, and beady eyes lasering into mine! My precarious situation bad enough, I all but soiled my camo pants when two cubs began Jack in the Boxing above the tall sage for a glimpse at whatever mother was looking at! Luckily, as most black bears do, mother guided her cubs up and away into heavy pine. Testing my personal fortitude to its limit, I called it a day.

Mexican Ridge. Muzzleloader season. Beginning with a smell so strong I could taste it, followed by the sound of hair scraping brush before perceiving the dark back of a bear ten yards away, I cannot describe the heart flaming exhilaration igniting my senses into full alert. Slowly regaining a semblance of composure, I pondered whether, or not, it sensed my presence and remained nearby.

Independence Mountain. Archery season. The bear stalking my tracks along a ditch bank after a September snowfall. A story worthy of a chapter of its own.

North Platte River Wilderness. Fishing. Frequent tracks and droppings along the riverbank ultimately twice rewarding me with actual sightings of the elusive beasts.

On several occasions I constructed spring bait stations for attracting bear using skinned beaver carcasses provided by retired warden mentor, trapper Sir Don Gore. Covering six to twelve beaver, gourmet bear food, with branches and heavy logs never failed to attract one or more bears. Checking the station, I would normally find it scattered in all directions with no sign whatsoever of the carcasses! My family, not fond of bear meat, I elected to not harvest a bear, even when I had one in my rifle sights. Not against hunting them, I personally preferred observing bears with a camera or binoculars in hand. Bill Kanode, our heavy equipment operator, frequently harvested bears in his spare time by searching open mountain ridges areas with scopes and binoculars. This ursiform man with an unmistakable laugh, savored bear meat.

The 'comedy of bears' can also be found in my tales of live trapping nuisance beasts:

MANWICH

A late-night call from Don Teem from his Rosebud store tattled the story of an African American man, Rudy Beckia, experiencing a terrifying bear encounter in the Arapaho Lakes area. Listening to Don's detailed story, I pictured Rudy arriving at a campground well after dark, finishing a bucket of Kentucky Fried Chicken and throwing the bones onto the ground. *Uh oh, get the picture!* Carelessly(unknowingly?) pitching his tent over the bones, Rudy crawled into his sleeping bag and fell asleep. Imagine the spine-chilling horror of a bear, scenting chicken, pushing its head under the tent, and rolling Rudy up while still in his bag. Hearing the crunching of bones, the helpless man must have figured he was next! DAMN! Self defensively, Rudy grabbed his flashlight and .22 pistol, squirmed out of his bag, stuck his head out of the tent and, finding himself eye to eye with the bear, fired twice. Considering Rudy's confinement, shooting his gun was a very bad idea. Conveying I would drive to Rosebud immediately, Don said not to bother because Rudy, in a state of total delirium, purchased a bag of junk food and headed home, announcing he was never coming back! Visiting Rudy's campsite the following morning, I found the neighboring campers more disturbed by Rudy's careless discharge of the firearm than the actual presence of the bear. Unfortunately, I never enjoyed the pleasure of conversing with Rudy! Brings a literal perspective of the quote, "Sometimes you eat the bear, and sometimes the bear eats you!"

BEAR SPRAY

The day following setting a live bear trap at a cabin near Gould, I received a call from the owners that a bear was in the trap. The nuisance bear's most recent crime was destroying several coolers, consuming all edibles, and drinking 24 cans of beer! Puncturing the cans with its teeth and holding them skyward allowed most of the beer to run down its throat, one might say he was high on the food chain. Hooking the trap to my pickup, a mother and her older daughter having witnessed the morning event from inside their cabin, tag teamed and severely aschewed me for not responding immediately to their calls. Both attractive, donning translucent shorty nightgowns, a bright sun glaring from behind, it was easy to pretend I was listening!

I stopped by the Sage Hen Forest Service Office to document the bear would be released along Damfino Creek along the Colorado Wyoming state line. The old game of 'Musical Bears', where wardens on one side entertain themselves by dumping bears on the other's side. Exiting the office, picture one of Sage Hens dearest widows asking if there was a bear in the trap. I replied there was, and she excitedly requested to see it. Carefully opening the peephole door, I warned her not to get too close. As her face drew closer and closer, predictably, the bear snorted a glob of snot and a paw full of excrement through the opening, scaring the absolute bejesus out of her and me! Nearly jumping out of her grannie panties, she glared as if it was my fault. Splattered with pungent bear bodily fluids coming from both ends, I asked if she needed a ride home. Curtly saying no, she wiped her face with a lacy kerchief and abruptly strutted away muttering undecipherable verbs and adjectives in a very unladylike manner. Now crap being what it is, there is nothing worse than the toxic, pungent mix of rotten bait, loose excrement, urine, snotty phlegm and barf found in a bear trap. NOTHING!

CROSS BEAR STITCHERY

August 1973. Now picture Sage Hens good veterinarian, his cheeky, hang dog eyes peering over small glasses off the end of his ruddy, bulbous nose into our culvert trap at a large bear with a significant L-shaped tear in one hind quarter. In his normal state of afternoon inebriation, I jokingly asked if he would sew up the wound. Head cocked to one side, speaking out of the corner of his mouth, Doc perplexingly drooled, "Are you asking ME to stitch it up?" *Priceless!*

ROPE A DOPES

Now picture a bear treed early morning by several blue healers behind Senator Dave Wattenburg's barn. When I arrived, several lariat swinging wranglers offered to rope the bear (cowboys have an affinity for roping wild beasts). *Seriously!* Smiling, I promptly answered, "Have you ever tried pushing on a rope?"

Just the sight of a bear track always stops me in mine. Bear spoor of any kind: the scarred etching of bear claws climbing a Parthenon aspen pillar; scat along a favored trail; consumed and covered entrails of harvested big game; an aspen or pine rub tree encrusted with bear hair; musky bear scent; and, of course, the Holy Grail of bear lore, actual sightings, always elicits time to pause!

The moral of my tales is to be bear aware. Better yet, when trekking the wilds, just be aware. You will be pleasantly surprised by nature's bountiful, often hidden treasures. And always watch your back. The beasts are there, watching you!

HOKA HEY!

KID'S STUFF

"As we grow older, Betsy and I have come to realize there is nothing more precious than raising children!"
SHP

My memoirs would not be complete without characterizing my son Marc Alan and daughter Annie Marie.

And there she was, my teenage daughter valiantly verifying,

without hesitation, the rumor circulating that she and some classmates were riding, after dark, the 'nodding donkey' oil well pumps north of Sage Hen. Giving her a high grade for honesty, (I would have done the same at her age), I played the father role and scolded her for making poor, unsafe choices. A similar confession came later for spotlighting and shooting porcupines with a ranching classmate! These two incidents exemplify Annie's spirited nature, commonplace events while maturing from a moody young child into an independent, motivated, charismatic young woman forging her trail to success.

While Marc spent considerable time with me hunting, fishing, Boy Scouts, 4 H Shooting Sports, and riding shotgun while I worked, Annie not so much. Showing little interest in hunting, she surprised me by attending my Hunter Education class. Annie, however, enjoyed fishing and on the limited occasions we fished as a family, I revered watching her peacefully cast away life's tensions and relaxingly concentrate on catching a trout. I miss that look! Living in today's complex harried world, Annie (everyone) should fish more.

Entering their teens, both acquired a strong work ethic mowing lawns and working for the Youth Conservation Corps on outdoor projects for state and federal resource agencies. Annie utilized her vibrant personality waitressing high-tipping tables during the early breakfast shift (5a.m.) at a popular Sage Hen restaurant, prudently banking enough to pay a large portion of her college tuition. Marc, saving up for college, worked summers for the school system and later for the Division of Parks on the Colorado State Forest stimulating his interests in resource management.

Betsy and I enjoyed watching both compete in high school sports; Marc playing baseball, football, and basketball; Annie, playing volleyball, basketball, and track. Annie, running dashes, relays, and low hurdles, ran like the wind.

Treasured memories of Marc and I hunting big game and teaching him flyfishing correspond with Annie and I searching for the perfect Christmas tree, trips to big city shopping malls with her friends to purchase homecoming and prom dresses, and my challenge of teaching her to drive on the backroads around Walden Reservoir.

In separate years, Marc and Annie individually joined me on our late summer inventory of bighorn sheep. Setting picturesque timber-line camps was a splendid way to end my summer season prior to working the chaotic four-month hunting seasons. Welcoming the breathtaking hikes over the steep wilderness terrain, we even managed to classify a few sheep.

On Annie's trip, we camped near Baker Pass in the aptly named Never Summer Range bordering Rocky Mountain National Park. After cooking a hearty supper over hot coals and enjoying time gazing into a blazing fire, Annie and I crawled into comfortable sleeping bags chitchatting about whatever came to mind. Falling into a deep sleep, we were brusquely awakened by incessant lightning bolts and booming thunder, followed by heavy rain pelting our tent. Lightning strikes much too close to our campsite, I watched in awe when the ridiculously bright flashes illuminated the inside of our tent, momentarily flashing Annie's face in stark detail revealing her wide eyes pleading for my nod that all was well. Greatly alarmed myself, I could only imagine what was going through her head. The intensity of the lightning strikes was verified in the morning by a splintered pine less than thirty yards from our tent. Luckily, morning dawned bright and sunny providing us an exhilarating day searching for sheep in the precipitous Never Summer basins.

Aware Annie and Marc tolerated incessant ribbing about having the 'game warden' as their father, I was honored knowing they held their ground and supported my place in the community.

To this day Annie swears she was raised on wild game; deer, elk, grouse, fish, ducks, pheasants etc. no doubt stretching the truth, I admit we dined on a lot of wild game. My answer, "You are what you eat and look at what you have become!" Once, when serving freshly fried elk liver and onions, I will forever remember her declaration to brother Marc, "Wait til you taste what dad wants us to eat this time!" As an adult, Annie refuses to eat the meat of anything wild.

Independent and self-driven, both were accepted to Colorado State University. Marc, following my footsteps, earned a degree in Wildlife Biology and later a master's degree in Wildlife Biology from the University of Wyoming. Annie, graduated with a degree in Human Development and Family Studies. Currently, Annie is the Executive Director of Teaching Tree Day Care Centers. Marc, after a distinguished career as a Conservation Officer with the Idaho Fish and Game Department, is steadily blazing a new career trail. Betsy and I are immensely proud of both.

"What Betsy and I have learned raising two children is to have them tell you what they want to do and encourage them to do it!" SHP

BUGLE BOYS

Archery Season. September 11, 1989.

Surrounded! Bulls bugling from all directions, concealed in morning's dark, Kirk and I were fervently living in elk heaven. Seizing a rare opportunity to hunt a section of private land crawling with elk, we were overwhelmed with great expectations. Day's glow bleaching through night's dark, we geared up and peaked over the ridge overlooking Conner Creek. Ghosting the meadow below was the breathtaking spectacle of a large herd bull resonating supremacy over challenging rivals, agitatedly attempting to collect his uneasy cows and calves. Once the herd melted into the timber, we crept down the ridge, crossed the trouser soaking, dew covered meadow and entered the forest. Eyes adjusting to the forest shadows, Kirk skirted the timber while I cat walked directly into the aspen pine mix. Our archery licenses allowing harvesting either a bull or a cow, we would be very happy to fill our freezers with the meat from either. Our ploy was to take a stand and patiently watch and listen, check the everchanging breeze, before stalking the bellowing bulls and chirping cows and calves. Mixing my bugles with cow calls while Kirk did the same, I crept to the far edge of the aspen and promptly spied a group of elk headed through open sage brush towards me! The spine-tingling sight of a heavy beamed five-point bull herding his harem while keeping two smaller bulls at bay was hard to process. Backing into a dense pine hugging a large aspen spire, I realized I was standing amid the fresh tracks these elk made entering the sagebrush during the night. *DAMN!* Senses on full alert, what could not go wrong, DID! The raucous sounds of rutting elk abruptly ceased and MY elk stood frozen in their tracks, eyes and ears intently focused on what I could not see but could hear; the rattling sounds of a pickup pulling a trailer. Quick as snake's tongue, the elk galloped back into the sage and disappeared. Kirk and I later discovered the landowner, forgetting we were hunting, had given a commercial aspen tree digger permission to harvest trees on the property!

A half hour passed, and I again recognized Kirk's bugle, at least I thought it was him. Nothing answered but Kirk bugled again, so I sat in some shrubby pine along a ditch, blew my bugle and waited. Three small bulls ghosted past but would not stop to my cow calls. Out of bow range, one momentarily looked back as if something was trailing behind, so I anxiously guarded their backtracks. Kirk bugled again and this time was quickly answered by an off-key bugle near my location. Detecting movement, I focused my binoculars on two face-painted bow hunters, dressed in full camouflage, evidently pursuing Kirk's luring bugles and unknowingly ruining our hunt! *DAMN!* Alternately creeping towards Kirk, like two grass spiders, one repeatedly bugled while the other cow called, both using hand signals to guide their tactics. Passing within twenty yards without detecting my presence, I gave them thirty yards before stalking the stalkers.

"There is someone walking behind you, turn around, look at me."
Bee Gees

Closing the distance like flies to bear shit, both entered stealth mode, intensely searching for the invisible bull, edgily preparing for what they believed was an imminent shot. Their senses so strongly focused ahead, a hungry grizzly bear could have made a camo lunch wrap out of both. Ten yards apart, one finally looked back and did a double take on the camouflaged, face painted apparition standing the ground they just stalked.

Cutting into their chase, I displayed my badge and announced I was a wildlife officer. Kirk, never letting a warden moment pass, audaciously resonated one last bugle before stepping out of his piney lair. The bowmen, noticeably humiliated by imagining they were pursuing a lonely bull (Kirk anything but), stood petrified in bewilderment. Glimpsing Kirk's bright teeth shining through his dark beard was priceless! Playing dumb and dumber, roles we practiced to proficiency, I nonsensically asked how their hunt was going, followed by Kirk's naïve inquiry if they knew whose property they were hunting on. One replied they were hunting **BML** lands, a lettered sequence misnomer of Bureau of Land Management **(BLM)** controlled public lands. Kirk asked what he meant, and the bowman replied he was not sure. The other fibbed they entered from public lands and crossed no fences. I switched his flip pointing out getting here from BLM was impossible without crossing properly signed fences belonging to two separate landowners.

Neither carrying licenses, Kirk and I ended our hunt and escorted them to their State Forest camp. Their licenses identified two Wisconsin hunters; Rene licensed to hunt deer and Gade for elk. *Imagine that!* Kirk informed Rene it was illegal to hunt elk without an elk license. *DUH!* Gaining backbone, Rene audaciously declared we could never prove he was hunting elk. Gade insinuating entrapment, insisted they had been illegally snared by Kirk's bugling. Gade also indicated he had a real problem with 'wardens' hunting private lands while obviously patrolling for wildlife violations. Kirk echoed we had a real problem with trespassers ruining our hunt.

Dumbing it down a notch. Kirk revealed we were quite familiar with their illegal ploy of purchasing one less expensive deer and one elk license with the intent of individually hunting both species. Predictably, Rene pointed out party hunting was legal to party hunt in Wisconsin prompting Kirk's reply not only were they were in Colorado, Wisconsin still required licenses for the species hunted. Enjoying the two suffering the gut-wrenching wrath of capture myopathy, their arrogant demeanor slowly transformed into miserable submission.

After confirming the landowner wanted to press charges, both were scratched tics for hunting private property without permission. Rene was also rewarded a tic for hunting elk without a license. Gade idiotically boasted they had trespassed these properties for years, their proficiency of playing 'Indian' allowed them to easily elude detection by being dropped off before daylight and picked up after dark, evading cattlemen and carefully avoiding fence lines and roads.

If they were Indians, we were Geronimo and Sitting Bull!

Rene questioned why we interrupted our hunt to ruin theirs. I answered, "It's what wardens do!"

What began a picture-perfect elk adventure ended, as our hunts so often do, with our innate magnetism of attracting the bad. Such is the life of a dedicated wildlife officer!

"Suppose you are a moron, then imagine you are a poacher. But I repeat myself."

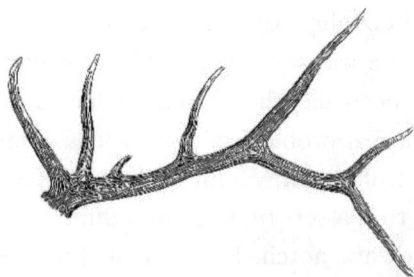

HEAD TRIPPER

A nd there I was, a late Friday August evening, regulating the night shift at Delaney Butte Lakes. Sitting in my vehicle hidden on the high ground between the three lakes, I gazed westward as the sun's fiery rays crowned the peaks of the Mount Zirkel divide, reflecting scarlet hues over the North Lake while a mischievous breeze shattered its calm into swells of sparkling garnets. A soul soothing spectacle indeed! The warm days and cool nights attracted large numbers of anglers from their urban agony. Fishing was good, very good, with tales of success luring all ages willing to travel the distance for a relaxing, late season getaway. Many, spending weekdays paying their vocational dues working for the 'man', worshipped these fleeting high-country summer weekends. *Everybody's working for the weekend!* I fully realized the treasures of cherishing one's work. Oh, what a lucky man I am!

All three lakes were a beehive of activity. A steady flow of vehicles streamed in while others hurriedly set up camps to join those already fishing the magic hours of dusking nightfall. Tonight, the mystifying songs of night birds, purring boat motors and generators, and the chatter of human voices were offset by the stereophonic broadcast of a Denver Broncos pre-season game from radios blasting over the waters of all three lakes. Three lakes teeming with fishermen on a mosquito free night, I was in a warden wonderland. Nightfall attracts intriguing creatures, including fish mongers otherwise disguised as law abiding fishermen during the day, and I was eager to root out any scofflaws veiling their misdeeds under darkness' security blanket.

As dusk smothered the western glow, I coasted my truck onto the county road and slowly drove between the South and East lakes. Head, tail and dash lights switched off, I spotted the silhouette of a man sitting in front of a strobing campfire above the bank of the South lake. Easing along a willow choked ditch I quietly pulled off the road and parked, undetected by the man and his large golden retriever. Standing up, he stumbled to the shoreline and tightened the line of his fishing pole held by a rod holder staked into the bank. Returning, the firelight revealed a rough looking, wild haired man, maybe in his twenties yet seemingly eroded beyond his years; one who may have never made it completely back from Woodstock. Sitting down in his lawn chair 'Woodstock' expertly rolled a joint, lit up and toked his way into a Rocky Mountain High. His grizzly-muzzled, well behaved dog attentively sat across the fire facing me and his master. Focusing my binoculars, I chuckled as the space cadet peacefully entered his happy place, enjoying music only he could hear. Allowing time for the late arrivals to begin fishing, it soon became clear Woodstock was several tokes over the line, very deep into his otherworldly stupor. Unable to resist using my truck's outside loudspeaker, I keyed the mike and in a crisp tone just above a whisper, announced, *"This is the Lord! Smoking pot on state property is against the law!"* In the firelight I saw the dog's ears perk, head cock to one side, and eyes transfix over his master's head towards my vehicle. Incredibly, Woodstock perceived the situation quite differently. His mind encased in a cloudy trance, he moved to the edge of his chair and, hazily staring into the eyes of his faithful companion, asked, "What did you say?" Assessing the situation, I reasoned anyone believing his dog had spoken deserved time on his personal cloud, I moved on. *Priceless!*

As a bold Comanche moon rose over the Medicine Bow Range, resembling a sand dollar floating through a black velvet sky, I decided to stalk the entire perimeter of the South Lake on foot. Listening to an unseen nighthawk's chirps and diving wing booms, I stuffed a ticket book, snacks and water into my backpack and began leap frogging fishermen, checking licenses and inspecting stringers and coolers. Pleasurably, I detected no violations, finding friendly families and individuals relaxing in the evening's serenity rather than exclusively focused on catching trout. Enjoying conversations with young and old alike, discussing everything from fishing regulations to weather, many stated they were glad to see a warden enforcing regulations. These people, the majority good, whose license fees pay my salary, are the outdoorsmen, women, and children I tirelessly worked for as an educator, mentor, and enforcer against the minority bad.

Heading towards the north bay of the lake, I shadowed the pitch-black of the west side willows and, would you believe, inadvertently tripped over an object I immediately perceived as alive! I had nearly stepped on a man's head! *WAUGH!* Jumping back with a ghastly shout, I switched on my flashlight, lighting up the face of a young man lying on his belly, head hovering over a smoking bong. His unseeing eyes attempting to focus on the bright light penetrating his ethereal head space, I could see he was in very bad condition; disheveled, soiled clothes, no shoes, matted hair, filthy face and hands. His imperceptive mind racing like a herd of turtles, he was unable to recognize who or what I was, and incapable of answering my questions. Grabbing the queue of hair loosely braided down the back of his neck with one hand and an armpit with the other, I helped him stand and leaned him against his vehicle. My request for his driver's license fell on unresponsive ears. Out of the blue, he uttered, "How did you know I was here?" Not knowing the contents of the bong, I began worrying about his health. Searching his vehicle, I found a registration and, running the name printed on it through the Sheriff's Office, yielded a driver's license meeting the description of my midnight toker. Lucky for me, and no doubt him, he had a warrant out for his arrest on a failure to appear traffic violation, and the Sheriff asked me to bring him in. I gathered up his drug paraphernalia, locked them into his vehicle for safe keeping, sat him down and hastily returned to my truck. Interestingly, Woodstock was now awkwardly stretched out on the ground by his campfire, only his faithful dog detecting my presence.

Hurriedly driving back to the drooping doper, I handcuffed his hands frontside and strapped him into my vehicle. On our way, taking a step back into his mind, he gathered a portion of his loose wits and, as we topped the high ridge overlooking Sage Hen's city lights, (population 800) uttered, "I can't believe we're already in Denver!" Smiling, I agreed we certainly made a high-speed trip (literally). Parking at the Sheriff's Office, I guided the lonesome loser to a gloomy, cold jail cell, happy to leave him knowing he had a warm bed and a not so good morning meal to aid his recovery and, no doubt, face charges for whatever drugs were in his vehicle!

"You step out of line, the man come and take you away..."
Buffalo Springfield

BAR STOOLIES - A BEETLE KILL?

The Bull Pen is often mockingly described as a small drinking community with a hunting and fishing problem. Sage Hen, with two bars and two liquor stores, nurtures a preponderance of gossiping barflies capable of drinking the creeks dry! Many died trying. Accommodating a peculiar mix of cowboys, ranch hands, loggers, miners, hunters, fishermen, hippies, drunks, misfits, retirees, wannabees, whores and out of towners, it hews a roughly spirited atmosphere bordering orderly joy and chaotic discontent. Hunting and fishing, of course, is cursed, argued, and deliberated on a regular basis. Occasionally, I found it necessary to contact one or more of the taverns' undying tenants for their 'inebriated intelligence' on an active case. Like squeezing blood from a turnip, I sometimes successfully harvested liquor induced testimonials placing me back in business. Imagine, opening the mid-morning door of a murky saloon to interview one suffering the previous night's inebriation; barstool row heads turning and eyes squinting my way as daylight lasered into their befuddled minds. Everyone looked guilty.

One August night in 1981, after the 2am bar whistle blew the barflies away, I was bell-rung from a deep sleep by an offensively ringing phone. Floundering in a mind-fogged stupor, it took time to comprehend the caller was one of my trustworthy gossipmongers. BEETLE??? My well cultivated grapevine ripe with the advent of early hunting seasons, this informant was vintage Chardonnay, his ability to distill the impurities of fermenting gossip was second to none! His proficiency of remaining anonymous, even to me, was surreal. Never voicing signs of inebriation, I found his accusations reliable as God's truth; not the chattering blabber of many snitches known as lying, thieving poachers themselves. Wardens, however, seek the facts no matter whose mouth it comes from!

"The enemy of my enemy is my friend."
Old Chinese Proverb

Tonight's evidence spilled from the loose lips of a sozzled man, Flake Chex, casting his liquor induced vainglory into the wind for all to hear, including my secret agent holding zero tolerance for those defiling the wild. Flake proudly announced he and ranch manager Hoss Cantright, poached a cow elk on Mexican Ridge. It was the season of making bank for ranchers and wardens alike. Recent heavy rains temporarily halted harvest of the native hay crop, providing time for some hay crews to parley, drink, poach, and drink some more. These predictable showers signaled the beginning of poaching season allowing some to exploit their access to private lands abounding with big game. Elusive warden prey, indeed. Flake belonged to a whole grain family of serial game thieves I called the 'Chex gang'. His brother Puff, and father Meat, repeatedly on our radar for poaching, trespassing and party hunting, were familiar with our office's 'wiggle room'; denying, listening to our evidence, denying again, listening to our 'deal' and finally admitting their misdeeds. The 'boys' also passionately chased down and killed coyotes for their valuable pelts with snow machines; an unethical, illegal means of killing any animal. But that, of course, is another story.

Hoss rationalized his out-of-season game thefts as reimbursement for private land forage grazed by big game at the expense of the ranch's cattle herds. Sustaining his and his extended family of friends and relatives with wild meat was viewed his warranted privilege for working on the ranch; a culturally distorted view of pilfering the wild's publicly owned bounty, unlicensed, out of season and undisturbed. Both Flake and Hoss wore their pre-season adventures proudly on their sleeve, boasting their cunning ability to hide their poaching escapades from clueless wardens. *Not this time boys.* Tonight, Flake blathered he was meeting Hoss at his ranch house after lunch to retrieve the elk from the mountain. My informant even detailed Flake volunteered to "bring his knives."

And there we were, I parked high on Pole Mountain and Wildlife Officer John Wagner veiled behind a haystack overlooking Hoss's ranch house As we chit-chatted on the radio to pass time, would you believe Flake arrived at the ranch fifteen minutes past high noon, exiting his vehicle carrying an armful of knives! *Hoka Hey!* Loading their pickup with a rifle, cloth bags, knives and a water jug, the two game gangsters drove up the winding dirt road towards Mexican Ridge, two wardens trailing twenty minutes behind. Following vehicle tracks in the red mud of the previous night's rain we, on a whim, parked below the crest of a ridge to stalk on foot for a quick look into the draw below. Sneak-peeking, we found the poachers skinning a fat cow elk hanging in an aspen patch fifty yards below. Both were frightfully ducking and swatting swarms of meat hungry hornets prevalent on the mountain this time of year. We literally caught them red-handed! As the mountain men used to say when good was about to turn bad, *"such a heap of fat meat was not going to 'shine' much longer."*

Returning to our vehicle, I swigged a mouthful of Mountain Dew and, before swallowing, my eyes locked with Wagner's causing an uncontrollable burst of laughter launching soda from my mouth and nose onto the dashboard. Indeed, a warden moment. Deciding again to walk rather than drive, we tracked the road leading to the unsuspecting elk skinners. Less than twenty yards away, Hoss turned around, whispered to Flake and, as the warden wolf howled, our thrill of victory contrasted sharply with the stinging ire of their defeat.

Realizing someone turned them in, you bet they wondered how we knew. To their displeasure, I tickled their minds stating simply I heard it through the grapevine. Recuperating from our gut-wrenching punch, the pair took their medicine quite well. They asked, of course, if we planned spreading word of their apprehension. *Embarrassing, aye? What would their peers say?* Professing our lips were sealed, we made no promise their poaching misdemeanors would evade the unremitting grind of the local rumor mill.

"Three may keep a Secret, if two of them are dead." Benjamin Franklin, Poor Richard's Almanack (1735)

In this case there were four of us, and their bloody secret would undoubtedly ooze into the attentive ears of a community hungry for tittle-tattling gossip. And, according to my worthy bar spy, it did!

Press hard boys, there's five copies!

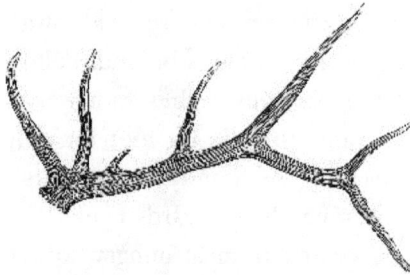

Poacher to warden: *"You are only writing me this ticket to fill your quota!"*

Warden to poacher: *"Oh, have you not heard? We can now write as many tickets as we want!"*

TWO SHOTS AND A WARDEN CHASER

Whether working or playing, I routinely sought quiet vantages or favored lairs to eat lunch, watch a sunrise or sunset, or simply absorb the immense natural landscapes of what I considered my field office, the Bull Pen. Those ever-changing, round the clock vistas provided soul nurturing landscapes transferring me far beyond what my eyes perceived!

"I could see for miles and miles and miles."
Who lyrics

One late September evening found me aimlessly biding time high on Independence Mountain. My justification of watching and listening for wildland illegalities veiled the actual ploy of satisfying my innate desires to witness the grand finale of another Indian Summer day. Comfortably parked overlooking the massive valley floor boldly guarded by high craggy peaks, I was in no rush to hasten the reflective silence of nightfall. As the evening's waning daystar prismed blazing crimson shafts through the clouded peaks of the west side granites, my eyes traced night's shadows crawling eastward across the basin. Feeling sundown's cold blades penetrate my shirt; hearing electrifying *peen*ts of a nightjar; and sniffing flares of ripening aspen leaves while stars mysteriously appeared as sparkling gems in the sky's fading azure is a very good time to take.

Eyes adapting with the fading light, the evening hush was curtly pierced by the shrill bugle of one, then another wapiti bull in aspens not thirty yards from my pickup. The high-pitched waning timbre of their calls implied juvenile loneliness. Mewing on my cow call, I received an immediate response from both stags. Imagine my anticipated surprise when two raghorns coyly ambled into the open searching for an unseen cow. *Donner and Blitzen* – thunder and lightning! The rut bewildered adolescents, hounded for weeks by larger bulls driving them away from cows and calves, were in a state of testosterone laced confusion and thus extremely vulnerable to the first days of the upcoming rifle season; literally dead meat standing if they did not change their ways. Leaving my truck with harsh yells and flailing arms caused the stags to trot to the timber's edge, stopping to stare momentarily before tiptoeing into the aspen. I decided then, barring any calls forcing me elsewhere, to begin the rifle season near this location.

The day before rifle season, weary from a week of administrative duties, I enthusiastically headed towards Independence Mountain to check hunting camps. Most hunters, having participated in the ritualistic foreplay of the hunt: purchasing local gifts for their wives; buying licenses; visiting bars and drinking copious amounts of liquor; setting up camp; sighting in rifles and scouting (thus pushing elk deep into heavy timber hidey-holes); telling old stories around campfires with some planning their first degree outdoor misdeeds; could now be found close to their camps. I greatly enjoyed surveying camp locations, identifying hunter miscreants currently on my radar or those having previously signed memberships into my 'club', renewing old acquaintances, and answering a cross fire of endless and often ridiculous hunter questions; the most predictable query, "Where's the elk?"

Walking into one well-equipped campsite of wall tents, wood stoves, meat poles, stacked wood and a large rock-rimmed campfire, I was greeted by an enthusiastic young lad beaming like a rising moon. Proudly producing his newly earned hunter education card and first ever bull elk license, I firmly shook his hand and wished him luck on tomorrow's hunt. There is nothing more nurturing to the values of hunting than the innocent excitement of a young boy or girl being constructively mentored into their first hunts. Father explained the boy had shadowed him on several big game hunts and tomorrow would be his first experience as a licensed hunter. Finding all camp members properly licensed, I said I looked forward to checking the young lad's bull hanging from their meat pole during the next few days.

So there I was, creeping up Independence Mountain in the pre-morning black, my headlights one of a multitude crawling their way to favored hunting lairs like ants with headlamps; armed assailants invading the mountain's tranquility. Maintaining my distance to prevent anyone 'Paul Revering' a warden presence, I topped out and hid my vehicle fifty yards into an overgrown hidey hole. Washing down the last glazed donut with stodgy black coffee, I stalked the darkness over a game trail to a familiar saddle and waited. In less than ten minutes two small bulls ghosted thru the pre-morning dawn less than twenty-five yards away. *Donner and Blitzen?*

Thirty minutes into daylight, thinking of moving to thaw my quickly chilling bones, a shot shattered the morning still, followed instantaneously by a second. All became deathly silent. I ascertained the shots came less than seventy yards below, most assuredly from the same rifle. Closing the distance, I knelt behind a clump of buffaloberry and was soon rewarded by movement below. Focusing my binoculars through dense lodgepole, a lone figure standing over the carcass of a raghorn bull materialized. Much to my surprise, the man walked twenty yards uphill to yet another small, and very dead, bull. *Donner and Blitzen!* Maintaining cover, I watched the man return to the first bull and begin field dressing it. Stalking in, I cleared my throat causing the hunter to stand, knife in hand, obviously quite startled to see a wildlife officer. With my signature smile I congratulated the hunter on his success then followed with the loaded small talk of possibly seeing this very bull a week earlier running with another not a quarter of a mile away. Pointing to the second bull, the hunter calmly replied it belonged to his son. *Donner and Blitzen!* Before asking the whereabouts of the second hunter, I detected a boy walking our direction up a narrow aspen draw. My heart skipped a beat upon recognizing the boy as the very one contacted in camp the previous day. The boy, eyes transfixed on one dead bull, was immediately steered upwards to the second by his father, now rapidly explaining both had killed bulls. Noting the bulls were dropped in their tracks by precise, below the ear neck shots; no blood, no blood trails and no sign of a struggle, I dove into warden mode beginning the routine questions of an obvious party hunting situation.

Testing the waters, I began questioning the boy. Predictably father threw him a lifeline, tersely answering my questions before the boy could respond. Firing my first warning shot, I sternly made it clear I believed father killed both elk. Father madly declared I had no right making such accusations in front of his son. Sensing where I was headed, the visibly perplexed but perceptive boy, under the telling glare of his father, agreeably admitted shooting the second bull. With a cold smirk, Father nodded with pleasure. Persistently, I quick fired bulleted questions at the defenseless boy; where he was when he shot; how many rounds he fired; had he picked up his brass; where he aimed when shooting etc. Stunned, the boy replied he could not remember. Advising the duo to field dress the bulls, I backtracked the boy seventy-five yards to a large aspen tree, where trampled vegetation indicated he spent considerable time. Scanning upwards, I noted this location was out of sight of his father and either of the two bulls. No brass was found.

Backtracking the bulls, I discovered they came in from above, neither crossing the visual path of the boy. Playing Columbo, I inspected the neck wounds hoping to dig out bullets, discovering only lead fragments in the through and through spine shattering bullet channels. Explaining I would bring in a metal detector sent father into another frightful rage. The disheartened lad, who only yesterday over-flowed with great expectations, was now overburdened with the heavy load of backing the bold faced lie of his devious father; swallowing the vile taste of being robbed of his sacred privilege to hunt and harvest his first bull elk. Staring into the boy's eyes, I fired point blank asking again if he had indeed killed the second bull and sadly watched the addlepated kid, eyes on father, dry mouth the exonerating falsehood, "Yes sir, I shot the bull."

Father, nodding to his son with a wink and a sneer, divulged the chicken shit man I was. Thinking of my own son, I knew the boy was damaged but probably fixable. Father was broken beyond repair. The truth could not be unraveled without firmly bending the boy to break his father. The scourge of party hunting defiles the sport in many ways; today a newly minted hunter - shiny, bright and uncirculated – became tarnished and worn by the crimes of a gluttonous father unwilling and incapable of manning up to his misdeeds. Mentally pondering winning the case against father in court without involving son testifying, I began weighing the options. My conscience whispered words of wisdom to **"let it be!"** Lightning flash fast I made a field judgment totally against the grain of my warden hardwood. Such impulsive decisions, right or wrong, are familiar to most wardens. Sometimes taking the long, less traveled road, rather than the rough journey to ticketville, can pay long term dividends. Today, I caged the hounds!

"I have always found that mercy bears richer fruits than strict justice."
Abraham Lincoln

However, not willing to let it all go, I turned to the father, Hardlee Aman. Arrogantly standing straight as doghair lodgepole, he was about to become my rub tree; nurturing the young sapling by giving father oak a verbal thrashing. I charged through the fundamentals of a well-rehearsed party hunting lecture, personalizing the truth and consequences of this situation by wittingly shaming father while mentoring his son. My words tracked these lines, "Personally I hate liars. Professionally, those entrapped in blatant untruths become a warden's fair game and are handled more strictly than those owning up to their misdeeds. While the truth does not always prevail, it often results in fewer charges, not losing license privileges, and less monetary fines. Bull elk are a treasured but limited resource. Colorado's one person- one license- one elk law is a means for equalizing harvest opportunities for hunters while providing sporting fairness for elk. It allows hunters to participate every year.

Increased harvest by legalizing party hunting mandates a reduction of the yearly number of licenses issued. In Colorado, party hunters are considered unethical, greedy game hogs defiling the very essence of fair chase sport hunting. My experience with party hunting often involves careless shooting, wounding loss, and wasted game; stealing from the wild's bounty. The majority of those playing the hunting game take great pride exercising their hunting privileges governed by written laws and covenants of morality and ethics they fully support. True hunter conservationists demand strict enforcement of party hunting laws, often policing their own ranks. The ability to develop the physical and mental skills necessary to harvest their own game on an even playing field, and turning it into savory table fare, is held in highest regard and maintains the dignity of sport hunting. Hunter behavior is based on the honor system where field conduct normally occurs undetected and unobserved, guided by one's personal moral compass. The tried and true modern-day hunter paves the way for the next generation of sportsmen to pass on the legacy, skills and traditions of a most noble sport."

Crosshairs on father, I explained while Colorado's Hunter Education Program provides the critical first steps for introducing new hunters to firearm safety, wildlife law, ethics, and care of meat, it is mandatory they be painstakingly mentored by seasoned hunters capable of reinforcing what it takes to become a true hunter conservationist. If father shot both bulls, he is a poacher. Having his son tag one with his license makes him also a poacher by participating in his father's illegal acts. The real tragedy clearly lies with father stealing the privilege for his son to continue hunting and possibly harvest his own bull elk. It also robs any chances of the second bull making it through the season and/or its availability to other hunters. If you shot both bulls, you failed miserably in mentoring your son to carry on the nobleness and legacy of the hunting sports to future generations.

Father, shaken but not stirred, displayed no interest in my words. More importantly, however, I notably had the lad's ear, intently listening and staring, as if I was a prophet. Instructing them to void their tags, I made it clear their elk season was over and left. Two days later, I checked their bulls hanging from the camp's meat pole; ner a word was spoken by father, son or camp member.

But wait, there's more!

Galloping ahead years later, I was contacted in Sage Hen by a young man who witnessed the unlawful killing of a doe deer early that morning on Independence Mountain. Peculiarly, he firmly asserted he always hunted alone before providing an extremely detailed map of where the deer was killed, the location of the poacher's camp and a clear synopsis of the poacher firing several shots before severely wounding the deer. Explaining, as he approached the struggling deer, the hunter asked for an extra 30-06 cartridge to finish it off. The older man offered a portion of the venison if he would help pack it out. The young man stated he helped the hunter field dress the deer but would not pack out an illegal animal. Returning to his vehicle, he immediately drove to Sage Hen and contacted the Sheriff's Office which, in turn, contacted me. Listening intently to his detailed story thinking who is this man, it was not until thanking him with a handshake did I recognize the face of a boy hunter from seasons past. Acknowledging their previous incident with his father and the two bulls, I praised him for taking time from his hunt and reporting the poaching incident, explaining he qualified for a monetary reward. Refusing compensation, he graciously expounded reporting the incident was a no brainer, exhibiting an innate sense of morality exceeding that of the most seasoned hunter conservationists.

Following the detailed map, I easily located the empty camp. Amazingly, I had once bugled in and harvested a raghorn bull elk near a wallow less than fifty yards from this camp. The map also led me to the kill sight where I found the deer hanging from a nearby pine tree. I also collected several empty 30-06 cartridges. Backtracking, I found the poacher, Rue Pilfer, in camp and small talked with him for thirty minutes. Offering no information about the illegal deer, I asked point blank if he had anything on his mind. Rue, without pause, admitted shooting a doe deer thinking it was a cow elk. Not wanting the meat to spoil, he hung it high against the trunk of a pine and planned to bring it out after his hunt. He seemed surprised when told I had already inspected the deer. Requesting he pack out the deer immediately, stating I would pick it up before dark. Later, while scratching the tics, Rue respectfully complimented the young man for reporting the incident, stating he was impressed with his extremely mature, seasoned behavior. I agreed, saying he had an exceptional, ingrained hunting ethic unwittingly instilled by his father very early in his hunting career. Rue, somewhat confused by my words, shook his head in the affirmative.

Days later I stopped by the witness' camp and was told by a camp member the young man returned home after taking a nice buck. Curious, I asked about his father and was told he passed away several years ago. The camp member explained the young man loved hunting this mountain and once old enough, always hunted alone. Peculiarly, I never again crossed paths with the witness, frequently pondering whether our encounter with the two bulls guided the boy towards becoming the ethically sound hunter conservationist he now was.

The moral of this tale is how an acorn can roll past the dark shadow of a miscreant father oak and thrive on its own. For me, what seemed the right thing to do so many years ago.....actually was.

"Once in a while You get shown the light in the strangest of places if you look at it right..."
The Grateful Dead Scarlet Begonia

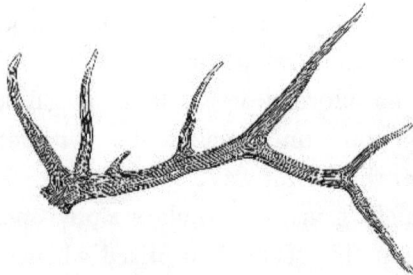

SECOND AMENDMENT

High Steak Surveillance

S eptember 1982. Another field escapade occurred during opening day of antelope season when I crossed paths with a trustworthy and highly respected friend. And there I was, side-scraping my vehicle through tall sage on a narrow private land two track in pre-dawn light below Buffalo Ridge. The warden friendly landowner granted unrestricted access through his locked gates. Concealing my vehicle in tall serviceberry on a limber pine bench I trekked to a rocky outcrop revering the first flickers of dawn. This elevated vista of the rolling sage dissected by a gravel county road sustained several herds of pronghorns; essential ingredients for a hearty warden stew. Season the pot with hunters, this open range theatre may proffer live performances of the hunting good, bad or ugly. For wardens, antelope season is a spot-on spectator sport.

As the morning's radiance warmed my core, I heeded a soaring raven family communicating my presence in undulating croaks and chortles. On cue, just when geese began honking their morning joy on the reservoirs below, my rolling guts rudely sabotaged my inner peace sending me on a tip-toeing turkey trot to retrieve 'paper'.

Balancing my posterior over a flexible limber pine branch offering a grand panoramic view, I detected two slow moving vehicles threading a narrow trail below my pine clad throne. *Damn, another crap shoot!* Habitually, warden 'scents' prompted bringing my binoculars and, in a bare-assed crouch, I focused on three individuals wearing hunter orange in the vehicles. When the 4X4s abruptly stopped in a grassy spring fed draw, I glassed a rifle barrel protruding from the passenger side window of the rear vehicle, apparently tracking several antelope weaving through the sage. The caravan continued allowing me to finish the paperwork and retrieve a spotting scope from my pickup. Returning to the outcrop, I set the 'Big Eye' in the lower branches of a limber pine. Steadying it against the tree's trunk, my eyes fixated on three armed hunters scoping the pronghorns over the hood of their vehicles. Turning up the power below the mark where the morning's solar waves interfered with my vision, I recognized them as acquaintances from Rosebud. Cody GranderStave, the elderly Bull Pen icon owning a prosperous restaurant and bar in the small town, was driving his old, familiar 'Scout'. Cody, a colorful raconteur, dynamically hosted a spirited lair for the multitudes of outdoor liars attracted by the ambiance of great food and liquor. Cody was shadowed by the 'Colonel', a drawling 'southerner' who recently built a trophy log house on a timber bench overlooking the willowy bottoms of Jack Creek. The third hunter was C.I. O'Dare, a brawny man who provided solid information on several poaching cases. In a flash, several shots fired by C.I. and the Colonel dropped a doe antelope. Cody, hastily scrambled to position himself for a shot at the fleeing herd but was offered no opportunity once the antelope disappeared over a ridge. After a short huddle around the carcass, C.I. began field dressing the doe while Cody and the Colonel retrieved the vehicles. Then, to my amazement, they drug the carcass well away from the gut pile and covered it with sage brush. *Hoka Hey!*

Leaving the concealed antelope, they opened a wire gate and drove onto the main county road, once again crossing paths with the antelope. C.I. quickly exited and, standing on the road, fired and missed a shot as a doe crossed, a dangerous and illegal misadventure indeed. Rapidly bouncing to the county road, I intercepted and greeted the nimrods with my warm warden smile, employing 'Columbo' style small talk as a diversion to unravel the threads of their current veil. *Dumb questions lead to incriminating answers.* A license check revealed C.I. and the Colonel both held doe licenses, neither tags detached, signed and dated as required by law upon harvesting big game species. Cody had no antelope license at all. I fired the proverbial loaded question, "Any Luck?" All laughingly responded they should have if they could shoot straight. They were clearly experiencing great pleasure in thinking they were duping me. Mentioning the stashed doe antelope, I copped their happy faces with the jolting statement I had witnessed their entire hunting endeavors- lock, stock, and barrel. Cody, the group's herculean mentoring guide, mis-fired his opening lie stating he had no idea what I was talking about. Aware I was pissing on Cody's post in front of two disciples, I politely opened the door to redemption by offering a chance to start over with the truth.

> *"In all lies there is wheat among the chaff."*
> Mark Twain

Cody, mistaking my attempt to steer them down truths short trail as a trap, continued scuttling the long road of lies and deceit, arrogantly declaring he would not tolerate being called a liar. Ambushing me with demeaning words, Cody 'showed his rifle', breaking the rules of my 'white flag' parley. I tolerantly listened to Cody crow a monotonous diatribe describing his high degree of hunting, fishing and trapping skills accomplished under his self-imposed, strict code of ethical and legal behavior earning him great respect throughout the community as an exemplary outdoorsman. "Had he not continually provided key information to the wardens on the illegalities of so many miscreants? Had he ever been accused of breaking wildlife law by anyone?" I trumped Cody's aces with two wild cards, stating the answer was 'yes' to both questions!

Cody's tirade silenced the song of trustworthiness in my soul, comprehending our mutual respect was a one-sided charade. Delving into the wild-eyed mind of a man I thought I knew, I suffered the sinking of yet another hollow friendship, pirated by the dark side of an aging local hero.

I held loyal friendships sacred; gilded treasures bearing a full measure of tried-and-true camaraderie essential for my ability to keep on, keepin' on. I expected my colleagues to follow a strict code of honorable outdoor conduct. Unveiled as a poacher, Cody no longer met these criteria. Not the first time I suffered the gut-wrenching wrath of fraudulent friendships, I nevertheless found myself stunned realizing I was a mere pawn in Cody's chess game of illicit outdoor behavior. Cody was a double agent, using his faux warden relationships to polish his stellar outdoorsman image to deceive all wardens of his fraudulent behavior. Practiced wardensmanship instructed me to check this mouthy king of the veld, curtly warning him to reel in his deceitful lines, emphasizing I witnessed the unlicensed Cody work hard for a shot at an antelope. The Colonel and C.I. stood pie-eyed and silent while Cody continued covering his tracks with additional dirt, stating his rifle was for hunting coyotes (legal) and to 'back up' his fellow hunters (illegal). Cody explained the doe was abandoned on his advice because they were unsure who actually killed it. I questioned Cody, a licensed guide and outfitter well acquainted with Colorado's tagging requirements, on what was gained by hiding the untagged antelope in the sagebrush? Cody clarified they covered it to protect it from crows, magpies and coyotes while deciding who would tag it. *Yeah, right!* Knowing Rosebud's elderly matriarch Judy Lichengal, a close friend of all three, held a doe antelope license and was infamous for tagging big game killed by others, I implied perhaps they were planning on bringing another licensed individual to the kill site. *Paydirt!* The shamefaced expressions worn by the Colonel and C.I confirmed their ploy for hiding the doe. The Colonel, an innocent player in this hunting game and heavily manipulated by Cody, took responsibility for not tagging the antelope. C.I admitted he too knew better and was sorry for shooting at an antelope from the county road. Both were good men. Cody, discredited in front of his compadres, showing no remorse for his guiding role in their misdeeds, ended his pitiful rant declaring what gave me the right to spy on them from private lands anyway. I delightfully watched Cody's mind ponder my meaningless answer; "I was watching because my Wheaties kicked in!"

The grapevine later confirmed Cody's plan to transfer Ms. Lichengal's license to the doe antelope. In fact, she ultimately was given the antelope by the Colonel. Cody continued publicly chastising me for utilizing unfair tactics and unprofessional behavior in rendering an unjust case against the naïve C.I and Colonel. But an unpredictable, pleasant surprise transpired when the grapevine fermented complementary wine by ratting out the rat; distilling countless tales of laws Cody bent and broke over the years, incessantly bragging about pulling the wool over the eyes of the witless wardens. Overtly exposed as committing mutiny on the public's wild bounty, he continued portraying himself as a persecuted hunting God, his perverted rationalizations approximating the poetic; lyrical fabrications of a whimsical broken old man, trapped in his own set of misbehavior.

Needless to say, the warm greetings my family and I family received while dining at Cody's restaurant chilled significantly, as did the size of my rib-eye; little did I know what was at *steak* by exposing a false friend as a miscreant.

One impulse from a vernal wood
May teach you more of man,
Of moral and evil good, Than all the sages can.
-William Wordsworth, "The Tables Turned," 1798

SWAN SONGS

"Death will come, always out of season."
Black Elk Omaha Chief

Death! Life's dead-on reality plays an emotive role in every enforcement officer's game. During my watch, I endured the disturbing reality of human demise in various scenarios, stark lessons of how quickly life's fire can be smitten. Murder/suicide, self-annihilation, drownings, vehicle fatalities, hunting accidents, and airplane crashes; individual tales narrating tragic stories of death and its impacts on families and friends suffering the worst of times. Managing the grief-stricken wrath of those anticipating death's heart-wrenching verification significantly impacted my life, providing lessons on slowing down, the importance of family and friends, paying attention to one's surroundings, driving safely, the values of first aid training, wearing life preservers, firearm safety, and watching my back.

SWAN SONGS
The wild swan's death-hymn took the soul
Of that waste place with joy
Hidden in sorrow: at first to the ear

The warble was low, and full and clear; ...
But anon her awful jubilant voice,
With a music strange and manifold,
Flow'd forth on a carol free and bold;
As when a mighty people rejoice
With shawms, and with cymbals, and harps of gold...
Lord Alfred Tennyson

Ancient Greek mythology spawned beliefs that swans, just before death, sing a tranquil song, after being relatively quiet (not musical) during their lifetime. This long-debated metaphorical proverb endures throughout modern-day arts, poetry, and writings signifying the rejoiceful chorus of one's final life performance. Studying these fables in academic literature classes prompted my imaginative contemplation possibly two individuals, approaching death, seemingly experienced the sense of tranquility articulated in the mythos of the Swan Song.

PEACEFUL PASSING

September 7, 1983. Hearing a Sheriff's Office radio call reporting a deceased fisherman at the Owl Creek Ranch, I answered I was nearby and would drive in and wait for assistance. At the ranch house, I spied a body lying prone in the gravel driveway. Strangely, there was no one around. Approaching, I discovered an elderly man whose ashen, clammy face divulged one who had undoubtedly met his maker. Dressed in waders, a fishing vest, and wide brimmed hat, a baited fishing pole at his side, was a solemn sight indeed. Looking small, as dead people do, eyes staring skyward, his calm expression disclosed his last breath was exhaled through a relaxed smile. Discovering numerous 10-12-inch butter browns in his wicker creel *(OK, I counted them!)*, the fisherman met his kismet drowning his last worm on a summer day on the Michigan River. Performing his final act as an angler, I pondered if dying bestowed him the serenity of the Swan's music. When Sheriff Cure arrived, the visibly shaken rancher and his wife appeared stating the deceased, fishing on their ranch property, was staying in Gould with his family. Cure asked me to deliver the bad news as he needed to wait for the coroner. Reluctantly, I agreed, and after suffering the mayhem of the fisherman's distressed family, requested they follow me to the ranch. Persevering a second round of family grief at the ranch, I returned home and spent the rest of the day with my family, brooding the fisherman's death.

BEHIND BLUE EYES

October 19, 1992. Late afternoon during elk season, a young man hiked off a rugged wilderness ridge near Red Elephant Mountain, drove the long distance into Sage Hen and reported he accidentally shot his friend while unloading his rifle. Believing his comrade was still alive, Sheriff Gary Cure, County Coroner George Crocket, Wildlife Officers Donnie Rodriguez, Kirk Snyder and I, drove to his camp behind Big Creek Lake and followed the distressed lad up the steep terrain dragging a 2-wheeled game cart. Topping the ridge three hours later at dusk and unable to locate the victim, we spent a sleepless, bone chilling night facing a blazing fire, roasting our sweat soaked bodies one frozen side at a time, melting the Vibram soles on our boots. At daybreak, we located the stone-cold victim propped against a fallen tree fifty yards from our firepit. Shot in the neck, he undoubtedly died instantly. Staring into the deceased hunter's crystalline blue eyes calmly focused on the boundless depths of cloudless, cerulean sky, I noted his facial expression revealed not terror, but peaceful serenity. Zipping his lifeless corpse into a body bag and binding it to the cart, thoughts of the young hunter's last hunt haunted my mind the entire two-hour trip down the mountain, their dead weight pulling me down the precipitous ridge. Suffering the wrath of his comrade's death, the young hunter spoke not a word until reaching camp where he cried his emotional grief with family and friends.

Sadly, I experienced many deaths throughout my career.

-The late-evening murder/suicide scenario at the bar/ restaurant in Three Way. The lone waitress, closing the restaurant late one evening, called and asked her husband to join her because her last customer was suspiciously hanging around. While her husband sat waiting, the customer shot and killed him. Attempting to rape the waitress, she managed to escape into the night's winter cold and reported the incident at a nearby ranch. The Sheriff, rounding up a posse, searched for and located the murderer's vehicle parked on the Saratoga highway near the state line, a fresh set of tracks crossing a fence and post holing through the deep sage snow. The Sheriff asked me to return to town and bring Division of Wildlife's Tucker Sno-Cat to chase down the fleeing felon! Luckily, before unloading the Sno-Cat, the murderer was discovered less than 100 yards from his vehicle. Lying prone, legs crossed, he killed himself with a self-inflicted gunshot wound. Imagine my relief of not needing to pursue the murderer with the sheriff and several armed citizens riding shotgun in the Sno-Cat!

-July 8, 1973. Scuba divers retrieving the body of a Lake John fisherman who drowned attempting to swim from his capsized boat against the warnings of family on shore. The victim, having a permanent tracheotomy and no business swimming, disappeared into the mossy waters. Divers, unable to located him, were directed by his wife to the exact spot he disappeared, instantly locating the body.

-May 16,1975. The drowning of a pre-teen lad thrown from a rubber raft floating the treacherous spring rapids in the North Platte River Canyon. His father, believing they successfully negotiated all rough water, allowed the boy to remove his life vest just ahead of the most dangerous rapids of their float trip. The weeklong search initiated my experience in consoling grieving family members, a proficiency I never fully achieved.

May 11, 1977. First on scene at a vehicle accident north of Sage Hen, I witnessed the contrasting damages caused by a head on collision between an economy car versus a large luxury size sedan. The small car, veering left of center, crashed into the large car, passenger side to passenger side. The man and his wife in the sedan, wearing seatbelts, walked away uninjured. The driver of the small car (no seatbelt) was critically injured and later died. The passenger and a small dog were killed instantly. The dead man (no seatbelt), legs crushed, knees forced under his chin by the car's battery protruding from the glove compartment, had smashed his head into the windshield, verifies the safety features of wearing seatbelts and the advantages of driving a larger car. The county's single ambulance transporting the injured man to the Laramie hospital, the state patrolman asked me to take the deceased, in a body bag, to the morgue's single cement slab at the State Highway Department headquarters in Sage Hen. Unable to close the tailgate, I white knuckled the steering wheel into town, extremely worried the body may slide out. That was a drive I will never forget!

July 6, 1978. The early summer drowning of a man camped with his wife at Lake Katherine, in the Mount Zirkel Wilderness. His wife hiked out and reported her husband left their tent at daylight and never returned. Searching the wilderness lake's perimeter, we found where her husband slipped down a large snowbank into the lake, attempted to scratch his way back up the icy slope, and apparently succumbed to the death grip of the glacial waters. After several failed attempts by scuba divers to locate his body, the victim haunted the lake for over 60 days before surfacing, nearly to the day predicted by forensic experts. The Sheriff, taking in his horses to pack out the body, Sage Hen Marshall Lee Pierce and I set up a command post at the Lone Pine trailhead using the county's milk truck converted into a search and rescue vehicle. Vainly attempting to calm the frenzied family members, we began hearing multiple gunshots high above our location. Soon, a hiker arrived stating the Sheriff was shooting rocks off boulders at the lake. *What?* Continued shots and eventually hearing someone hollering, another hiker reported the very inebriated Sheriff was nearby, leading his horse with the body draped over its back. Not wanting the family to witness the pending events, we instructed them to meet us in Sage Hen where they could peacefully identify the victim. In old school, Bull Pen style, the coroner met the rescue party, minus the Sheriff, at the local gas station where the body bag was laid on the bay's hydraulic rack, unzipped and gravely identified by the family.

August 25, 1988. First on scene at a rollover car accident on a gravel road near Seymour Lake, where a man had been thrown through the windshield. The driver, unable to locate his friend, hitched a ride to Rosebud and reported the accident. Following a hard target search, I located a grossly greasy mass of hair. Thinking it was a scalp (later identified as the victim's hairpiece), I soon located the broken corpse of the hairless man in thick willows, dead as the rocks around him.

December 4-6, 1978. Answering a report of a commuter plane, a 7pm flight from Steamboat Springs carrying 24 passengers, going down in blizzard conditions 'somewhere' on the west side of the Bull Pen, the Sheriff organized an unorganized posse from the local bars. Turning loose a herd of highly spirited men into the night's blizzarding grim with no clues of the plane's whereabouts, was a sight indeed. Understandably, a few wandering searchers became lost and returned to their vehicles. Others, wrecking their snow machines racing through zero visibility conditions, I volunteered to transport the nearly frozen wounded back to Sage Hen. While three county Search and Rescue teams and the Civil Air Patrol concentrated on the downed planes transmitter signal, the exact location of the plane remained unknown until six survivors hiked into the Grizzly Creek Guard Station at daylight and directed rescue teams into the crash site. As snowplows opened the road into the Guard Station, a caravan of rescuers, driving snowmachines and Tucker Sno-Cats, headed to the crash site located on the open powerline corridor cut through heavy timber on USFS property. I remained at the Guard Station to aid medical personnel care for the wounded. The injured and uninjured survivors, some lashed to the Sno-Cats side, is a memory I will never forget. Welcoming the medical experience, I quickly learned those with in the most serious condition remained relatively quiet while those with less severe injuries wailed loudly. Miraculously, 22 of the 24 survived. One passenger was found dead at the crash scene and the pilot, after hero-ically landing the plane in the snow-covered opening of the power lines, later died of head injuries.

Date not found-The tragic tale of a young boy separated from his father while hunting elk in the remotely wild Old Roach area on the north end of the Bull Pen. A search party located the boy's frozen body the following morning, leaning against a tree, a victim of hypothermia. Water soaked from slogging through a beaver pond, he died during the night less than a hundred yards from the road search teams travelled, calling out his name all night.

. . .

Of course, not all outdoor mishaps end in death: the Grim Reaper's scythe failing to slice his fatal blow;

-Packing out a west side hunter suffering a severely mangled shoulder from a gunshot wound inflicted by his hunting companion who mistook his orange vest for the back end of an elk.

- Outfitter Don Bourbeau Sr. and I, utilizing horses to pack out an injured man camped at Blue Lake in the Zirkel Wilderness area. The victim, breaking a leg while 'recreationally' sliding down the lake's steep snowfields, crashed into the bare boulders at the bottom. Floating the injured man across the lake in a rubber raft, Don and I hoisted him onto my horse (I hiked out on foot) and returned to the trailhead with the victim in good spirits and experiencing little pain. His campmate, however, after an early morning hike into the lake and setting up camp, hiking back out to report the accident, riding horseback to the lake and back to the trailhead, ended the day extremely exhausted and very saddle sore. Barely able to walk, he was unquestionably in worse condition than his campmate

-Rescuing a man in a Flight for Life helicopter from the remote Wolverine Lake in the Zirkel wilderness. His campmate hiked out and reported his fishing friend had suffered a heart attack. Landing the chopper on rugged terrain below their camp, the nurse and I carried the two-hundred-pound man on a stretcher over the craggy seventy-five yards to the helicopter. Weighing no more than one hundred pounds herself, she was one tough nurse. We later found out the victim suffered an extreme case of altitude sickness and had no heart problems.

I also have tales tattling the lighter side of human misfortune:

CONCRETE OBSTACLES

The Bull Pen's good Doctor France often found himself remedying the assorted ailments and injuries suffered by members of the outdoor community. One incident, involving three young Nebraska archery elk hunters who annually packed in a wilderness camp on the west side of the Bull Pen making the critical mistake of packing in only freeze-dried meals. After several days consuming the colon binding 'feasts', their hunt was crudely interrupted by a vital trip to Sage Hen seeking medical treatment for extreme bloat and what they described as the tremendous difficulty of evacuating stools having the dimensions and sharp edges of cement blocks! Dr. France curing their near terminal constipation with strong laxatives, advised drinking plenty of water, and refilling their backcountry larder with plenty of fruits and vegetables. Given time, they recovered and successfully harvested two elk.

BUTT SHOT

There I was, interviewing a hunter who 'accidentally' shot himself in the buttocks one Friday afternoon before elk season. Contacted by our good doctor David France after he had stitched up the hunter's rear end, I grabbed the proper investigative forms, recorded Doc's information, and headed to the hunter's camp on Independence Mountain. Finding the wounded man, Dopey Keister, standing in front of a blazing campfire with two comrades, I noted the holstered big iron hanging from his right hip. Asking how he was doing, Dopey jokingly admitted he would not be sitting down the next few days! Filling the blanks on the Accident Report, I found his account matched those provided by Doc France; accidentally dropping his pistol causing it to hit the ground and fire, the bullet grazing his left buttocks. His camp mates indicated they were absent when the accident occurred. When asked if the pistol was cocked before it fell to the ground, the victim said it was not. Checking the firearm, a western style Ruger single action revolver, I found it in good working condition. Suspicious, I finished the report, told Dopey it could have been much worse, to be more careful, and take diligent care of his wound.

Not entirely satisfied, I walked to a nearby camp and asked a hunter if he witnessed the hunting accident, who rudely declared he never spoke to anyone involved in law enforcement. *OooKaay!* Next, I knocked on the door of a giant motor home and was greeted by a quaint, older lady fixing supper for her husband who was out scouting for elk. Accepting a cup of coffee, I asked if she witnessed the hunting accident in the nearby camp. With a warming smile, she reiterated the story of observing the victim drinking beer while quick drawing and shooting his pistol at empty beer cans. Suddenly, she heard the gun fire and watched Dopey fall to his knees and cry out in pain while holding his backside. Running over and asking if there was anything she could do, Dopey, packing a shirt into the back of his pants, exclaimed he was driving to Sage Hen to find a doctor. Returning several hours later, Dopey said his wound required ten stitches, but otherwise he was OK.

The reader needs no imagination to comprehend the theatrics involved when I again contacted Dopey. Listening to the very humbled man confess the details of his self-inflicted wound enhanced by the facial expressions of his camp mates; a narrative of a drinking man's bullet finding a worthy victim.

"There is no cure for birth and death save to enjoy the interval."
George Santayana

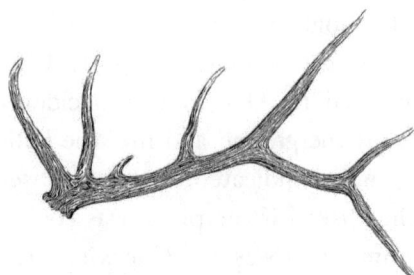

Hunter phone call to Warden: *"When do deer turn into elk?"*

Warden to Hunter: *"Just before deer season."*

LICKEY SPLIT - RIDE A BIKE GO TO JAIL!

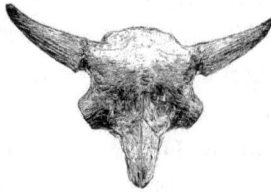

September 10, 1983. My day began picking up a trainee at the bunkhouse and patrolling the opening day of Sage Grouse season. Finding few hunters, we received Rout County radio traffic requesting assistance at the Rabbit Ears restaurant/bar to investigate damages caused by individuals attending an afterhours party. Seizing the opportunity to introduce my trainee to incidents not related to wildlife, we headed towards Rabbit Ears Pass.

Arriving before the Rout County deputies, we surveyed the demolished dining area. Broken beer bottles, glasses, plates, and tableware mixed with busted tables and chairs covering the wood floor, my eyes locked on a frizzled ball of brown hair. *What?* Deputies arriving in separate vehicles, two were immediately dispatched to investigate an elderly couple's early morning discovery of a 'hippie' (their words) passed out on the kitchen table of their nearby cabin. The remaining deputy briefed us on the early morning complaint made at the Routt County Sheriff's Office: a young woman, Teasie Barrett, specified she had been beaten by her boyfriend during a late-night party at the restaurant. Displaying face and arm bruises, Teasie indicated she wanted to press charges. Admitting drugs and alcohol were involved, she explained a fist fight broke out between her boyfriend, Henry

Hairball, and friend, Warp Oglebush, after she began table dancing in the nude. When Warp began licking her legs, Hairball began beating her! Warp, defending Teasie, jumped Hairball instigating a whole house brawl. *I am not making this up!*

Staring through the shattered glass of the broken picture window, I observed a man's head pop out of the grassy highway right of way. After looking around, the man, wearing a ponytail, belly crawled across the pavement and disappeared into in the brush on the other side of the highway. Alerting the deputy, we went outside and intercepted the man slinking towards a Harley Davidson motorcycle parked next to the restaurant. Displaying the detoxing hyperactivity of a long night of mixing drugs and alcohol, the man's driver's license identified him as none other than the infamous Henry Hairball, later discovered as the same individual breaking into and discovered passed out in the elderly couple's cabin. The deputy, informing Hairball he was under arrest for assault, ordered him to kneel and place his hands on his head. Returning to his patrol car to retrieve handcuffs, I safeguarded the mentally frayed Hairball. Asking about the mass of hair protruding from his rear pocket, Hairball replied someone had pulled it out and he hoped he could put it back. *Wow!* When the deputy returned, Hairball, noticing the cuffs, panicked, scraped a handful of gravel, shoved it into his mouth and warned he was going to swallow and commit suicide. Astounded, we momentarily stood back and watched the stoned man gag out his woes. Then it really got interesting,

Hairball, choking, screaming, sweating, off balance, and waving his arms to keep us away, I, having recently completed a course in self-defense and learning wrist control techniques, believed I could restrain his eccentric behavior. Grabbing his extended arm by the wrist, I placed my right palm over the back of his hand, secured his wrist with my left hand and twisted. Powerfully wrenching his straightened arm down placing immense torque on Hairball's wrist, elbow, and shoulder joints, I brashly ordered him to spit out the rocks. Without hesitation, Hairball expelled the gravel with the force of a shotgun blast! Face planting him into the ground, I straddled his back, handcuffed him, and helped him to his feet. Escorting him to the passenger side of the deputy's car, we fastened his seat belt while he repeatedly wailed, "Ride a bike, go to jail!' Hairball, repeatedly kicking the glove box, I secured his ankles with several zip ties retrieved from my vehicle. Because Hairball had a deep scalp wound matted with bloody hair, the deputy indicated we would transport him to the Steamboat Springs hospital before booking him into jail. *We?* Asking me to ride in the back seat of his patrol car to control the madman, I asked my trainee to follow in my pickup.

In only a few miles it became obvious the deputy could not have made the trip alone. While Hairball continued detoxing, conversing with someone in another world, I attempted controlling his constant struggling by pulling his ponytail. The harder he fought the harder I pulled, to the point I could feel hair breaking free of his scalp. Continuously chanting, "Ride a bike, go to jail," Hairball's mental state frequently switched from extreme depression to overwhelming happiness. Pulling into the hospital, I opened Hairball's door, watching in awe as he instantly pulled up his knees and, with a thrusting strike, kicked out the deputy's windshield! Infuriated, the deputy and I roughly pulled Hairball from the vehicle, set him on his knees, hoisted him up by his armpits and ankles, and hauled him into the hospital. Passing three elderly ladies sitting in the waiting room, Hairball glared them down and screamed, "What the f...k are you looking at!"

A nurse directed us to a room where we placed Hairball on a table, strapped him down and stood back while a doctor administered medicine to calm him down. Listening to Hairball grossly refuse stitches, his girlfriend Teasie peaked through the door, gained his attention, said, "I love you!"

This is where the trainee and I rode away, leaving the deputy with what would surely be another rodeo!

Hi Yo Silver, away!

TATTLETALE HEART

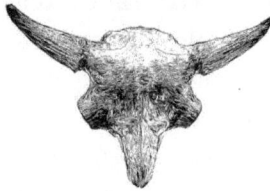

Late October 1980, I was doggedly harvesting the bountiful fruit from a grapevine thriving on the Bull Pen's fertile hunting grounds. Today's grapes shot word of several illegal elk kills on a large section of private land where a blend of unscrupulous hunters and abundant elk distilled both warden wine and nimrod whines. Wildlife Officers can legally enter private lands to check hunters or fishermen without the landowner's permission, stimulating a superfluity of rabble-rousing discussions and field escapades. Numerous 'Friend Ships' are wrecked when wardens cannonball hunters violating wildlife law on private property. Appreciated or not, I unwaveringly performed my duty-bound forays onto the private hinterlands, where the security of fences and locked gates provide some a deceitful sense of security to defile the furtive wild. Working for wild beasts and the sporting good against the cunningly bad, no matter what side of the fence they were on, made my day.

During my watch, private land hunting was significantly changing. In the past, Bull Pen residents and their friends enjoyed undeterred access across most private lands. However, increasing elk populations triggered more elk using private property year-round as well as large numbers of elk driven off public onto private lands during the hunting seasons, resulted in landowners discovering there was good money in leasing access rights to the private sector. 'Hatfield-McCoy' feuds developed between landowners and hunters as trespass and illegal hunting increased. Old relationships became mired in the stinking sty of tipster against tipster, providing wardens a leap into the squealing pigpen. One grunt of misbehavior led to incessant hogwash, often resulting in unfavorable results on both sides of the fence.

And there I was, while weaving my vehicle in 'grandma' gear over a frozen private two track through low-growth harvested pine, I spotted a familiar vehicle parked along a property boundary fence line. The driver, Angst Gunner, was a well-known rancher recognized for his hunting deeds and misdeeds throughout the community, and more-so to the wardens. Angst owned or had legal access to large tracts of land supporting sizeable populations of big game. The wardens knew him as the leader of the well-known band of native and imported nimrods renowned for corruptly killing large numbers of elk, their misdeeds rowdily telegraphed by their own boastful bragging. As a result, wardens were grilled relentlessly about our inability to capture these blatant poachers pilfering the public's bounty. And, in due time, we did. But that is another story.

The fence separated Angsts' ground from what he could not hunt. Walking up to his pickup window, his furrowed brow and squinting eyes already questioned why I was on his private land. I cut to the quick explaining I was working a solid tip of several illegal elk kills occurring in this vicinity. I enjoyed firing loaded questions at the overly suspicious to witness the unpredictable 'ricochets' they echoed. Angst hang-fired, "What exactly are you are looking for?" As his mind processed what he knew versus what I may or may not know, I interrupted his thoughts probing who in his party had filled their elk tags. Angst conceded having several elk hanging in his barn, a couple harvested by wives of his hunting party. Women are known throughout the hunting world for the ability to fill their tags afore their men; amazingly killing game without leaving their abode or workplace.

Pointing out a murder of crows erratically fluttering over a glossy gut pile croaking caws of culinary fulfillment from feasting on rotting entrails, Angst admitted witnessing a hunter standing there over the carcass of a raghorn bull elk on opening day. Strangely breaking the sacred hunting code of silence, he identified the man as Hansel Elgrande, a highly respected emigrant known for his jubilant personality, stellar work ethic, and sensational esteem for life. Hansel and his wife Gretel represented the Bull Pen's finest citizenry; products of their overseas wartime experiences surviving the grasp of mankind's very worst. Like Angst, Hansel was frequently accused of illegally filling the licenses of others. Unlike Angst, whenever queried, Hansel was always steadfastly upfront and honest. In one instance he provided detailed information leading to a rock-solid charge against the actual perpetrator involved in the illegal elk case Hansel himself was implicated in. However, knowing well that party hunting was deeply embedded in the local hunting culture, and Hansel was licensed to harvest only a cow elk, it was imperative I speak to him in person.

Pondering why Angst violated the sacred brotherhood code by snitching on Hansel, believing they were good friends, I entered my Columbo mode and, while checking his elk license, annoyingly queried leading questions regarding members of his hunting party; what they were licensed for, where he hunted the previous day etc. Driving away, leaving him in an uneasy state of paranoia, I checked my rearview mirror and smiled; Angst already on his two-way radio, no doubt 'Paul Revering' my presence on their mountain.

Contacting Hansel at his Sage Hen home the following morning, I found him curiously nervous but, as always, pleasantly chivalrous. Gretel amiably served coffee and scrumptious homemade muffins and joined us at the kitchen table. When confronted with shooting a bull elk on Conner Creek, Hansel resolutely denied the accusation, admitting only to walking up to a critically wounded bull lying along a fence line, shot by a hunting comrade. Gretel suddenly stood and stoically left the room without a word, Hansel's eyes intently following. The air, thickened with the discernible stillness of deception, signaled it was time for me to let the sleeping bear lie. *This is where the warden rides away!* I stood offering Hansel my hand stating because of the high respect I held for his family, I believed his story and needed no further information, despite sensing this would not be our final conversation.

Good wardensmanship allots time for the meat of the hunting game to marinate.

My warden instincts precisely accurate, it was no surprise when a highly emotional Hansel knocked on my office door that same afternoon. I tried calming him by emphasizing our time-honored friendship could resolve whatever was on his mind. In short breaths, Hansel said after I left his home, Gretel and his son admonished him for dishonoring the family's covenants of truth and honesty, sending him on a conscience driven guilt trip to my office. His moral compass, haunted by a 'tattling' heart drumming deafening messages to his moral code, conquered his ability to continue hiding behind his lies. Valiantly falling on his sword, he told the woeful tale of killing a bull elk along the property boundary that seemed unable to jump the fence. Believing the bull was wounded, he killed it and a hunting compadre tagged it. Field dressing the bull, they found a 50 caliber round ball in one hind quarter apparently inflicted during the September muzzleloader season, and another bullet wound in its neck, possibly triggered by a member of his hunting party. Not certain who wounded the bull, he believed pursuing and killing it was the right thing to do. Vowing to never again lie to me, the sincere 'mea culpa' expression covering his face made it crystal clear he never would.

Looking straight into Hansel's eyes, I sternly affirmed killing a bull elk on a cow license is illegal. The uncertainty of who initially wounded the bull was, in my mind, highly suspicious. I explained an unlicensed hunter putting a critically wounded animal out of its misery enters hunting's grey area but, under certain conditions, is considered ethically right in the eyes of most wardens. This situation was certainly not the case as there was background evidence Hansel also had taken shots at the bull. I emphasized failing to divulge the entire truth this morning was Hansel's biggest mistake. His lies defined his misdeeds. Calculating due process, I scratched out a sizeable tic before explaining with a firm handshake, his truthfulness, as late coming as it was, substantially increased my admiration for his entire family. Experiencing the tranquil peace of a clean conscience, Hansel was now visibly at ease, our friendship remaining strong and secure.

Citizens like Hansel and Gretel, living under self-imposed, strict moral codes, render living the Bull Pen so distinctly special. Their rich European background blending with the Bull Pen's abounding western spirit of freedom and independence, are one of many strong chords tightly binding the community's socio-cultural fabric. Hunting American style provided Hansel treasured male bonding recreation with friends and family while delivering highly nutritional meat Gretel prepared in a manner putting the finest restaurants to shame.

Angst, for reasons unknown, steered me towards his good neighbor Hansel. Was he diverting me from the misdeeds of those hunting his side of the fence, or perhaps getting even because he no longer had permission to hunt the other side? Maybe he was greedily jealous thinking the bull could have been his if it jumped the fence. But this I know, implicating Hansel had nothing to do with field justice for the bull or Angst's respect for wildlife law, and everything to do with spitefully avenging a grudge over a boundary fence.

"There is no witness so dreadful, no accuser so terrible as the conscience that dwells in the heart of every man."
Polybius

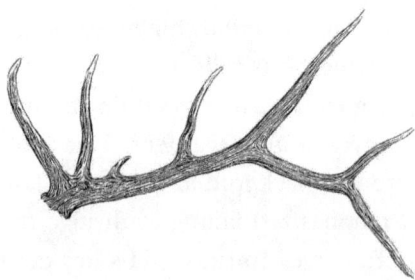

RED VELVET BLUES

There I was! Crossing, before daylight, the Colorado/Wyoming state line north of the long-abandoned mining town of Pearl. Driving through the clearcuts below Blackhall Mountain, deer seemingly everywhere, I snaked my way into the narrow, tree lined two-track paralleling Damfino Park. It was archery deer and elk season and knowing both were abundant on both sides of the state line, my gut told me time invested here area would pay dividends. Stopping frequently, I heard bulls bugling their testosterone driven chorus' across the Damfino Creeks puzzle-pieced meadows. Periodically spotting anxious bulls herding groups of nervous cows and calves made my pre-dawn venture very worthwhile. It was in this Park many years ago, while bowhunting with Cousin Tim, we discovered the buffalo skull pictured on my books' front covers. The tip of its horn protruding from a floating, sod covered bog revealed this bison may have succumbed by sinking into the bog; or trapped from migrating to the lowlands and starving due to heavy early snows; or killed by a Native Americans projectile point. Not knowing is the wild's haunting mysticism. Truth be told, Damfino Park was a better place with the buffalo.

At that time, Damfino was remotely accessible from the North by meandering two tracks, and easily accessible from the south off the well graveled Colorado State Line road connecting Pearl and the Encampment River. Aimlessly patrolling all morning and finding no one, I shared lunch with several gray jays before weaving my way out, electing an early return home for a rare afternoon and evening spent with family.

Predictably, driving once again through Pearl, I received a call from the Sheriff's Office reporting concerned archery hunters hearing multiple gun shots on Independence Mountain near Wills Reservoir. My family evening quickly disappearing , I turned onto the steep, dirt road, slow tracking my vehicle upwards to the head of Wheeler Creek and hid my vehicle. Passing time visiting an isolated elk wallow and photographing Fairy Slippers around a hidden spring, detecting no sights or sounds of human activity, I began patrolling the rim road. Locating a pickup parked above Threemile Creek, I ran the license plate through the Sheriff's Office, finding it registered to Bane Bowman, an archery hunter I routinely checked in years past. Deciding to stretch my legs and stalk down the rough two-track into Threemile, I was instantly lured by the bugles of two, if not three, bull elk. Mesmerized by the fluctuating timbre tones floating through the forest, I echolocated one bull fast tracking my way. Stalking towards Sugarloaf Mountain, I spotted Bowman crouched in thick Buffalo Berry, his face painted the color of his camo clothing. Acknowledging each other's presence, we had no time to speak as the bull quickly closed the distance, his last bugle less than thirty yards away. Motioning Bowman to stay down, I backed away and softly bugled. The wind in our favor, the incoming bull instantly responded. Countering with several chirps from my cow call, gaping in heart pounding astonishment, Bowman and I witnessed the bull raucously crash out of the brushy timber and come to a screeching halt, scanning all directions for a rival bull herding cows. *DAMN!*. Close enough to taste the bull's pungent scent, my knotted guts and cramped knees, I could only imagine the thrilling agony Bowman was experiencing. Violently raking his hormone fueled aggression against a small aspen foe, the bull bellowed a guttural bugle, pissed on his underbelly, and commenced shredding the remaining velvet from his heavy 5X5 antlers. My eyes on Bowman, not 20 yards from the raging bull, I deliberated why he was not driving an arrow into the elk's heaving chest. Hell, he was not even at full draw!

Suddenly, Bowman's head turned my way and, his white, luminescent eyes beaming through a dark painted face expressing extreme urgency, he faintly mouthed, "Is there any chance you could sell me an elk license?" *WHAT?* Shrugging a negative, I resisted another cow chirp thinking the rutting bull might violate the dignity of the cow urine scent-soaked, Bowman. Once again, the bull bugled, posing a few minutes before hound-dogging into the timber to face his blaring challenger .

Approaching, I found Bowman shaken and quite stirred, chastising himself for purchasing only an archery deer license, electing to hunt elk later during the rifle season because of so many unsuccessful years bow hunting elk. Picking slivers of red velvet from the demolished aspen, I asked what he would have done if I had not been there and he said, "Honestly, I do not know"!

There's a million stories in the naked woods!

PINK OPS

June 1990. Understand, or not, I acquired a habit of wearing pink baseball caps whenever fishing. Initially nitpicked by my comrades (why would a man wear pink), donning glowing headgear was accepted as one more of my peculiar attributes, and quite handy for tracking my whereabouts when river fishing.

And there I was, capped in pink, float tubing South Delaney Butte Lake, fly casting a Hornberg dry trailed by a weighted emerger mimicking a colossal hatch of large caddis skittering across the lake's surface. Hefty, broad shouldered rainbows voraciously snapping caddis emergents and walloping the adults, the stars aligned for an evening of topwater fishing delight. Missing strikes, losing flies, or hooking and releasing trout on almost every cast, I sculled past two boat fishermen, Heckle and Jeckle, cackling about the incredible fishing. Watching Jeckle slip a fat rainbow into a submerged wire basket hanging from their boat, I noted it held several more. Their legal limit being two trout apiece, they had my attention. *Someone' knocking at my door, someone's ringin' my bell .... Let em in!* All too often I ran into worthy warden turmoil on personal time. If these two thwarted my rare fishing time by pirating the lake's bounty, I would share my misery with a dose of warden wrath. With a smile and a nod, I re-entered my fishing stupor.

Shortly, Heckle cawed to a group of spirited partygoers on the bank. Two young men paddled out in a canoe, merrily retrieved four trout from the wire basket, and returned to shore. *HOKA HEY!* Fifteen minutes later, the fishing magpies crowed bagging another limit and the canoeing pair transported four more trout to shore. Overhearing swagger about a stash of trout in their Sage Hen motel room, I allowed the fish filchers another illicit round before putting on my warden face. Understand, while they fished their way towards ticketville, I too was catching and releasing a wealth of trout, warden multitasking at its finest!

After they sent another limit to shore, I paddled up to their boat and asked, "Don't you guys worry about being caught by the game warden?" Heckle giddily replied, "Hell no, that son-of-a-bitch never checks boat fishermen!" After a thoughtful, eye searching pause, he sheepishly replied, "Surely you're not the game warden?" *Don't call me Shirley!* Displaying my badge, I requested fishing licenses and explained I would retrieve my personal pickup and meet them on shore. Joining the somber young men and women, their party was obviously over. Tallying Heckle and Jeckle's illegal trout, collecting several fishing licenses from their stone-faced comrades, I escorted them to town. Finding an abundance of iced trout in several coolers, the other license holders fibbed catching their limits earlier. One, having flown his private plane into Sage Hen from Utah, offered to pay the boatmen's fines but I, an equal opportunity warden, increased the poaching pair's agony by scratching tics to both. A worthy case, indeed!

Returning to fish dusk's magical hour, the waning caddis hatch supplying less competition for my flies, the ravenous trout continued hammering my imitations. The Utah pilot, flying home, buzzed the lake twice tipping the plane's wings, enhancing the ambiance of my evening's good fortune.

Of course, word of my crimson disguise quickly entwined its way through the fishing grapevine. But can you believe, my exposed clandestine operation was greatly obscured when several angling friends began wearing their own pink hats, creating the paranoiac perception of a persistent warden's presence. *Priceless!*

Warden: *"How's the fishing?"*

Fisherman: *"Pretty good."*

Warden: *"How many fish have you kept?"*

Fisherman: *"That depends on the limit."*

CAT CANYON ELK MASSACRE

Sheriff's Office: *Wildlife 164.*
Wildlife 164: *Go ahead.*
Sheriff's Office: *We have reports of 70 shots fired near Cat Canyon needing immediate attention.*
Wildlife 164: We will *be there in thirty minute!.*
Sheriff's Office: *Copy that!*

SERIOUSLY? **70 shots?** October 17, 1987. Opening morning of elk season. There we were, Regional Wildlife Manager Walt Graul and I parked above Mexican Ridge appreciating the morning calm afore the inevitable storm of complaints triggered by hunters thundering through elk country. On cue, around noon, my radio blared the above details followed by State Parks Officers Kurt Mill and Mike Hopper confirming similar reports and were responding from the Mountain's east side. Answering we would drive in from the west, knowing immediate response was critical for intercepting what was described to the Officers as an elk slaughter. Racing east on Highway 14, my mind tracked the incessant complaints of illegal hunting activity annually occurring on the Mountain by a well-known gang of local and out of town hunters. Gunner Stockman, owner of a longstanding family ranch, allegedly directed a party hunting game on State School lands he leased for grazing and on his privately controlled ranchland. Proudly flaunting their illicit transgressions, Stockman and his hunters greatly offended the hunting good as well as non-hunting citizens, who relentlessly hounded us to snag the crowing game thieves. Today may offer the opportunity to catch the infamous poachers red-handed in the security of their private hunting lair. Well acquainted with those playing starring roles, I understood their seasoned skills of deception would deliver significant warden challenges. *Round up the usual suspects!*

Bouncing over dirt roads on the Mountain's west side, Graul and I encountered six nervous hunters transporting two properly tagged and skinned cow elk in their pickup beds. Claiming the elk were killed on BLM lands north of Cat Canyon, they denied knowledge of any illegal hunting activities. Their jittery demeanor told me otherwise. Stating they were staying in the town of Gould, separate from the main pack hunting the State School lands. Scent heavy with illicit hunting activity, my gut growled we were rousing a hornet's nest. Officer Mill and Hopper, relaying additional information hunters were killing elk (legally and illegally) driven from the School Lands, triggered my call for additional enforcement backup from the Division of Wildlife, Division of Parks, Arapaho National Wildlife Refuge and the Sheriff's Office. Wildlife Officers Kirk Snyder and Ray Varney radioed they checked 3 bulls and 3 cows, all properly tagged, belonging to Stockman's hunting group also denying knowledge of illegal activity during their morning hunt.

Entering Cat Canyon, we coordinated with Mill and Hopper who discovered the untagged carcasses of 2 cow elk, a spike bull and a 3-point bull. Neither bulls meeting the required minimum antler restrictions of four points on at least one antler and/or a 4-inch brow tine, were thus illegal. The edgy demeanor of the remaining hunters clarified we interrupted their attempts to cover the abandoned cows with additional licenses and to sneak out the illegal bulls. Those who transported tagged elk prior to our arrival had shielded, at least for now, any roles they may have played in the surplus elk kills. Running out of daylight, Snyder and I contacted Stockman's hunters and clarified we would return early tomorrow morning to meet with them and continue our investigation. Acknowledging they heard a lot of shooting not belonging to their hunting party, they reiterated their elk were harvested legally and suggested we focus on the illegal activity of the Gould hunters.

Rendezvousing for supper in Gould, our team shared information and discussed tomorrow's game plan. Team members retrieved the four elk on the mountain and transported them to the Division of Wildlife headquarters in Sage Hen. Re-contacting the Gould hunters at their cabin, Kirk and I found them belligerent and uncooperative, incriminating Stockman's group for setting them up to disguise their illegal behavior. Fingers pointing in all directions, all were craftily playing the lawyer game creating reasonable doubt and confusion to mask their misdeeds. That evening, Kirk and I reviewed the phone messages recorded at the Sheriff's Office and taken by our wives (the uncompensated members of our team). News had spread like wildfire; locals demanded justice, newspapers and TV stations requested firsthand interviews, and the grapevine shook vigorously, significantly obstructing our ability to concentrate on the field investigation. Administrative staff took up some of the slack by managing the media pressure. Our challenges encompassed resolving the four unclaimed elk, answering questions regarding the legality of the tagged elk of both hunting groups, tracking reported blood trails leaving the State School Lands, and documenting eyewitness accounts on adjacent properties. Cleaning up this bloodbath would involve considerable time; a rogue bronc Kirk and I bucked in more than one rodeo! We were probing a case where undetected lawbreakers killed an overabundance of illegal elk while hunting the same ground at the same time as those professing their innocence! *Saddle up wardens!*

Daylight the second day, Graul, Snyder and I teamed up for another assault on the Cat Canyon hunters. Graul, playing devil's advocate, pointed out weaknesses in our investigations, his comprehensive notes greatly aiding our thought processes as we pieced together the extraordinarily complex hunting puzzle. Grab you pen and watch, Graul! Meeting the hunters at the Ranch Headquarters, it was obvious they devoted considerable time blending and reinforcing their stories. Driving into Cat Canyon, successful hunters self-assuredly led us to their kill sites, claimed one (legal?) elk and denied knowledge of other elk killed nearby. Experience dictated Kirk and I focus on the minutia. To the trained eye, nothing is trivial. Circumstantial evidence often obscure, is frequently clarified by combining evidence with hunter statements. Graul's 'devil' would be found in the details. Entering Columbo mode, our sweet and sour personalities blended into a fortifying investigative ally. Individually skilled interrogators, together we could make a mime talk. No brag just fact! We methodically mapped hunter locations, kill sites, unclaimed elk, while meticulously collecting, bagging and labeling evidence; bullets from elk carcasses, cigarette butts, rope, and wire samples from kill sites and pickup beds. Boot and vehicle tracks were photographed, and plaster casts made of well-defined imprints. Rifle serial numbers were entered into law enforcement data bases by the Sheriff's office. Live rounds collected from rifle magazines were compared to empty cartridges left at kill sites. Inspecting the final three kill locations, we discovered an illegal 2-point bull and a calf hanging in nearby timber. Hunters, never missing a chance to shut up, shrugged off any knowledge of who killed them. *Yeah, right!* Slowly, evidence, interviews and cross examinations spun threads of mistruths weaving a web of contradictions. Culprits became entangled in their own deceitful tales. Utilizing the Law of Holes, the old adage, "if you find yourself in a hole, stop digging," Kirk and I eagerly helped shovel until some were unable to crawl out without admitting guilt and/or unwittingly incriminating others.

We now had clear-cut evidence their annual ritual of illegally killing elk until all licenses were filled backfired into a catastrophic elk slaughter, far beyond what we or the hunters could have possibly imagined. Not anticipating the incredible number of elk, reported as 200 or more, driven from heavy timber into a large block of recently harvested timber and open sage, the shooters haphazardly opened fire causing the confused herd to scatter in all directions towards two separate hunting groups. Firing no less than 70 shots, they wantonly ambushed and killed 21 elk and wounded many more in a killing field of approximately one square mile. The initial shooting lasted approximately fifteen minutes, ending when there were no elk left to shoot at. After the initial barrage, sporadic shooting on adjacent properties persisted for over an hour. The mushrooming impact of yesterday's carnage bulleting through wardens and hunters alike, we detected Stockman was strikingly troubled. Initially referring to the incident as an unavoidable mistake, he now realized we were witnessing the collateral damage of first-degree poaching massacre!

Eyewitness interviews continuing into the third day confirmed the opening morning chaos of swarming elk aimlessly gunned down by shooters firing in all directions, a dangerous environment for elk and hunters. A legal hunter, sitting high in a private blind along a property boundary fence, observed one shooter firing at elk from the hip! Some hunters admitted having no idea how many shots they fired or the number of elk they shot at. Hunters adjacent to the School Lands were reported joining the illegal carnage while others legally harvested and tagged wounded elk with their licenses. Reports of severely wounded elk, one with its jaws shot off and several with broken legs, and blood trails tracked by team members leading to the spoiled carcasses of dead elk on adjacent properties further described the overall butchery. The day ended with Kirk and I crashing Stockman's outdoor cookout. Graul worriedly suggested it was a rude ploy for extracting additional information. *Once a warden, always a prick!* Entering the celebration, the group became intensely quiet, their serpentine eyes glaring sensations we were walking into a den of snakes. Amazingly, Stockman approached and expressed he would accept responsibility for all illegal elk. Kirk and I curtly clarified his offers were totally unacceptable, explaining the great injustices of ignoring the heinous behavior of all other poachers. Stockman settled on admitting illegally killing 1 cow elk (to fill his wife's tag) and provided firsthand knowledge of an illegal 4-point bull killed by a Gould cow hunter. His honor amongst thieves was a game changer, initiating some to accept responsibility for their personal wrongs. In a flash of wild justice, their confessionals led to four charges filed against Stockman's poachers (1 illegal cow elk, 1 hunting elk without a license, and 2 illegal bulls), and one charge for an illegal bull in the Gould hunting group. All, including the tongue-tied truthfully challenged, remained unwilling to implicate any of their own. Our evidence exhausted and neglected cases needing our attention in all corners of the Bull Pen, Kirk and I backed off, allowing time for the ever-ripening grapevine to whine fresh incriminating details. This was not the end game of the Cat Canyon Elk Massacre, the Fat Lady had yet to sing her song.

The fuming beast, of course, continued raising its ugly head. The hunting good, dissatisfied with our investigations, demanded more citations and heavier fines. Nonhunters who normally supported hunting, questioned the validity of the sport. Hostile assertions chastised not only the poachers but also wildlife officers for not pursuing additional charges due to our friendships with and/or fear of the perpetrators. Anti-hunters had a field day annihilating the integrity of the hunting sports using this inhumane slaughter as prime examples of the cold-hearted killing hunting encompass. Such violently toxic hostility, specifically targeting Stockman, plus strong recommendations to finalize the incident from owners of agricultural land leased by him, led us to reopen the case. By mid-November, the grapevine fermented additional evidence providing significant pieces to our complicated puzzle. Extremely upset by negative media coverage reaching national levels, threatening phone calls, hate mail and even death threats, Stockman wisely brokered our latest evidence to the hunters. Turnabout is (un)fair play resulted in hunters revealing poaching misdeeds in both groups, instigating four additional illegal elk charges against Stockman's poachers and a charge for another illegal bull killed by a Gould poacher. New information also revealed the names of individuals opening locked gates, allowing Gould hunters quick access to their kills, substantiating the two groups coordinated efforts to cover their misdeeds.

It was now time to put the Cat Canyon Elk Massacre to rest!

In the end, out of the 21 identified hunters 10 citations were issued to 8 individual poachers totaling $6,232 in fines. Of the 21 elk killed, ten were determined illegal. Of the 15 elk initially tagged by hunters claiming they were legally harvested, three were proven illegally killed by others. No less than ten additional elk were found wounded and/or dead on surrounding properties. Several wounded elk were legally harvested, tagged, and formally reported to us by the hunting good.

Understand, pushing elk to strategically posted hunters is a legally acceptable hunting practice. I have stalked my share of heavy timber towards waiting hunters as well as posting myself in front of hunters doing the same. However, the illegal, unethical, and irresponsible slaughter of elk in Cat Canyon cannot be considered hunting. The participants were poachers, killers firing a shooting gallery scenario at confused, milling, and fleeing elk with no regard to numbers or sex they killed or wounded. This behavior, so ingrained into their hunting culture, ended in a scandalous massacre epitomizing the carnage inflicted by party hunting. Mob psychology at its worst, it portrayed totally unacceptable behavior in modern day hunting.

One member of Stockman's group put the incident into perspective by admitting, "if you hunt with this gang long enough, no matter what values you thought you may have, you will eventually actively play your part in their party hunting game." Also, I ponder to this day what the youngest member of Stockman's hunting pack, a wide-eyed lad always present in the shadows, thought of our brazen determination to interfere and resolve the party hunting culture he was being mentored into.

Make no mistake, more charges would have been filed if positive identification of those Cat Canyon poachers breaking wildlife law had been accurately documented. With such reliably precise field information rarely available, we relied on persistence, evidence, and statements to finalize the cases. Cooperation and attitude play major roles in wildlife law enforcement decisions. Although slow in developing, the collaboration of violators, arbitrated by Stockman, determined our final citation decisions. Without it, resolving the senseless slaughter would have taken a great deal more time resulting in fewer citations against less individuals. Understand, with possibly one exception, the poachers involved were otherwise good men, ultimately displaying remorse and embarrassment for their illegal behavior. However, Kirk and I brusquely made it crystal clear we were shockingly disgusted by their disgraceful misdeeds, knowing it would be cussed and discussed by hunters and nonhunters for a long time.

The last full measure of the Cat Canyon Elk Massacre weighs far heavier than the number of tickets written or the dollar amount of fines. The opening morning of the 1987 elk season on Cat Canyon was a bad day for the hunting good, severely tarnishing hunting's historical legacy evolving into modern-day sport hunting. But on that day, what happened on the Mountain did not stay on the Mountain. The atrocities witnessed by principled hunters, immediately reported to law enforcement authorities, initiated the ensuing downfall of the hunting bad. Justice often not black and white, hunting being no exception, was equitably served by the resounding voices of the hunting and nonhunting public demanding strict wildlife law enforcement and adherence to high-level moral codes dictating the ethical hunting behavior of modern-day sportsman.

"So let it be written, so let it be done!"
Ramses II

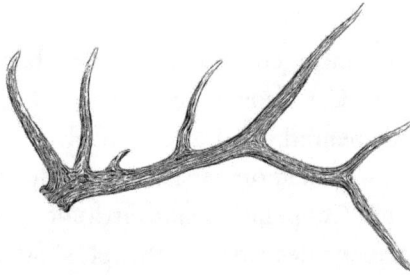

PRODIGAL SON

October 1987. Saturday, opening day of deer and elk season. The time when blood runs high. There we were! Wildlife Biologist Steve Steinert and I parked along the rutted two track bordering Lost Creek awaiting daybreak. Windows down, we absorbed dawn's tranquil stillness domed by an inky sky splattered with a bajillion spangling stars. The morning's icy chill mingling with scents of aspen, sage, and pine, invigorated our purpose. We were steered here by a midnight phone call from an anonymous informant hearing two 'faint' shots just before dark. Stating he was calling from Rosebud and, based on the lively background chatter, I knew the tipster was in the town's five-star restaurant/bar. Saloons are warden treasures, and this lair for liars routinely whispered secretive truths of outdoor wrongdoings. The informant's fervent sense of urgency hinted he knew much more.

Inevitably, dawn's serenity was rudely shattered by a single rifle shot from the ridge above. On full alert, we 4-wheeled up the steep trail described by last nights informant. Cresting the ridge, we spied two hunters standing over a field dressed 3X3 buck. Greeting them, noting a carcass tag wrapped around the buck's antlers, I requested their hunting licenses. Both licensed for deer and elk, one identifying

Tommie Dadaboy, anxious as a morning bird dog and the other Will Hanover, warily watching in total silence. Last night's report haunting my mind and a deer field dressed before the morning sun washed the ridge, I suspiciously pulled out my meat thermometer and sank it's prong deep into the buck's hindquarter. Explaining body temperature approximated the time the deer was killed, I closely scrutinized the hunters' demeanor. Focused on the thermometer's dial, Tommie went from anxious to uneasy while Hanover remained quiet. The thermometer reading warmer than I expected, Tommie affirmed he shot the deer 20 minutes earlier, corresponding with the time Steinert and I heard the shot. We needed more. Tommie, bragging about the accuracy of his 6mm rifle, Steinert responded the lack of blood indicated the deer must have died instantly. Asking the pair if they heard shots in this area the night before, Tommie declared they had not, a clue they were here at that time. Hanover's silence murmured time may tattle his thoughts. Scent of illicit behavior wafting but not yet enough to track, I inspected the deer for additional evidence. Discovering nothing, I congratulated Tommie on his success, shook his hand and left him happy as a woodpecker in beetle kill. Too happy! Driving away, we concurred Hanover was undoubtedly our informant, wardensmanship advising patience may ultimately reveal the real story.

And it did, but not in the way I anticipated. An urgent call Sunday morning from the Sheriff's Office sent me to the Buffalo Ranch to meet Kent Crowder (County Administrator/Deputy Sheriff) concerning the illegal shooting of a fawn deer. At the ranch, Crowder articulated the implausible details of discovering a young man beating a fawn deer's head with a large rock! *Seriously!* Crowder, while tracking deer on Buffalo Ridge, heard and traced two rifle shots leading him to the hunter. Asking what was going on, the hunter replied his day was not going well, explaining he accidentally wounded the fawn when shooting at a large buck. Crowder identified himself as a deputy sheriff and instructed the hunter to field dress the deer and drag to the road going into the ranch. At Crowder's request, the hunter revealed his name was Tommie Dadaboy! *Hoka Hey!* Indicating Tommie was trespassing, Crowder said his predicament needed investigation by wildlife officer Steve Porter. Tommie, now very upset, divulged he'd been contacted by Porter the day before. Pleading with Crowder not to turn him in because killing the fawn was an accident, Tommie said he would make sure it did not go to waste. He also stated he did not want his comrade to know about the fawn. Helping Tommie drag the fawn to the road, Crowder followed him to his truck parked on the public side of the gated private property. Watching Tommie's hunting comrade (yup, Will Hanover) walk off the public section of the ridge, Crowder loaded the fawn into his vehicle, and escorted the pair to the ranch house. Hanover, having no idea what previously transpired, Tommie had a lot of splainin' to do.

Requesting the hunting and driver's licenses from both men, Crowder detected the carcass tag was missing from Tommie's bloodied deer license and questioned if he had killed another deer. Tommie, not able to explain why the tag was detached, professed he had not. *Yeah, right!* Crowder, noting Hanover's agitated silence, said his anger increased as Tommie's misdeeds were revealed. Crowder continued trying to contact me while ranch manager Steve Story and Tommie hung and skinned the fawn in the barn. Recording the make, model, and license plate number of Tommie's vehicle, Crowder asked where they were camped and Tommie said on Green Ridge. Retaining Tommie's licenses, Crowder escorted the pair to the locked gate, thanked Tommie for his cooperation, and turned them loose. Arriving at the ranch soon thereafter, one cannot imagine my astonishment once again holding Tommie's deer license, knowing its tag was on the 3X3 buck killed early yesterday! Sometimes you eat the bear...!

Searching Green Ridge until dark, finding no sign of Tommie or his camp, I began calling his front range home. Reaching the renegade early Monday morning, I found Tommie eagerly cooperative, agreeing to meet that afternoon at the Sheriff's Office. In the interrogation room, Tommie thoroughly detailed his misdeeds, accurately matching Crowder's in-depth account. Looking into the youthful man's cobalt eyes, his flattened pugnosed bull dog face, locks of brown hair curling upwards from his ball cap, and soft patchy, youthful facial hair, I almost felt sorry for the apologetic lad. Almost! Questioning why he continued hunting deer after filling his tag on opening morning, Tommie said he was hunting elk, hoping to push deer or elk towards Hanover. Jumping a large buck running with does and fawns, he could not resist taking the shot, knowing if he killed it, Hanover had a license to tag the deer. Whimpering like a newly weened puppy, he repeatedly expressed regret, awkwardly stumbling over the rubble of his misdeeds. Tommie admitted breaking hunting and fishing laws not only kept him out of trouble *(What?)* but also increased his ability to kill game, greatly pleasing his father. Known as a 'bad ass' poacher, Tommie's father apparently cast a long, dark shadow greatly influencing his son's behavior. Obviously, Tommies idea of trouble did not include poaching. Here was a twenty-six year old boy, craving the respect of an irresponsible father, willing to break wildlife law to imitate the great hunter his father was not. Acknowledging he could not control his behavior, Tommie asked if I would help him do something about it. Momentarily speechless, I sensed there may be enough good in Tommie impelling him to change his ways. Maybe. I advised correcting his illicit behavior was the first step in becoming the hunter he seemingly wanted to be.

Due to his cooperation, ranch manager Steve Story judiciously waived filling trespass charges and, for the same reason, I charged him only for the illegal fawn, skipping the additional charge of hunting deer without a valid license. Tommie, noticeably relaxed, conceded he was relieved to have the incident behind him. Realizing sincere confessions are made by the truthful as well as the deceptive I, once again, cautiously turned him loose with a handshake, predicting this was not the end of Tommie's story.

THE BEAR BITES TWICE

And it wasn't. Receiving another late night call Monday evening from the informant, now openly identifying himself as Will Hanover, wanting confirmation we filed charges against Tommie for the fawn. He also tattled Steinert and I had overlooked crucial evidence at the kill site of the 3X3 buck, specifying it had been illegally shot by

Tommie's .22 rifle on Friday evening, not on opening morning. The high powered rifle shot Steinert and I heard early Saturday morning was Tommie shooting the already dead buck in the neck to simulate a morning kill. Asking Hanover why he remained silent at the kill site, he admitted killing the paralyzed deer with a shot behind its ear with Tommie's .22, (a customary method for killing a downed big game animal) and not wanting to incriminate himself for killing an illegal deer. His admission validated his phone call reporting hearing two 'faint' shots on Friday evening. Enraged by Tommie's blatant, illicit behavior occurring twice in two days, Hanover ended their friendship and commanded Tommie to drive him home Saturday evening. This explained why I could not locate Tommie on Sunday evening.

Searching again Tuesday morning and not finding Tommie, I contacted Denver area wildlife officer Pat Tucker who, accompanied by wildlife officer Dave Lovell, contacted the runaway Wednesday morning at his home. The head of the 3X3 buck in the back of Tommie's truck, the officers listened to the identical story Steinert and I heard on opening morning. However, after firing a few loaded questions based on my information, Tommie confessed to illegally shooting the 3X3 the evening before the season with his .22 rifle and signed a written statement detailing his misdeeds. Tucker scratched tics for hunting out of season and illegally taking a deer, reporting to me he was amazed by Tommie's extreme cooperation and remorse for committing both violations. Tommie also told Tucker he would have immediately confessed illegally taking the 3X3 if Steinert and I had only asked. *You bet!* Tommie pled guilty to all charges in Jackson County court, paid over $1300 in fines, and ultimately had his hunting and fishing license suspended.

In my view, Tommie mimicked a Jack Merridew (Lord of the Flies) boy hunter. True to his nature and nurture, he hunted illegally to please his feckless father, conflicting with his self-proclaimed desire to become a legal, ethical hunter. A prodigal son encouraged by a conscienceless father, Tommie could not outrun his father's demons. Proposing Tommie the Shakespearaen chance 'To Be', I realized, given the opportunity, he would decide 'Not To Be'.

Here's lookin' at you kid!

Hunter phone call to Warden: *"When do caribou migrate through the Bull Pen."*

Warden to Hunter: *"Right ahead of the Polar Bears."*

THE GALVANIZED TRUTH

And there we were, working elk season on a sun-bursting October morning exploring the Big Creek backcountry in the northwest corner of the Bull Pen. Dawning hoarfrosts melding into comfortably warm, windless days kept elk widely scattered throughout their high elevation, inaccessible hidey holes. Most nimrods hunted the morning and early evening cool, taking advantage of the mid-day warmth to enjoy the finest fishing the Bull Pen offers. Mentoring Trainee Candidate Jackie Clay, I was anxious to introduce her to the incomprehensible enforcement scenarios common during big game hunting seasons; how switching direction often leads to unpredictable adventures.

Maneuvering my vehicle over the rocky, narrow road on the east side of Big Creek Lake, I veiled it into a patch of thick scrub; a ploy to catch-dog fishermen along a remote section of the lakeshore. Bushwhacking the trail ridge above the lake's steep bank, we stumbled upon a man and a woman fishing a stone's throw below us. Lady Luck, the matronly ally of warden work, instantly greeted us when the man said (I kid you not!), "Watch for the wardens while I go up the hill and take a leak." Passing within twenty feet, he failed noticing us. After the grizzly whiskered gent returned to his two poles, we took a pine duff seat to peruse our prey. His stoop shoulders, long arms and large, knobby hands resembled those of a worn-out farmer. Dressed in a greasy baseball cap, a long-sleeved red plaid shirt, knee-high black gum boots, and loose fitting jean coveralls cinched by a brass buckled belt holding a huge Bowie Knife, the belted kingfisher depicted a picture-perfect Norman Rockwell watercolor of a timeworn fisherman.

His helpmate, a sturdy beldam with a cheeky, hog-jowled face, starkly white hair and fleshy, round ears, resembled a weathered Cabbage Patch Doll. Behemoth, unbound, drooping breasts in a heavy rag wool sweater divulged gravity was indeed her worst enemy. Heavy, loose sweatpants starkly contrasted with her black leather old lady shoes. Her dead-fish eyes and ashen skin gave me the heebie-jeebies. *Not a woman one would slay a dragon for.* Relentlessly jabbering, she actively fished with her own two poles while standing guard over a proverbial galvanized water-filled tub crammed with a preponderance of perishing trout. Both were landing fish although the man was outdoing his wife two to one. We watched the woman 'cherry pick' larger trout caught, releasing those smaller from the tub, some floating belly-up in the lake in front of them; illegal because of the high mortality rate of released, bait hooked fish. The old man's paranoia working overtime, he nervously paced hither and thither, repetitively searching the lakeshore and into the forest, while we hid in plain view.

The two-handled tub flaunted an indisputable over bag limit of rainbow trout. No need to dawdle, it was time to pounce. Walking downhill I cleared my throat, sending the fish hogs into 'deer in the headlight' stares enjoyed by all wardens. Trainee Clay cut to the quick and asked for their fishing licenses, identifying the pair as Hank and Henrietta Hubris. Obviously aged beyond their years, both just over fifty, Henrietta unsurprisingly also produced her daughter's licenses, stating she would soon be returning. Trainee Clay queried why she did not have the required stamp to fish with two poles (husband Hank did) and Henrietta shrugged it off stating she did not think it was a big deal. She sternly clarified half or more of the trout belonged to their 'kids' currently hiking the lake's perimeter. Specifying we needed to check their camp for additional fish, Henrietta turtle-snapped back all their fish were in the tub. To our astonishment an osprey plunged into the lake fish-hawking a dying trout from the water, initiating my reprimand for releasing deep-hooked trout back into the lake explaining fish caught and not immediately released or fish dying after release must be counted in their bag limit. Henrietta scoffed at the ridiculousness of such a complicated law stating, "What's the big deal if some of the trout die?" Hank spoke not a word. Pouring water out of the tub, we grabbed its handles and escorted the pair to their camp. Additional trout were found in a cooler under the camper bringing their total to thirty-five. On cue, Henrietta admitted she (conveniently) had forgot about them. Suspicious, I stated we would wait for the return of the missing hikers causing Henrietta to storm a flurry of expletives demeaning our distrusting behavior. Hank said not a word. While waiting, a young couple unexpectedly drove up and after a huddle with Henrietta, weakly claimed fourteen of the trout. The two novices admitted not understanding fishing laws, relying entirely on Hank's guidance for filling their licenses. They further explained they were on a day trip, planning to return home with their limits. Henrietta, revitalized by the arrival of two additional licenses, babbled the remaining trout belonged to her daughter and granddaughter, and requested we leave. I cantankerously clarified we would continue waiting for the missing pair sparking another fiery eruption of noxious profanities from Henrietta broadcasting their right to catch as many fish as there were licenses. Hank said not a word. Sifting Henrietta's filthy rationalizations for hidden grains of truth, I was amply rewarded when she blamed her husband for catching most of the trout. Hank's pot now stirred, the fighting tomcat broke his silence with a diatribe of 'God Damn' driven justifications for breaking the 'pathetic' laws preventing them for making up for the times they caught few or no fish, and for trips not made because they were busy working. His self-confessing excuses buzz-sawed through my personal fortitude; it was time to release the hounds.

I singled out Hank in a vain attempt to admit his daughter and granddaughter never made the trip. The hickory knot-hardheaded old man, firmly anchored in his wife's lies, would not know what to do if common sense bit him in the ass. Next, I separated and curtly questioned the naïvely trustworthy young couple, who innocently conceded Hank's daughter and granddaughter were not there, adding Henrietta purposely brought her daughter's license to cover excess fish if checked by wildlife officials. *Hoka Hey!* Their deception unveiled, Henrietta and Hank suffering a bad case of foot' n mouth disease, shamelessly listened as I articulated my well-rehearsed lecture delineating the woes of their wrongs, securing their full attention when I labelled them poachers. Hank accepted responsibility for all of the illegal trout. Trainee Clay scratched Hank's tic, leaving Henrietta for my personal enjoyment. Rewarding her with a citation for the illegal use of two poles, I waived the charges of 'providing false information to a wildlife officer' while making clear I was seriously considering citing her daughter for illegally transferring her license to transport their filched trout. For the young licensed couple's honesty, I rewarded them the fourteen trout claimed earlier *No doubt most caught by Hank!* Henrietta, in turn, compensated me with a word class ass-chew, a discourse of blaspheming smutty dialogue that would frighten a corpse.

This is where the wardens rode away!

Unfortunately, Trainee Clay later found the Hubris' licenses in her contact book. *DAMN!* The next morning, we made the long trip to Big Creek only to find the scoundrels gone. Nobody answering my Sunday evening phone calls, I left a message stating their licenses would be sent Registered Mail on Monday. Predictably, a few weeks later, I was required to respond to a scathing complaint letter addressed to my supervisor from none other than Henrietta, describing Clay and I as badged crooks who purposely stole their licenses.

No good deed goes unpunished!

As luck would have it, I crossed paths the following summer with Hank and Henrietta's son Duff fishing Cowdrey Lake. I 'Big-Eyed' Duff remove a bag of trout from his cooler and hand it to another fisherman leaving the lake. When contacted Duff rudely denied it, stating there was no way I could have seen him give away fish from across the lake. Flaunting my notes, including notations made when Duff peed in the lake (illegal but a tic never scratched because of the free-ranging livestock around the lake), Duff gave it up after expelling a bucketful of verbal excrement proclaiming me to be the 'worthless prick" his mother had so well described.

Paybacks are a bitch!

Realizing this nature-nurtured lout reflected the very personage of 'mommy dearest', I scratched out his tic for an over limit of fish. Taunting his psyche, I once again labeled his entire family as poachers. They were a deceitful clan stealing off the public common always proclaiming innocence when mired in guilt. Muzzled, the red-faced Duff retreated in blazing rage; poachers simply hate being called... poachers.

I heat up, I can't cool down
My situation goes 'round and 'round
'Round and 'round and 'round it goes
Where it stops nobody knows ....
Abra-abra-cadabra by the Steve Miller Band

SOUTHERN EXPOSURE

There I was, eyes glued on a Louisiana hunter's wallet as he shuffled through a wad of one-hundred-dollar bills. It was elk season and I, parked on a remote Owl Mountain Road, had stopped him to check his hunting license. The hunter, Billy Hill, expressing amazement of crossing paths with a warden so far off the main road, I answered, "Yeah, I get that a lot!" Chit-chatting, Billy's distinct southern drawl and courteous demeanor was a pleasant way to start my morning. Until it was not. Noticing a hunting rifle leaning against his right leg, I explained I needed to check the firearm to make sure it was not loaded and asked him to carefully open the rifle's bolt. Billy obeyed, exposing a cartridge in the chamber. Requesting him to exit the pickup, I retrieved the live round while explaining the possession of a fully loaded firearm in a motor vehicle was a strictly enforced safety violation requiring the issuance of a citation. Billy, expressing serious southern discomfort, flashed a king-sized Fireman's badge, curtly insisting I exercise professional courtesy and ignore the violation. Making clear that was not how I worked, he switched gears, showed me the money, and bribed, "How much would it take for me to look the other way?" Having hunted this dog before, I unblinkingly replied, "A million bucks! That's what my job is worth!"

thoroughly enjoying Billy's mouth gaping glare as I dug out my ticket book.

The Bull Pen grapevine frequently complaining about a clan of 'Cajun' outlaws invading 'their' neighborhood, this contact with Billy was my initial introduction to the southern states hunting culture. Subsequently, I and my colleagues repeatedly caught them defiling the legal and ethical codes of outdoor behavior. Time invested in field contacts or unannounced visits to their cabins routinely paid dividends of criminal mischief, their flagrant behavior so blatantly transparent, contacting them became an effective training exercise for new recruits:

-Discovering several deer tagged with Wyoming licenses hanging from a meat pole at a Cajun cabin, I discovered a buck tagged by the absentee wife of hunter, Huck Peewaddle. Phoning his wife and introducing myself as a Colorado wildlife officer, I asked if she had recently killed a Wyoming deer. The puzzled woman replied, "I'm not sure, but since you are calling, I must have!"

-On the day before elk season my supervisor, Don Benson, and I tracked a distinct, elk hair infused drag mark on a well-traveled county road leading to a five-point bull hanging from the meat pole of a Cajun cabin. Two men in camp, one, Gunner Bagemwrong, courteously confessed and counted out the hefty fine from a container filled with cash reserved for payment of their inevitable misdeeds.

-Checking licenses at another Cajun cabin, I spotted a gadwall duck blown to smithereens on their porch. Asking who murdered the duck, the father unhesitatingly confessed his son, Beau Diddley, made a great, long-distance rifle shot (illegal) as the duck swam across a beaver pond below their cabin. Unsurprisingly, after scratching a tic, another Cajun, Daniel Boondoggle, was cited that evening for an illegal deer.

Repeatedly violating wildlife law, it was evident outdoor misbehavior was in their DNA. Paying fines never a deterrent, they righted their wrongs with money, never showing remorse or changing their behavior. Antlers meaning more than meat, they once donated cash to the local Boy Scout troop in return for the racks confiscated from their illegal elk (approved by my supervisor against my wishes).

And so it was, citations issued for loaded firearms, hunting out of season, tagging violations, wasting meat, trespass, use of motor vehicles to hunt game, illegally taking and possessing game, spotlighting etc. continued, their fines accumulating to levels we jokingly referred as our version of the Louisiana Purchase.

Cajun contacts also delivered events not related to breaking wildlife law:

-Pulling into their cabin, I was once greeted by several 'painted lady's' showing great interest in having a uniformed officer visit their camp. As I naively pondered the situation, one Cajun father explained the 'girls' were high school graduation gifts for their sons!

"I give you the boy. Give me back the man." Paint Your Wagon

-An incident occurred when the clan stopped at our office with the carcass of a bull elk, legally shot during the rifle season, with a steel broadhead (arrowhead) buried deep in its hind quarter, apparently wounded earlier by a bowhunter. I found the injury healing well but bearing an unpleasant odor. The remaining meat looking and smelling good, I suggested they discard the damaged hindquarter. Not buying what I was selling, I offered to donate the elk to welfare and issue the hunter a new license. The hunter, Klux Dilrod, accepted my deal on the condition he could keep the antlers. Based on their previous misbehavior, I explained the antlers would remain the property of the state. Choosing to keep the elk, Klux caught me completely off guard when he declared, "I'll take the elk home and feed it to the nig...rs!."

RUN AND GUN

RUNNIN' ELK LIKE LAKOTA WARRIORS CHASING BUFFALO!

November 1990. Late elk season, the cold, snowy weather pushing elk to lower elevations instigated increased harvests and a corresponding rise of hunter misbehavior. The grape vine loaded with fruit, and officers tied up in their own investigations, we were forced prioritizing violations, leaving a preponderance of hunting wrath unharvested. Multiple complaints of hunters chasing elk with motor vehicles across the sagebrush flats on the south end of the Bull Pen was an annual occurrence when heavy hunting pressure pushes elk off the timbered public and private lands. Road hunting the open sage, legal when laws are followed, proffers the hunting good a sporting challenge to spot, stalk, and fill their tags. However, a select group of poachers take road hunting to low levels by chasing down and killing elk utilizing trucks, ATVs, snowmachines, often using portable radios to direct colleagues to the elk. Some hunters spend the entire season sitting in vehicles on high points or driving the open sage searching for elk. Chasing big game with motorized vehicles, unethically violating the spirit of fair chase, provokes additional illegalities involving party hunting, shooting from roads and from vehicles, trespass, and wounding loss. Extremely unsafe for the shooters and all living things within the range of their bullets, wildlife officers exercise zero tolerance for these illicit hunting tactics. 'Run and gun' episodes taking place within the home range of the Cajuns, it was only a matter of time before we captured them and others red-handed, as wildlife officers continue doing every elk season.

Raucous misbehavior rampant, we called in the troops, assigning trainees, the fish guys, wildlife biologists, Arapaho National Wildlife Refuge personnel and state wildlife officers from the eastern plains to cover all corners of the Bull Pen. U.S. Fish and Wildlife Service Agent, Terry Grosz, was strategically placed to work Owl Ridge undercover. Grosz, a formidable 270 pound 6'7" law enforcement warrior had the uncanny ability of detecting trouble before the troublemakers triggered it! Driving his large diesel Dodge pickup displaying magnetic signs of a drilling company on its side doors, Terry treasured exercising his extensive wildlife law enforcement field roots working covertly portraying a hunter or fisherman. Always requesting a task, whether for a specific assignment or directing him into a place to fish or hunt, Terry crossed paths with bad guys. Frequently visiting the Bull Pen to get away from his never-ending administrative duties in Denver, Terry became a treasured friend, fixing full course dinners of gargantuan grilled steaks and chops while bunking at the Refuge headquarters. No longer with us, Terry spread his wildlife law enforcement legacy across our nation. There will never be another Terry Grosz!

But I wander!

There we were, Kirk Snyder, Supervisor Scott Hoover and I working a complicated illegal outfitter case, Agent Grosz radioed he was hearing radio traffic on his scanner tattling a herd of elk was being chased and shot at by vehicles across the open sage flats below Owl Ridge. Alerting all available personnel, we quickly had a formidable corps headed Terry's direction. The Sheriff's Office, relaying similar reports from concerned hunters, we were headed into good warden trouble.

Wildlife Biologist Steve Steinert answering a report of elk killed illegally on Verl Brown's private ranch, I joined Officer Hoover's interrogation of Cajun hunter, Skeeter B. Wilderd, claiming a freshly killed spike bull (illegal) lying nearby in the sagebrush. Confused, Skeeter was unable to explain a dead cow elk within view of 'his' spike bull. After considerable debate, he vaguely indicated another group of hunters were also shooting at the running herd and admitted he was unsure who killed either elk. Picking up fresh brass from five different rifle calibers, one possibly matching Skeeter's, Hoover instructed him to field dress the spike and we would contact him later. A group of very upset hunters drove up, the driver declaring they witnessed several hunters firing shots at the running elk from this location, dropping at least two, before racing off in pursuit of the remaining elk.

Steinert, radioing for assistance, reported Rancher Verl Brown, extremely mad, had cornered a group of Cajuns on his land transporting five elk in their pickups and believed there were more dead elk taken on his property. On our way to join Steinert, Hoover and I observed an abandoned bull lying within view of the road. Meeting Steinert, we escorted the Cajuns away from the infuriated rancher to a remote gravel pit. With the aid of Agent Grosz, Snyder, fish guys Kehmeier and Van Buren, and Steinert, we unloaded seven elk, after discovering two additional calves the Cajuns claimed were killed earlier on public (BLM) land. Interrogating each man separately, listening to them bumfuzzle their way through contradicting stories, they admitted killing and not retrieving two other elk. Rudely arrogant and unremorseful, the poachers did not blink when we discussed the possibility of confiscating their vehicles illegally used to chase down and kill the elk. One, T-Bo Jangles, danced his jingle, "go ahead and take them, I own a car dealership and we'll get new ones!"

Long story short, our interrogations, combined with witness interviews and the appalling evidence imprinted in the blood-spattered swath left by the fleeing elk in six inches of fresh snow, we puzzle-pieced their outrageous criminal behavior:

Early morning, two Cajuns, Bush and Wack, driving high over the rough Owl Ridge two track, jumped the herd and radioed their compatriots the direction the elk were headed. Following the elk to a fence corner, two calves unable to cross were abandoned, allowing the pair to intercept and fill their antlerless licenses. Another hunter, Fluky Road-roamer, unaffiliated with the Cajuns, filled his antlerless tag when the fleeing herd paused at another fence. For reasons unknown, Fluky drug the elk behind his vehicle to his cabin (miles away) without field dressing it. *Seriously!*

Next, the entire group of Cajuns intercepted the herd, put down the spike bull and the cow, dropped off Skeeter, and continued chasing, shooting, and killing elk until the herd disappeared into the Owl Mountain timber. During the five to six-mile chase over public and private lands, a total of ten elk were killed, eight considered illegal (the two calves believed to be legal) and confiscated. Before we arrived, the poachers assessed the aftermath and sorted their tags to cover their criminal carnage.

Rancher Verl Brown made crystal clear his problems with the Cajuns extended over ten years and was pressing trespass charges against all of them.

Assembling the elk killers in Sage Hen, we summarized their pending charges and heavy fines - 24 charges totaling $10,331.00! The seven elk killers wisely elected to avoid the publicity of court and paid their fines on the spot. Understand, no amount of money can erase the damage inflicted by their tragic assault on hunting's long-term legacy. This clan defiled the legal, moral, and ethical codes devised and demanded by the hunting good for over 150 years.

Unsurprisingly, I am told by the local Bull Pen wildlife officers the unsportsmanlike conduct of the coonass Cajuns continues to this day. The same holds true for the annual 'run and gun' elk chasing outbreaks, featuring many card-carrying members of the illegal hunting fraternity I captured during my watch. *Round up the usual suspects!*

"Stupid Is, As Stupid Does!"
Forest Gump

Warden to Hunter Ripley at his mountain cabin: *"Did you see anyone spotlighting last night?"*

Ripley to Warden: *"No, and I was up late sitting by our campfire."*

Ripley's young son: *"Maybe he means when you shined our spotlight last night driving to our cabin and shot the porcupine!"*

Out of the mouths of babes!

THE COLD HARD TRACKS

October 1990. Visualize two teenage brothers savoring the freedom and independence of hunting bull elk behind the ranch managed by their hard-working father and mother. A cold day after a blizzarding storm, the frozen ground blanketed with fresh snow, elk were fast tracking towards their traditional wintering grounds. Spotting a group of cows, calves and a spike bull skirting the timbered edge of Custer draw, the young hunters could only watch because harvesting spike bulls was illegal, their licenses good only for bulls having antlers with a minimum of 4 points on at least one side.

Imagine their amazement when four hunters standing next to a jeep fired a burst of shots at the elk, illegally gunning down the spike bull and wounding at least one cow. Incredulously, the boys watched in awe when the elk killers approached the spike bull, momentarily inspected it, and returned to their jeep making no attempt to track the wounded cow.

Consider the audacity of the two brothers when confronting the elk killers, politely questioning them about the spike bull, and listening to them haughtily brag about their flagrant misdeeds. Memorizing the jeep's license plate number, the worthy young hunters returned to the ranch, informed their highly principled father of what they saw, who immediately contacted the Sheriff's Office.

Receiving the information late that evening, Wildlife Officer Kirk Snyder and I questioned the brothers the following morning before accessing Custer Draw from the ranch headquarters. From a distance, the location of the dead spike bull veiled in timber at the meadows edge, was tattled by the black and white wing flashes and scratchy *wick-wick* calls of three magpies. Searching where the jeep had been parked, we picked up shell casings from four different rifle calibers.

Walking into the chaotic crime scene we found the spoiled bull, a blood trail disguised in multiple elk tracks disappearing into the timber, and a spider web of man tracks. Pausing to puzzle piece the information gleaned from the brothers and the evidence in front of us, Kirk and I realized we were looking at what no amount of money could buy – the open book test of reading relatively fresh snow. Remarkably, in plain sight, we discovered something never encountered or, for that matter, ever heard of – distinct, single bullet trails tunneling just below the snow's surface. Online with the elk killers' jeep, the bullets arced over the meadow and entered the snow, traveled fifteen yards or less, apparently losing energy and stopping without exiting! Skeptically, we discussed the possibility of retrieving the expended bullets using a metal detector!

As Kirk and I worked the crime scene, imagine the idiocy of the elk killers returning and parking their jeep in the same spot as the day before. *Hoka Hey!* Taking them by surprise, we scurried across the meadow and made contact. Kirk immediately announced, for their benefit, the jeep's plates matched our report. Checking their hunting licenses, we found the four licensed to harvest legally antlered bulls (neither cows nor spikes). Arrogantly denying our accusations of killing and abandoning the spike bull and wounding a cow(s), they deviously refused to answer our questions. As a team, Kirk and I normally could make a mime talk, but not today! Bonded in deceit, they attempted bumfuzzling us with verbal attacks, their catch-us-if-you-can attitude hell bent on having our jobs for criminally making false accusations without any proof. Threatening to report our reprehensible behavior to our superiors, one hunter, shaking a fist in my face, declared they were prepared to fight!

"Don't stand, don't stand, don't stand so close to me!"
The Police

Kirk brashly ordering him to back off, made it clear if they did not settle down their arrest was imminent. Peculiarly, they did! Fueled by the strong possibility of retrieving expended bullets from the spike bull and/or the snow-covered bullet trails and (hopefully) matching them to the elk killers' rifles, our demeanor shifted from politely friendly to tersely professional. To their amazement, we took charge and methodically confiscated, tagged, and recorded serial numbers on their rifles, bagged and recorded the loaded cartridges in their rifles, and carefully secured them in our vehicle. Providing them phone numbers of our supervisor and our agency's Director, we ordered the four elk killers to leave.

Taking pictures of the elk killers' boot prints where the jeep was parked, we matched them to those at the crime scene. Photos of the spike bull and the mounded snow trails were also taken. Kirk, a metal detector wizard, began scanning the terminal ends of the burrowing trails while I necropsied the gut-wrenching bull. Hitting paydirt, Kirk recovered a perfectly intact spent bullet! Chortling his good fortune, he discovered another as I, encased in a toxic cloud of reeking rot, traced a bullet channel tracking deep into the bull's neck. Hearing footsteps, I stepped back for some air and was greeted by good friend and State Park's employee, Jay Wenum. Recognizing my dilemma, Wenum admitted he smelled the putrid scent long before spotting me. Explaining our situation, he could not believe my personal resilience while knifing through the maggot gagging carcass. *My thoughts exactly!* Dry heaving my way through meat and bone, Kirk rudely heckled me to put on my big boy pants! While Kirk continued retrieving additional bullets of varying calibers, I finally dug out an intact, perfectly mushroomed bullet displaying rifle barrel markings that could potentially match one of the confiscated firearms. *HOKA HEY!*

Admiring our cold, leaden evidence, we photographed, packaged, and recorded each bullet in sequentially numbered envelopes. Wenum, displaying great interest, was regarded by Kirk and I as a worthy candidate for joining our ranks as a District Wildlife Manager (DWM) with the Colorado Division of Wildlife. Steadfastly persuading him to apply, I am proud to announce Jay successfully made the move, thriving as a DWM and retired as a supervisor in the Gunnison Valley.

November. Transferring our evidence to the Colorado Bureau of Investigation (CBI) in Denver for technical analysis, we were given a grand tour of their facilities, their personnel eager to help resolve our case.

As unbelievable this story may seem, even to this day, our perseverance and preponderance of evidence was rewarded the following spring when the CBI scientifically matched our bullets to the elk killers' rifles. After lengthy legal arguments between our District Attorney and their lawyer, Dewey Screwum, including insinuations of Kirk and I's professional incompetence and blatant disregard of client rights, Dewey finally waved the white flag and openly confessed, "sometimes a lawyer is forced to admit his clients are blatant liars."

The combination of fines for hunting elk without proper licenses, the wasted spike bull, the wounded cow, and lawyer fees substantiated our efforts, providing justice the four poachers sorely deserved. Once again, the hunting good prevailed! A hearty thanks to the young hunters, two honorable boys willing to bring the poacher's blatant acts to our attention.

"Justice will not be served until those who are unaffected are as outraged as those who are."
Benjamin Franklin

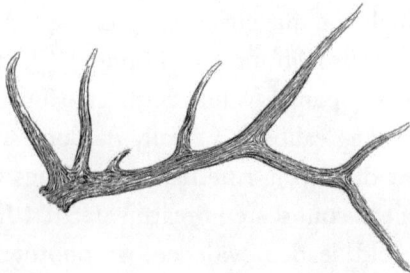

THE LOCH KATHERINE MONSTER

S ummer 1982. Belly laughing during a phone call from comrade
Cliff Pabst, a blue-ribbon jokester, as he described his late-night
awakening by a distraught neighbor detailing an encounter with a
'monster' rising from the depths of Lake Katherine. Scaring him and
his buddy enough to break camp and hike out in the dark, Cliff assured
me this man was dead serious, stone sober, and not a pothead. Lake
Katherine, a high elevation lake in the Bull Pen's Zirkel Wilderness,
and her sister lake Bighorn, were two of my favorite destinations for
working and playing. Unconvinced, I considered Cliff's call one of the
million stories imagined when humans interact with the mystifying
wild. A week later, another report of late evening, unexplainable sightings at Katherine tweaked my imagination enough to hike in and
spend the night. After all, who would pass up two similar reports
expressing the presence of a "dragon' like beast emerging from the
depths of Lake Katherine. And a great excuse to work and fish Bighorn
Lake the next day!

Parking at the trailhead the following afternoon, I trekked upwards
into Katherine, pitched a comfortable camp above the lake, boiled a
delectable, freeze-dried supper. and reclined against a log to enjoy the
evening. No one at the lake, the solitude of the darkening wilderness

ignited a ridiculously star-studded sky, fervently enhancing my aloneness. Spellbound by a silence found only in wilderness, I disremembered my woes and concentrated on my life's perpetual fortunes. I even forgot why I was there. Then it got weird! Somewhere in the eerie gloam came a splash and, believe it or not, the 'beast' appeared, disturbing the lakes surface as it swam by. Excitedly focusing my binoculars, the alleged 'dragon' materialized into a sizable flock of young and adult mergansers (a fish eating duck) swimming in V-formation! With a loud hoot, my echo resounded over the cirque's mountain amphitheater, replicating my delight. Mystery solved, comatose after an hour staring into campfire flames, I crawled into my down bag, slept like a winter bear, rose with the sun, feasted on oatmeal and raisins, and contoured into Bighorn. Once again, no human activity, I reveled the waterfall's song as cutthroat trout rose to my handtied muskrat fly. Blessed with over 24 hours of solitude, I strolled out revitalized, invigorated to face whatever issues awaited. I was not only in the wilderness; the wilderness was within me.

Greeting a group of backpackers at the trailhead, noting their fishing gear, I asked if they had fishing licenses. Their blank stares answering my question, I waved goodbye and said, "I'll catch you later."

"And into the forest I go, to lose my mind and find my soul."
John Muir

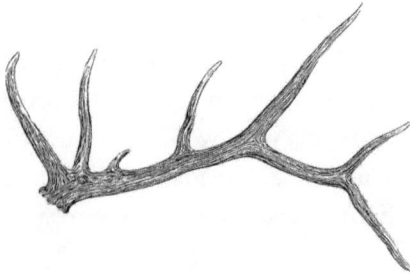

GULLIBLE GUIDES AND AN OUTLAW OUTFITTER

OUTFITTER: A person providing, for compensation, services for hunting or fishing on land the person does not own.
GUIDE: An Outfitter or his employee leading or assisting person(s) to and from a place where such person expects to take fish or wildlife.

Outfitting/guiding services require licensing by the State of Colorado and are governed by strictly enforced State and Federal laws and regulations.

Midwinter 1991. There I was, staring at a pair of skidmarked untidy whities, the last recorded item in the massive inventory of one of the most consequential cases filed against an illegal Colorado big game outfitter. The October 1990 case emerged after receiving multiple complaints of trespassing hunters, on foot and horseback, accompanied by guides wearing camouflage clothing. Wildlife Officer Kirk Snyder uncovered our first tangible clue resolving a fiery trespass altercation between a landowner and three men (a hunter, a man wearing camo, and a black hatted 'cowboy') caught packing out an elk across his private land. After considerable debate, Kirk cleared the air resulting in the landowner not filing charges. The 'cowboy', Jack S. Shyster, cordially introduced himself as a licensed Colorado

OUTFITTER leasing the Robertson Ranch for <u>his</u> commercial hunting operation. Shyster also acknowledged the man dressed in camo was one of <u>his</u> GUIDES. Reviewing Colorado's legally licensed outfitters that evening, Kirk and I found no record of Shyster or his business.

The next day, I was summoned to Rosebud to address a hunter complaint regarding the use of 'his' personally constructed public land hunting blind by a hunter and a camo garbed guide. Clarifying it was legal for anyone to use the vacant blind, the disgruntled hunter detailed descriptions of the two men, and the private properties they trespassed near dusk to meet a black truck parked along a Forest Service boundary fence before driving into the Robertson ranch.

The following week, I received another trespass complaint involving a hunter and a man wearing camo picked up by a black truck along the same Forest Boundary fence. The infuriated landowner wanting to file charges, it was time to pay Shyster a visit. Accessing the leased property through its 'back door', Colorado Parks Officer Jay Wenum and I entered from the south through 'Coconut Grove', named for its tall, large crowned aspen trees. Unbeknown to us, we were headed into worthy warden turmoil. Opening a taut barbwire gate and driving into the property, we passed a parked tractor trailer rig before encountering a sizable hunting camp swarming with highly spirited men; some dressed in full camo, several wearing daylight fluorescent orange, and a black hatted 'cowboy'. Parking at a distance, we scrutinized the men and their weaponry; several brandishing large Bowie knives, most wearing holstered pistols, and multiple rifles propped against surrounding trees. Carcasses of elk were scattered across the camp, and a large bull elk filled a pickup bed. Singing and dancing to loud country/western music, some sharing a bottle of whiskey, others holding red solo cups, three knife bearing men were butchering a bull elk spread across a makeshift table of unhewn boards. In my mind, a real-life drama depicting the merriment of an early 19th century mountain man rendezvous. Time taking a break, their unrestrained revelry lapsed into dead silence as they dazedly focused on Wenum and I. Abruptly milling and spreading out, several retreated into thick aspen. Wenum, eyes glaring like a mouse-snatching owl, took a stand behind my opened driver's door while I prepared confronting the rapidly approaching 'cowboy'. Violating my comfort zone with a strychnine grin and excessively firm handshake, he introduced himself as Jack S. Shyster, this time as a GUIDE hired by a legally licensed outfitter. I distinguished this declaration an attempt to cover his tracks after previously describing himself as an outfitter to Officer Snyder. Thwarting the camp's toxic atmosphere, I requested identification and licenses from all present and, while Wenum recorded the information, I began asking questions. The three men dressed in camo introduced themselves as GUIDES, another as a camp hand, and one stated she was the camp cook. Three properly licensed out of state hunters were also present. Shyster, producing his First Aid card, a legal requirement for guides and outfitters, apologized for not having a copy of the outfitter's license he was GUIDING under. He described the three wearing camo as apprentice guides, receiving their First Aid training later as part of his outfitting/guiding school. Requesting the mandatory Federal permits for guiding and outfitting on public lands, Shyster specified they were not required because they worked as photographers when on public lands! *THAT'S ONE FOR THE BOOK!* Mentioning the hunting blind and trespass incidents, Shyster affirmed no person in his camp ever entered any private land other than the Robertson property. Explaining we had witnesses stating otherwise, Shyster became incredibly angry. Questioning the two men involved in the hunting blind incident, Shyster rudely interrupted and blew up when I sternly instructed him to back off. The guide, Scout N. Truder, explained he worked for OUTFITTER Shyster since September as an apprentice GUIDE, attending Shyster's school at a cost of $700 and laboring free gratis as part of his training. Because Shyster called the shots, he could say no more. The hunter, Drew LeBlanc, remained silent until Wenum indicated the tag on the bull on the butchering table was his, triggering LeBlanc to disavow any and all knowledge of his hunt, including the location of the kill site! *Seriously!* Shyster asserted he would lead us to the kill site, but quickly recanted when Wenum revealed LeBlanc's tag specified the bull was killed on the day of the hunting blind incident. Obviously, LeBlanc could not have killed the elk that day because of the testimony provided by the hunter confronting LeBlanc and his guide at the blind and watching them trespass to meet the black pickup at dark. Wenum complicated their dilemma by specifying the presence of snow would allow us to easily locate the kill site. Shyster, steering Scout and LeBlanc into the cook tent, desperately attempted to describe where LeBlanc's bull was killed.! Hearing every word, I pulled back the tent flap and advised any illegalities would jeopardize the alleged OUTFIT-TER'S license Shyster claimed they were GUIDING under. LeBlanc, reaffirming he remembered nothing, the visibly shaken Shyster screamed harassment and ordered everyone to quit answering our questions. A bull hanging from a meat pole, tagged by hunter Tommy Gunner, plainly wearing a guilt-ridden face overripe for an imminent, fruit bearing interview.

Welcome as coyotes at a wolf kill, we faced the oxymoron of gaining intelligence from a pack of rogue, inebriated nimrods. The noxious mix of potentially serious wildlife violations, weapons, and booze signaled it was time to leave.

"A man's got to know his limitations."
Dirty Harry

Backing out, the camp members cheerily high fived our departure, believing they won a war barely into its first battle! On the way out we intercepted another man wearing camo, Shag Henchman, driving a black pickup along the reputed Forest Boundary fence with fourth hunter, Shaky Wheedle. Asking Shag if he was guiding for Shyster, he stated he was not a guide, only a camp hand. Shaky, notably confused with Shag's answer, nervously produced a nonresident elk license. Turning them loose, we backtracked their vehicle tracks in the melting snow and located Shaky's boot tracks trespassing private property before crossing onto public land to meet Shag.

Further investigation revealed Shyster's OUTFITTERS LICENSE had been revoked for committing multiple wildlife crimes. Several kill sites of Shyster's trespassing hunters were located. Robertson, sensing trouble, complained Shyster had not paid for his lease. The next morning supervisor Scott Hoover, Kirk and I alerted available officers to standby while we organized a raid on Shyster's camp. Leaving Sage Hen, we intercepted Shyster's four out of state hunters stealing through town. Distressed with their detainment, we guided them to our office, discussed their options, all wisely agreeing to cooperate. Out of the blue, Gunner stunned us with his shamefaced confession of killing three bulls while GUIDED by Shyster. Asserting Shyster directed him to tag one bull, the other would be tagged by Drew LeBlanc, the amnesiac involved in the hunting blind altercation. Shyster ordered LeBlanc to tag the extra bull, clarifying LeBlanc did not kill the bull they were butchering in camp. The third elk, a spike bull not meeting the minimum 4-point antler restrictions, was abandoned.

With Gunner riding shotgun, we easily located the kill site tracing hovering magpies and crows and chasing away two loping song dogs. There, on a section of State School land closed to public hunting, the sight of two devoured gut piles and the rotten, dismembered carcass of the spike bull really pissed me off! Everything here was wrong! Gunner, emotionally distressed by the coldhearted spectacle of his misdeeds, honorably accepted total blame for his illicit behavior.

Returning to Sage Hen, tics were scratched to Gunner for one illegal elk and to LeBlanc for tagging the 'extra' bull. Our focus predominantly on Shyster, leniency (a written warning for the wasted spike bull) was provided for their cooperation. Paying their fines, all four hunters penned statements detailing Shyster's countless crimes. Victims of the 'OUTFITTER'S' misguided behavior, they delivered firm handshakes, confident their information would take Shyster down.

Calling in the troops, while Shyster and crew silently watched, we confiscated the ENTIRE CAMP; the tractor trailer, pickups, tents, lanterns, fuel, clothing, trailers, horses, saddles, bridles, stoves, cooking utensils, food, coolers, elk - EVERYTHING! Interviewing Shyster's 'guides', and 'camp hands' at their camp, most remained arrogantly uncooperative, unwilling to incriminate Shyster in wrongdoings they were tied to. Later interviews, when free of Shyster's influence and our guarantee of immunity, the guides acknowledged believing they were legally GUIDING hunters on the private Robertson ranch and public lands as students of Shyster, allegedly a legally licensed OUTFITTER. Instructed they had permission to cross but not hunt on surrounding private property, Shyster coached them to falsely claim they were trailing wounded game if caught in a trespass dispute. 'Camp hand' Shag Henchman disclosed the location of stashed illegal elk meat killed by Shyster trespassing on private land. He further incriminated Shyster for killing elk for clients and transporting a large, illegal bull to a front range taxidermist. Mucked in serious criminal crap, Shyster had no one throwing him lifelines.

The case acquired a life of its own after Shyster lawyered up. While his attorney vainly searched for threads of injustice, our tireless team (District Attorneys, Sheriff Office personnel, Brand Inspectors, State and Federal Officers, and Colorado State Outfitting Licensing Officials), unraveled the pack rat's illicit nest. Both sides rejecting the terms of a settlement for nine months, just before the scheduled September 1991 jury trial, Shyster's charges were plea bargained to one felony and six misdemeanors, and no jail time. District Court accepted Shyster's guilty plea and ordered the following:

- Fine amounts to be paid in three yearly installments.
- Four years supervised probation
- Lifetime forfeiture of his Colorado hunting and fishing privileges.
- Lifetime forfeiture of his Colorado Outfitter and Guide licenses, including his right to engage in any such activity the remainder of his lifetime.
- $1,000 paid to the Colorado Division of Wildlife for prosecution costs.
- $8,000 in restitution payments to five individual hunters.
- Forfeiture of all property seized by the Colorado Division of Wildlife except for his three horses and tack.
- Reimbursing the landowner leasing his property $3,000 and a horse trailer.

Beginning with reports of trespass, this case ended with the elimination of a blatant criminal abusing Colorado outfitting and wildlife laws for personal gain. Shyster's convictions justified the necessity for protecting the rights of paying clientele; insuring they are provided qualified guides, safe and comfortable living quarters, good food, and the privilege to legally hunt in areas accessible to wild game. Shyster's downfall also safeguarded the integrity of Colorado's legally licensed Outfitters, law abiding, hardworking, dependable, highly qualified men and women. Shyster's hunting and fishing license suspensions secured the privileges of credible hunters and fishermen, maintained the integrity of the hunting and fishing sports, and endorsed the spirit of fair chase for man and beast.

During our watch, we worked with the majority good, (Redfeather Outfitters, Whistling Elk Outfitters, Buffalo Creek Outfitters naming a few) as well as the minority bad (trespass, fist fights, poaching, poor service, uncomfortable accommodations, etc.).

Shyster unquestionably sank to the lowest end of ugly!

Carpe caput lupinum – Seize the wolf's head

FLIES BY THE BLOODWOOD

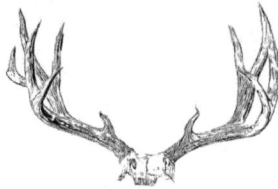

There we were, answering a trusty spy dogs bark, Wildlife Officer John Wagner and I cautiously drove into a remote cabin site in the Grizzly Creek Subdivision. Wardens are routinely diverted into secluded lairs where high numbers of thieves congregate, and the scent of misconduct can be whiffed most any given day. This subdivision, a Hatfield/McCoy horde of rowdy rascals squabbling incessantly over the boundaries of their illicit activities, was a warden's nightmare. Greed and jealousy running amok and no honor among these thieving pack-rats, we often reaped worthy intelligence from the wanton idiocy of their own ranks.

The subdivision, platted beneath the Rabbit Ear's Range, was marginally successful at best, being buried in snow seven to eight months a year and a long distance from the popular Steamboat Springs ski resort. Lots, therefore, sold at reduced rates to bargain buyers chasing dreams of owning a piece of mountainous Colorado. Attracting an assortment of middle income, non-conforming outdoor miscreants, the subdivision also lodged principled residents suffering the wrath of their neighbors' scandalous activities. One, actively serving as a reliable informant, routinely provided worthy information detailing critical pieces for our enforcement puzzles. Based on his information, we repeatedly visited a family clan of misfits, citing them for poaching, trespass, and licensing violations; two and threepeat offenders becoming card carrying members of our select club of outdoor scoundrels. Routinely gasbagging homicidal threats to anyone getting in their way, my life was twice threatened by these numskull scofflaws. But I wander.

Today's informant possessed zero tolerance for illegal behavior of any kind. The misdeeds he prattled today were serious violations defiling the wild, landing Wagner and I on solid ground. Observing the violations firsthand at the poachers' residence less than two hours before, our mole immediately called the Sheriff and reported his neighbors had illegally killed and hid two fawn deer in their woodpile! It was archery season and killing antlerless deer was illegal. How could anyone, even a poacher, shoot one, let alone two, spotted fawns?

The tip arrowed us towards an unfamiliar residence veiled in thick conifers. Stalking a steep, rutted driveway we discovered a crude dwelling sided with unmatched plywood remnants. Smoke billowed out of a crooked pipe chimney and, judging by the large amount of scattered firewood and wood scraps, keeping the shack warm was an endless chore. Energized with rock-solid information, we opted playing *Columbo*; annoyingly questioning and worrying the miscreants before taking them out. They were essentially dead poachers walking.

While I guarded the large woodpile accurately described by the informant, Wagner pounded on the cabin door gruffly announcing our presence. Hearing movement, an elf-eared, long nosed, weak chinned, mousy grey-haired man opened the door. This person, Bo N. Hed, aptly described by our informant, was olden ugly, flogged hard by Father Time. His cadaverous face tattled a chain smoker; pallid yellow with thin, crinkled lips hiding nicotine-stained, unevenly spaced teeth. His son Dick Hed, a ripening version of his father, stood silently in the doorway shadows. As Wagner explained we were investigating a poaching case involving two fawns, Bo garbled a hollow diatribe proclaiming his total disapproval of poachers. Casting the proverbial warden line that we regarded those providing information concerning wildlife violations as first-class sportsmen, I watched Bo rise to the bait. Oblivious, Bo vainly believed I was referring to him, affirming we would be the first to know if he was aware of anyone violating wildlife law. His lying logorrhea, powered by a low caliber IQ, were the defecating words of a man hiding his own misdeeds. *Release the badgers!*

Winking at Wagner, I tracked the edges of the woodpile, picked up a blood-stained board and fired two loaded questions,

"What's up with all the flies? Is this blood on these boards?"

Bo, realizing his pilfering culpability was about to be revealed, shock gobbled a series of head bobbing, neck stretching, red faced, one-eyed stares putting a distressed wild turkey to shame. His son, remaining silent, grimaced like a possum with a mouthful of wasps! With a final kick to his cul de sac, I instructed Bo to help me remove the firewood to see what was attracting so many flies. In a blink, the diminutive carcasses were revealed, a pitiful sight indeed! Both fawns obviously killed by a high-powered rifle, their shoulders shredded, bloodshot, and totally unsalvageable.

Bo, resembling a snake attempting to crawl back into its shed skin, knew even his hollow conscience could not justify killing the two spotted fawns. Like a bobcat hacking a hairball, Bo expelled a mass of vile words rationalizing his (mis)behavior as that of a poor man justly poaching to provide his family winter's meat supply. Mindlessly adding if the doe had not bounded away, he would have shot her and spared the fawns. His stinking rationalizations dangling like crap on a dung beetle's mouth, exposed a nowhere man headed in the same direction.

Predictably, Bo switched guns and began firing obscenities at his double agent, attempting to soil the informant's reputation by asserting 'squealing' was a far worse offense than poaching deer for his family's sustenance. Having hunted this dog many times, I fed his paranoia declaring three separate people turned him in, his misdeeds were known throughout the neighborhood. Fat tics scratched; we left the hapless pair whining their woes.

Cursed with stool sample personalities, Bo and Dick Hed were uneducated, lower-class misfits who relentlessly cheated their way through life... you know, morons! The informant, Barrett Grinnen, lived a quarter mile downhill of the feckless game thieves. With no intention of stopping, Barrett would have it no other way. Waving us down, he read our smiles while staring at the two fawns in the back of our pickup, high fiving his extreme pleasure of bringing down the Heds. A wildlife warrior willing to openly advertise his intolerance for anyone filching Nature's bounty, Barret respectably refused the monetary reward offered for turning in his neighboring game thieves.

"So let it be written, so let it be done."
Ramses II The Ten Commandments

Warden to Poacher: *"Would you please stick with the facts?"*

Poacher to Warden: *"This is my hunting story. There are no facts."*

WASTE NOT, WANT NOT

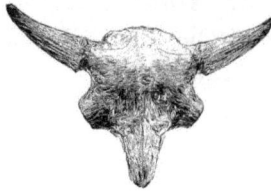

October 23, 1980. Checking elk licenses in an Indian Creek camp, Regional Fish Biologist Steve Puttman stared in awe as I handcuffed a hunter wanted for assault on a Denver arrest warrant. After the Sheriff arrived and transported the man to Sage Hen, Puttman and I headed towards Hidden Lakes.

Patrolling backroads towards the Grizzly/Helena trailhead, we located a camp on Whalen Creek with a skinned and quartered bull elk wrapped in black plastic hanging on the sunny side of a pine tree. Oddly hearing sporadic popping sounds, I pulled away the plastic and discovered the bull's neck colored an olive fluorescence, a gut-wrenching smell, the noises caused by rupturing ulcers oozing a pea green pus. Pulling away the rest of the plastic and overwhelmed by the pungent stench of warm, spoiled meat, I ascertained the entire carcass unfit for human consumption. Puttman agreed. Finding a <u>deer</u> tag attached to the bull's antlers, it was obvious someone had some 'splainin' to do!"

Waste of game meat is considered a serious offense by hunters, nonhunters and wildlife officers. Caring for and providing for human consumption of all edible portions of wild meat is a sacred covenant maintaining the integrity of the hunting and fishing sports. Wild meat cannot be wasted, period. My experience, however, required handling potential waste cases cautiously, first speaking with the hunter(s) involved to interpret their rationalization. In the past, I crossed paths with some hunters purposely allowing meat to decompose to a predetermined level for making chili and other cultural dishes. The tale behind this elk, greatly exceeding my standards for spoilage, needed to be told.

Waiting several hours, a nimrod named Retch Blewitt arrived telling his woeful story of killing the bull in an open meadow before sunrise on opening morning. He and his buddy, having no experience field dressing elk, waited until late evening for their hunting partner, described as a professional meat cutter, to properly take care of the meat (ten hours after the kill). An unseasonably warm October, today the third full day after the kill, the bull was destined to spoil. Asking Retch why the bull was tagged with his deer license, he had not yet realized his mistake. Later, two hunters walked into camp, one the 'meat cutter' and the other not wearing the legally required daylight fluorescent orange (hat, vest, coat etc.), admitting he simply forgot.

Checking licenses, I discovered only the meat cutter, Butch Skinner, to be an experienced hunter. While I informed Retch his bull was criminally unsalvageable, Skinner arrogantly challenged my expertise, declaring the elk edible, would be professionally cut and wrapped at his butcher shop, and divided amongst all the hunters. *OK!* Providing them the benefit of my doubts, I requested Retch to load the elk into his vehicle and follow me to our Sage Hen warehouse, fully equipped to process the bull, where we would all determine the meat's condition. A quick stop at a local meat shop, the butcher indicated he could not accept Retch's rancid bull for processing. Skinner and Retch adamant the bull was not spoiled, I guided them to our warehouse, helped place the foul-smelling carcass on clean plastic outside the rear garage door, provided clean knives, water, and saws, and stood back as they began boning the meat. The reeking stench more than my scent hardened nose could handle, Puttman and I retreated into our office and opened the entry door for fresh air. Within minutes, a chalk faced, grimacing Skinner joined us and, swallowing his pride, admitted the bull could not be salvaged. Asking what changed their minds, Skinner uttered,

"RETCH THREW UP!" Breaking through the malodourous warehouse smell, I found Retch on his knees, sweating profusely, in a state of near terminal dry heaves. Recuperating (not really) in our office, I schooled Retch on the legal responsibility for taking care of harvested game and cited him for wasting the elk. Shaking hands, Retch heartfully apologized and Butch humbly expressed remorse for not mentoring his hunting gang on the proper care of game meat.

This I know, harvesting an elk is a major accomplishment, one normally not coming easy, and requiring field expertise and hard work. Inexperience denied Retch the pleasure of successful harvest. Retch and Butch, extremely distraught over the loss of the savory meat, would never again waste wild game.

The spoiled carcass was strategically placed in tall sage away from a remote back road, to be recycled by crows, ravens, magpies, eagles, and coyotes. In less than a week it would be reduced to scattered fur, hide and bone, Nature's efficient scheme for salvaging death to sustain the wild.

Scent 'em out, Warden!

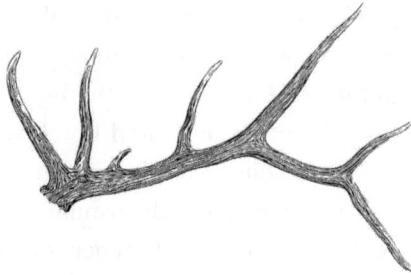

ICE BREAKER

A
nd there I was, a week after Thanksgiving checking ice conditions at Cowdrey Lake for the Division of Wildlife's weekly fishing report for fishermen eager to participate in the great fishing normally occurring with freeze up. Today the lake was entirely covered in ice, although completely ice free a few days prior. Suddenly, a pickup roared over the hill, sped down the boat ramp and cruised twenty yards onto the ice! *DAMN!* Judiciously watching the driver exit the vehicle, take a manual ice auger from the truck's bed, and promptly began drilling a hole. In only a few revolutions the auger broke through the ice causing him to lose his balance and clumsily sprawl forward on all fours over the hole. Quickly standing, he retrieved the submerged auger, its offset handle wedged above hole, pussyfooted to his truck, and slowly backed it onto the boat ramp. Driving down to meet him, we had the following conversation:

Warden: "I saw that!"

Fisherman: "SON OF A BITCH!"

Warden: "That was really scary!"

Fisherman: (louder) "SON OF A BITCH!!"

Warden: "It could have been much worse!"

Fisherman: (even louder) "SON OF A BITCH!!!"

After this intellectual discourse, the man glared into my eyes and said, "Why in the hell have you not posted a sign warning of THIN ICE! I smiled and explained one should always carefully check the ice thickness before walking or driving onto any water. I drove away allowing the distraught man to recover from what he no doubt envisioned as a near death experience.

Cowabunga!

Warden to man standing on riverbank holding a fishing pole: *"I need to check your fishing license."*

Man to Warden: *"Oh, I am not fishing, I am just looking."*

Warden to Man: *"Ok, can I see your looking license?"*

LEAVE IT TO BEAVERS

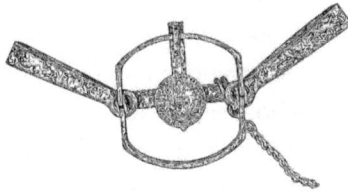

My initial training included field instruction on trapping beaver and the use of explosives to clear out beaver dams causing water flow problems. Trapping problem beaver in those times was a responsibility of the state's District Wildlife Managers to aid landowners experiencing damage to their irrigation ditches. Our instructors, the last of the State's 'Beaver Men' hired during the '40's to control beaver statewide, provided basic trapping skills for trainees.

Most of these trappers were later hired as Wildlife Conservation Officers (later promoted to District Wildlife Managers), continuing to trap problem beaver in their assigned districts. While the training was good, my beaver management expertise was sharply honed when assigned to the Bull Pen and teaming with fellow District Wildlife Manager, Sir Don Gore. Don, one of the 'Beaver Men' mentioned above, claimed a lifetime catch of over 10,000 beaver! Don, stationed in the Bull Pen until his mid 80's retirement, was a legendary icon. I took great pleasure listening to Don and his confederates, Sig Palm and Johnny Hobbs, imbibe their early trapping adventures during the wildlife agency's early history, while sharing a bottle of Black Jack. The 'Beaver Men', long since passed, have taken their stories with them and, as the saying goes, when an old man dies, a library burns to the ground.

The Bull Pen's agricultural economy is dependent on one crop of irrigated native hay. Irrigation ditches and headgates are, of course, waterway magnets for attracting the industrious beaver instigating requests for our assistance. Assigned to the Bull Pen in 1973, Don and I became close friends, and he eagerly shared his trapping skills with me. Eventually, Don trusted me with the well-guarded formula of the old-time trappers' scent recipe. Using the musky blend, traditionally poured into pint whiskey bottles (I still have one on my bookshelf), I became a successful beaver trapper but failed miserably on skinning and fleshing pelts. Don, who cleanly (no nicks) shaved off a beaver hide with a razor-sharp Green River knife in fifteen minutes, calmed my frustration by politely stating one must skin 1000 beaver to become proficient. Don, never a fan of law enforcement, proudly claimed the title of trapper til his dying day. Nothing provided Sir Don more pleasure than uncoiling a dead beaver from the drowning pole set in deep water, caught in a 41/2 Oneida Newhouse using his secret scent. Nothing!

After Sir Don's retirement, I was summoned by the good doctor France to trap problem beaver on his Indian Creek property. The doctor, not wanting the beaver killed, I obliged by setting two live traps on a beaver pond below his stately cabin. While standing on the dam, would you believe a beaver surfaced, beelined to my mud dob bearing a few drops of the secret recipe, and trapped itself just yards away. Luckily having a holding cage in the back of my pickup to transport captured beaver to a new location, I placed the beaver in it, reset the trap and continued conversing with the good doctor. Shortly, a second beaver surfaced and, unable to resist the scent, was promptly trapped, *Damn, I'm good!* Thoroughly amazed, the good doctor compared my skills to those of Sir Don. Standing proud, I humbly admitted I learned from the best.

DAM BEAVER

Early in my career, the use of explosives to blow out beaver dams was quite common, solving irrigation problems and proffering good landowner/ agency relationships. That is until the state' attorneys deemed explosives carried too much liability (imagine unsupervised field men roaming the outback using explosives!). But until this responsibility was taken away, I must admit it was a very entertaining task we conducted responsibly and professionally. *Damn, it was fun blowing beaver dams!*

And there I was, attentively listening to Mr. Angst Castor pleading I blow out a beaver dam backing up water close to his Gould cabin. Unwittingly constructing his abode in the flood plain next to the Michigan River, Angst was delirious! Doing my best to convince him the dam was too close to the cabin for using explosives, I suggested he hire someone with a backhoe to dig out the hefty dam. Not buying what I was selling (after all my services were free) I reluctantly agreed to blow the dam with the restriction he lights the fuse. Angst, accepting this absurdly ridiculous, nonbinding agreement not liberating me or the state if things went wrong, I prepared the explosives.

Luckily, the dam, luckily faced away from the cabin. I set what I considered a light load of explosives (two sticks of dynamite), deep into the dam after making a hole in the dam using a long, sturdy tree branch. With the heavy water pressure against the dam, I believed the exploding debris would travel up and away from his cabin. Stringing a long fuse rope, Angst lit it and we scampered to the cabin for shelter and impatiently waited, and waited, and waited.

KABOOM! Gazing at exploding mass of sticks, mud, rocks, and water blasting skyward, only a few branches and gobs of black mud harmlessly hit the cabin's windows and roof. Happily watching acres of backwater gush through the gaping hole in the dam, I began gathering my supplies and saw Angst grab a walking stick and begin wading towards the blast sight. Warning him to be careful, Angst suddenly disappeared into the depths of the blow hole, only his hat visible swirling through the rushing torrent. Dashing below the dam, after what seemed like forever, Angst launched from the whirlpool like a rocket, arms flailing, spitting water, and floated downriver. Wading into the backwater, I grabbed his collar and pulled the water-soaked wreck to shore. Giving Angst several moments of silence to recover, we honored his ordeal with high fives and hearty belly laughs. Asking me to keep his drenching episode secret, especially from his wife, I explained, "What happened at the dam, stays at the dam!"

OK, I never divulged this incident to Angst' wife, but .....!

THIRD AMENDMENT

October 1987. Yet another crap shoot materialized during the opening day of elk season when I was contacted by westside rancher John Stamison who overheard a rogue hunting gang's plan to ambush a Butler Creek elk herd. The remote Butler Creek/Coburn Draw area was an elk honey-hole during the August/September rut and later when heavy snows drive deer and elk from the high country. Public land access was limited to foot or horseback. Stamison granted me permission to cross his hay meadows providing expeditious private land access to the draw. Leaving SageHen well before daylight, I bushwhacked across the vast hay-land following harvest equipment trails avoiding wet areas and deep irrigation ditches on my way to the Forest boundary. An early morning ground fog of rolling vapory mists mystically swirled through my headlights. At the Forest fence I opened a tight wire gate and drove a narrow ATV track into an aspen grove. Parked, I cranked my window down to marinate in the silent unworldliness of the eerily late, foggy mountain breaking dawn, waiting nearly an hour before the aspen spires surrounding my truck began taking form.

Predictably, I sensed the rumbling snap, crackle and pop of my morning Rice Krispies, prompting immediate evacuation of my vehicle and thereafter my bowels (hopefully in that order)! And there I was, seated comfortably on a skillfully selected, fallen aspen 'throne' for another invigorating backwoods movement. Now imagine this warden nearly tumbling backwards when a gunshot's thundering echo cracked the morning's miasma! The ear splitting, sphincter tightening after-shock wholly interrupted the relief of relieving myself. Habitually, warden 'scents' mandated wearing binoculars and, once again bare-assed, I scanned the foggy hillside across the draw immediately detecting the blazing orange of a hunter shooting at a bull elk dashing into heavy aspen. *Damn!* After several minutes, the hunter pointed his rifle skyward and fired three successive shots.

Leaving his rocky vantage, the hunter cautiously stalked down the brushy hillside, eyes fixated on something I could not see. Creeping, he stopped, stretched his rifle bearing arm and poked the barrel into the heavy brush. Imagine the blood curdling shock we both experienced when a heavily antlered bull elk reared its head from the sage, aggres-sively attempting to hook the man with its sur-royal daggers. Severely wounded, the bull's head dropped forcefully out of sight. Setting his rifle down, the hunter removed a huge bowie knife from his belt, guardedly approached the bull from behind, grabbed a hind leg and began field dressing it! Thinking the bull dead, I marveled when the beast's head again arose, terrorizing the hunter with another hostile antler swipe. This incredible event repeated itself several times until the bull presumably expired, allowing the hunter to cut its throat. Next, the hunter began tracking the running bull I observed earlier, disappearing in the aspens for a short time before returning to the dead bull. Witnessing this entire event from my thunder log, I finished my end of the paperwork and began stalking the harried nimrod. On my way I spied another hunter posted high on ridge above, probably another witness to the entire incident. Additional proof hunting can be a spectator sport.

If you are thinking this amazing adventure cannot get any better, do not be fooled. The hunter, immersed up to his elbows in blood and guts, bolted upright upon detecting my vigilant approach. His words defied him, "Where in hell did you come from?" Calming the knife wielding hunter with small talk while testing the air for a whiff of warden scent, I grabbed one of the great stag's hind legs to aid field dressing the magnificent 6-point bull. The hunter nervously mumbled and made no eye contact as I eased into my investigation by congratulating the man on his successful harvest. The hunter replied it was the largest elk he ever killed and wondered how he could pack it to his distant cabin below Livingston Park. I stated I would help after checking his license and investigating the kill site. Shell-shocked, the hunter gazed the tell-taling 'thousand-yard stare' of a gut queasy miscreant. Without hesitation, he confessed having no elk license because he had never, ever, been contacted by a game warden. Requesting his driver's license, the self-proclaimed poacher curtly refused, stating he was not driving so I had no right asking for it. Shifting into overdrive, I crassly made it crystal clear producing legal identification was mandatory and cooperation from this point on would ensure the rest of the man's day would go much smoother. And it did.

Inspection of the poacher's driver's license identified him as Chaff Brumbaugh, a grain farmer from eastern Colorado. Curiously, I questioned why he attempted to field dress the elk while it was still alive. Brumbaugh awkwardly explained he ran out of bullets! My puzzle began piecing together realizing the additional shot at the fleeting bull plus the three shots fired into the air emptied Brumbaugh's magazine. Questioning the three shots, Brumbaugh decently confirmed he was alerting his buddies he put 'some' elk down and needed assistance. I tracked the deep hoof prints of the second bull through the aspen up a steep hill finding no trace of the elk or blood. Returning to the kill site, a crestfallen Brumbaugh solicited a monetary assessment of his misdeeds, stating he understood wildlife violations were very costly. Parboiling the poacher's mind, I said they would discuss economics later. Returning to my vehicle and winding through a narrow cow trail, I maneuvered below the bull allowing a short downhill drag into the truck's bed. The game thief heartily apologized all the way to his cabin, claiming never again to hunt or fish without a license. *Yeah, right!* He rationalized no one would ever pass up a shot at such a large bull. In Chaff's words, "What would you have done?" I explained I would never hunt without the required licenses and certainly hoped Chaff learned his lesson well. At the cabin, I calculated Brumbaugh's transgressions to be $1300. Brumbaugh promptly pulled a huge wad of bills from his wallet, counted out the fine explaining he cashed a large wheat check a few days ago, **luckily** mad money his wife knew nothing about!

> *This guy comes up to me*
> *His face red like a rose on a thorn bush*
> *Like all the colors of a royal flush*
> *And he's peeling off those dollar bills*
> *Slappin' 'em down, one hundred, two hundred...*
> Bullet In The Blue Sky –U2

All semblance of the poacher's luck vanished when I disclosed the elk would be confiscated; the hapless game thief believing his significant monetary investment justified a return of the highly desired trophy bull; a first degree poacher suffering a third degree warden burn.

Another one bites the dust!!!

MISTAKEN IDENTITY

October 16, 1976. There I was, working as an undercover warden seeking hunters on the opening morning of elk season. Bushwhacking through heavy timber and cussing myself for forgetting a head lamp, I wiped my bloody nose scratched by a pine branch. Breaking out of the timber, I gained my bearings, crossed a brushy draw, climbed to the top of a ridge, and sat on a rocky outcrop. The frosty morning's chill reinforced by a slight breeze, stinging my face and already penetrating my clammy long johns, I yearned the pending warmth of sunrise. Fortunately, the heartwarming 1974 memory of bugling in and harvesting a raghorn bull elk with my muzzleloader and packing it out with Betsy, Marc, and Anne, lessened the bite of the predawn cold.

Sugar Loaf Mountain peaking to the east, I treasured the panoramic view of ridges, draws, aspen, pine, and sage forming the headwaters of Three Mile Creek; good ground for a hunter or warden. Heavily garbed in plain clothes, including a vest and hat beaming daylight fluorescent orange and a rifle strapped to my shoulder, I was a warden play-acting the role of an elk hunter.

Just before sunrise I detected the orange vest of a hunter sitting 100 yards below, focusing his binoculars on me. *BUSTED?* Interrupted by sounds of animals shuffling through aspen leaves, I watched the hunter aim his rifle, turn my way and wave, and fire at something I could not see. Seconds later, a cow and calf elk appeared and, with a second shot, he dropped the cow in her tracks. Standing, he waved again, crept up to the cow and began field dressing it. Walking down the steep hill and approaching the hunter, I witnessed his smile wither and his face pale, surefire signs of capture myopathy. Having met during past seasons, we instantaneously recognized each other. I knew him as Chap Fallen, a front range police captain. Stating he thought I was his hunting partner, he inquired why I was not wearing a uniform. *OOPS!* Replying I often worked under cover, I probed if he hit another elk with his first shot and he acknowledged both shots were fired at the cow he was field dressing. Requesting Chap's antlerless elk license, he uttered it was in his vehicle parked above. While he finished field dressing the cow, I searched for signs of another wounded or dead elk. Finding the calf and another elk had escaped unscathed, I suddenly realized Chap was no longer around the dead cow. Glancing upwards, I observed him fast tracking up the ridge before disappearing over the bench where I had been sitting. *WHAT!* Shifting my legs into over-drive, I chugged upwards, soon gulping in heart pounding breaths wondering how Chap could be in better shape than I. *The chase was on!* Cresting the bench, I found him lying face up on the ground, gasping for air like a beached carp. Inquiring if he was OK, Chap replied he was not, confessing between breaths he was licensed for a bull elk and killed the cow elk for a comrade having a cow license. Extremely distraught by my veiled buzzkill, Chap slowly calmed during the mile hike back to our vehicles.

At camp, Chap's cow hunting buddy, Guy Wisely, angered I was citing a fellow officer for a meaningless offense, vulgarly degraded my character, pedigree, and avocation, insinuating game warden rhymes with asshole. *No, it doesn't!* Affirming, "I get that a lot," I menaced his masculinity by asking if he lacked the skills for killing his own elk. Sensing the situation was getting out of hand, Chap judiciously requested Guy to leave. Humbled, Chap conceded he, as a law enforce-ment officer, had no excuse for violating any laws and apologized for putting me into such an awkward position. After scratching the tic, I advised he recruit Guy to help pack out the elk and I would return the following afternoon to confiscate it. Loading the cow into my truck the next day, Chap stated Guy was in their tent recuperating from packing out the elk. Chap, informing me he already reported his misdeeds to his supervisor and was worried the charges may impact his employment, I clarified his over-all cooperation would be well-documented in my written case report. After a firm handshake, Chap praised my professionalism and acknowledged he would never again disobey wildlife law.

Aye, aye, Captain!

TO KILL A WARDEN

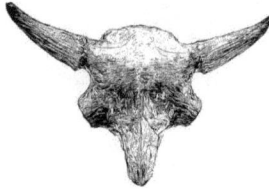

"Whoever fights monsters should see to it that in the process he does not become a monster. And if you gaze long enough into an abyss, the abyss will gaze back into you."
Friedrich Nietzsche

May 1986. There I was, one warming spring day investigating a report from a worthy hunter regarding an illegal, unmarked bear bait on public land near Arapaho Creek. Hiding my vehicle off-road, I bushwhacked through lodgepole pine into brushy aspen bordering the grassy sage meadow described by the informant. Scanning the timber with binoculars, an indiscernible breeze worried the aspen leaves tattling the putrid scent of a bear bait. A swallowtail butterfly wafting over the sun-drenched meadow caught my eye and I impulsively hesitated to admire its bright yellow wings embroidered in symmetrical black veined panes. Sensing something amiss, I ignored this fluttering forewarning and carelessly walked into the open meadow, my survival instincts kicking in just before hearing the gunshot!

"Something's happening here. What it is ain't exactly clear. There's a man with a gun over there telling me I got to beware."
Buffalo Springfield

Heeding the unmistakable buzz of a bullet whir above my head and thud into the aspen soil across the meadow, I instantly hit the ground. Heavy footfalls scurrying through the timber kept me down until I regained enough grit to backtrack into the timber. On full sensory alert I drew my weapon and stalked, tree to tree, towards where the shot was fired. Detecting a tree stand above two separate bait stations-spoiled hams, twinkies, molasses, sugared donuts, rotting carp etc.- I could not locate the legally required identification of the bear hunter(s) displayed within sight of the station. Baiting to attract and harvest bears, lawful at that time, was banned in 1992 in Colorado. Tracking the scuff marks made by the runaway shooter, ending on a narrow two-track next to fresh vehicle tracks, indicated the shooter had escaped. Pondering how I failed hearing the vehicle, I returned to the bait station, verified there was no posted hunter identification, and patrolled the area until dark. Returning early the following morning and discovering the tree stand had been removed, I scolded myself for not confiscating it. Patrolling the area, I pulled over and checked two haughty bear hunters who sneeringly denied knowledge of the bait station. This incident remains a mystery to this day. An after season visit to the bait station revealed only empty Twinkie wrappers, grease-soaked pine duff, and fish scales. There was, however, plenty of bear signs: claw marked trees, scratched off bear hair on tree bark, and a mess of bear crap. Marginally confident the incident involved someone purposely firing a shot over my head to scare me or amuse himself; it provided me ample warning to never let my guard down.

It is well documented that wildlife officers experience relatively high rates of bodily assault, injury, and death associated with their unique brand of law enforcement. Officers nationwide are familiar with the grim story of an Idaho rogue poacher, Claude Lafayette Dallas, who murdered Idaho Department of Fish and Game officers Conley Elms and Bill Pogue in an execution-style slaying in the remote

Owyhee desert on January 5, 1981. The details surrounding their murder is used as a real-life training scenario in many states depicting the vulnerability of wildlife officers often working alone in secluded areas where most perpetrators are armed with guns, knives, bow and arrows etc.

Throughout my career, I and my associates were routinely instructed in defensive tactics, firearm training and qualification, arrest techniques, laws pertaining to search and seizure, de-escalation of volatile situations etc. Nevertheless, I initially gave little thought to my susceptibility to bodily injury. I quickly learned, however, the arrogant behavior of certain egotistical officers instigated variable levels of public rage.

De meanor the officer, De meanor the public.

Unquestionably, my self-protective communicative skills and/or knowing when to back off, deescalated and prevented many potentially detrimental contacts. Contacting the public with a courteous smile and pleasant greeting thwarted most threats. Regularly working a little north of nowhere, normally alone, I understood avoiding conflict rested with my ability to effectively communicate with stressed individuals involved in wildlife crime. My tongue was my strength.

"In matters of truth and justice there is no difference between large and small problems, for issues concerning the treatment of people are all the same."
Albert Einstein

Like all wildlife officers, I too experienced various levels of threats from an assortment of criminal degenerates, ranging from threatening my personal space, bluff attacks, aggressive verbal threats, to individuals seriously contemplating attacking me with fists or a weapon. As I seasoned with age and experience, my youthful immortality waning, certain incidents increased my skills to identify and control those capable and willing to inflict bodily harm:

- My first life-threatening event came from a young man working in the local sawmill. Captured shooting cottontail rabbits without a license he declared, "where I come from (Arkansas) no one purchased hunting licenses and would rather shoot a warden rather than receive a ticket!"
- Two separate field contacts involved miscreants facing arrest warrants. Disturbingly focused on their nearby handguns, with one hand covering my holstered pistol, I verbally warned, "Don't even think about it!" Ordering them to move away from their firearm, I secured and unload their weapons.
- Enjoying a beer at a local bar, Buzz Sawyer, a logger, forewarned if I ever investigated him for poaching, he would kill me. Sniping vile quips through lichen-rough beard stubble, Buzz took a shortcut from careless to stupid threatening to do the same to anyone turning him in. Nodding at the attentive bartender, I stared into Buzz's eyes, reminded him of the stupidity of making death threats in front of a witness, and clarified his remarks would be reported to the Sheriff's office.
- The Bagscum Duo. Father Turdy Bagscum and his son Flatus, were two feral pigs illicitly wallowing in their boar's nest mountain acreage above the headwaters of Grizzly Creek. One early fall afternoon, while I scratched tics to both for poaching deer, Sheriff Cure dealt with their accompanying trespass. Turdy, a burned-out dimwit, warned he would shoot me on sight if he ever encountered me alone in the woods. Infuriated, I suggested settling his threat immediately. Cure, guarding my back, warned Turdy he would be the first one contacted if I turned up injured or dead. The following year, after I cited Flatus for fishing without a license, he was later caught illegally hunting on private ranch property by two cowboys (brothers). Flatus, having the mentality of a stool sample, demanded a court appearance. Idiotically presenting erroneous winter photos depicting the public land where he was contacted by the

cowboys, his snowmachine clearly parked on their private land, the impassive judge accepted the cowboys' testimony and declared Flatus guilty. After court, following his father's path, he warned of my imminent death. Stupidity, a strong swimmer in their gene pool, Turdy defended his son shouting, "there's a place for you, but it ain't dug yet." Again, I recapped the insanity of making death threats in front of Sheriff Cure. One year later patrolling above Grizzly Creek during archery season, I crossed paths with the two cowboys who testified against Flatus. Mounted on sturdy steeds, six guns on their hips and rifles in scabbards, I smilingly asked what they were up to. Mindful of Bagscum'st death threats, they replied, "We're hunting Turdy and Flatus." Scrutinizing the two gritty ranchers, I had no doubt if caught trespassing, the Bagscum Duo would be in deep trouble.

- March 1982. A man and his wife, Dume and Clara Belle, losing their Colorado residency case in court after I proved both were legal residents of Kentucky, Dume suggested I wear body armor. Overextending his privileges to be stupid, Dume warned he was going to hunt me down and kill me with his semi-automatic rifle. Sheriff Cure, hearing the threat, severely aschewed Dume down in front of a crowded courtroom. Curiously, future contacts with Dume were pleasantly cordial.

- August1983. Investigating a report of two drunks crashing their vehicle through a locked gate and destroying fifty yards of fence, I headed towards Wade's Lake. Inspecting the damage, the informant disclosed he had warned the men he was calling the game warden. Well after dark and from a comfortable distance, I watched the inebriated morons jibber-jabbing around a blazing campfire discussing 'taking out' any warden stupid enough to show up. Calling in backup, Sheriff Cure arrived an hour later, awarded the blooming idiots an ass biting lecture, cited them for trespass and destruction of property, and made clear they were liable for the fence repair.

- Another episode occurred while investigating a truck parked next to a dilapidated, homestead cabin north of Seymour Lake. The driver's door open, I spied the distinct shadow of an individual, pistol in hand, standing behind the cabin. Retreating, I drove to a high spot, ran the vehicles plate number through Sheriff's dispatch, and waited. After the vehicle and its owner were cleared, I observed a man enter the vehicle and drive away. Intercepting him, I discovered a very scared young man who thought I was an angry landowner intending to inflict harm. His driver's license matching the vehicle registration, I turned him loose with a warning not to be so eager to use his firearm.

- Frequently checking the creel or cooler of a well-known Rosebud resident, Lewie Claptrap, I received word he was barroom boasting, "the next time I put my hands on his property would be my last." Not perceiving this stalwart man as my enemy, I confronted Lewie who humbly asserted he was only kidding. Interestingly, Lewie later provided detailed information leading me to several solid poaching cases.

- Fall 1985. I gained another chilling lesson from an undercover officer covertly working an illegal outfitter. The agent's late night campfire tale of listening to the outfitter boast he had passed up a great chance to kill a warden parked in a remote section of Arapaho Creek. Hunting a timbered ridge above the warden, the outfitter divulged centering his rifle's crosshairs on the warden's head. Realizing that warden was me, I asked the undercover officer if he believed the outfitter was serious. The officer replied, "Dead serious."

Granted, most threats were the deceiving dribble of craven cowards, I treated them as genuine and personally responded to them whenever possible. This I know, more now than ever, there are unstable people stalking the wilds. Unable to decipher what is going on in anyone's head, and realizing the offenders have the timely advantage of executing the first move to inflict injury, a wildlife officer must always remain on full alert, prepared to quickly react, and skillfully utilize his/her training to control threats to their wellbeing.

Guard your topknot, warden!

LEADING LINES

ugust 16, 1987. My late father's birthday. There I was, taking this special day to enjoy what wardens describe as aimless district patrol (ADP). No target, no real purpose other than cruising the outback on a dazzling August day!

Bouncing over the gravel road paralleling Indian Creek, I passed a local cowboy sound asleep in a shady aspen grove, only his horse showing any sign of life as I passed by. Peculiarly, this was the second time this summer I saw this cowboy sleeping, verifying cowboys, like bears, 'nap' in the woods.

Clanging over the heavy metal cattle guard entering Arapaho National Forest, I soon discovered a large camp. Tent flaps open and a smoldering campfire (dangerously illegal), I presumed the occupants were not far away. Nosing around, I spotted a note under a Nebraska pickup's wiper blade. Apparently written to an absent camp member, it tattled his friends were fishing the upper drainage beaver ponds and to grab a fishing pole and join them. Placing the note back under the wiper, I sensed the beginning of a warden treasure hunt!

Driving on, I located another Nebraska truck at the gated road closure described in the note. I parked and tracked the heavy boot traffic leading to the beaver ponds. Spying five young men, I bushwhacked into a dense string of subalpine fir to veil my approach. Confirming all were fishing, I observed one placing their catch into the burlap sack. Stepping from the shadows, my presence immediately impacted the man holding the bag. Warning his comrades, all eyes focused on me, they provided great entertainment stumbling in muddled confusion over the uneven, water-soaked marshland. Approaching the bag man, emptying the sack into the stream below the beaver dam, I cheerfully warned it was too late. Amazingly, grinning like possums crapping razor blades, all five surrendered respectably admitting they did not having fishing licenses. Counting the trout back into the sack, I escorted them to their vehicle. On the way out we met the young man the note was written to. Appreciating his comrades' predicament he chuckled, thanking his lucky stars for drawing the short straw to purchase supplies in Sage Hen. At their camp, I equally divided the illegal trout, scratched tics charging each for 3 illegal trout and not having a fishing license. Conceding they foolishly risked not crossing paths with a wildlife officer, they paid their fines ($105 each) on the spot. Allowing them to keep the trout, I told them to feast on the delectable, $50/lb. brook trout, a gift from the State of Colorado for their outstanding attitudes.

One, asking what led me to the beaver ponds, I replied, "I rely heavily on the written word!"

> *"Honesty is the best of all lost arts."*
> Mark Twain

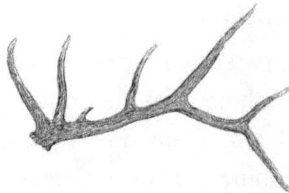

ELUDING

"Where ain't they?" (Popeye)

U nsolved crimes haunt the minds of law enforcement officers long after their careers end. As a retired wildlife officer, I had my share, and while elusive game thieves tendered a challenging chase, those never captured, the named and the nameless, ghost my thoughts to this day:

-Those illegally killed moose, some with antlers removed, rotting into a pile of hair, bones, and rumen; others salvageable but neither providing suitable evidence to track the poacher(s) down.

-The tragedy of discovering **eleven** rifle killed male sage grouse blatantly stacked on their spring breeding ground: a malignant message to wildlife personnel censusing grouse populations. Tracing the days old vehicle tracks for miles to an empty cabin, I contacted the owners and their guests throughout the summer, all asserting their clan would never commit such a heinous crime.

-A winter camp above the North Platte River, below an ancient Indian burial tree, where I discovered a warm fire, signs of a recently poached deer, and fresh boot tracks leaving the well camouflaged juniper wickiup. Following the tracks, an instinctive sensation warned someone was close, maybe too close. Noting the clear view of my vehicle parked below, I returned early the following morning, hid my truck, and crept into the camp from above finding the foot travelling poacher gone with the wind.

-An incident where an intimidated informant provided firsthand information on who, what and where an elk was poached, but because of her apprehensive reluctance to testify and my carelessness, the poacher evaded capture. The offender, Dupe Beguile, a pearly man with a bullying, self-centered ego, blatantly boasted his misdeeds, basking in his freedom of unrestrained misbehavior. A savvy outdoorsman and killer of wild game, Dupe was high on my bad guy list. My informant testified Dupe would return the following morning to tag the elk with the license of another hunter. Stealing into the kill site in pre-dawn darkness, I found the elk had been skillfully field dressed and dragged uphill to the ridge saddle for cooling by the mountain's thermals. A heart and liver hanging in a cloth bag in a nearby pine, validated my alleged foe intended retrieving the bull. Hiding in thick downfall above the glassy eyed carcass, I enjoyed a dazzling sunrise rouse scurrying glimpses and spirited sounds of birds, chipmunks, and squirrels making their wild living from the forest's bounty. A magpie flitted over the gut pile and landed like a kite pulled tight on a string, foolishly advertising its feast with scratchy songs inviting several camp robbers and a raven. A spike bull elk walking through the saddle balked at the carcass and quickly bolted up the ridge. But after three hours of restricted movement the morning's chill cold stoned me to the bone. Sensing no human activity, I exited my lair, stretched, and took a spine shivering leak. Suddenly the forest became eerily silent. Thinking bear, I scanned the area with binoculars and spied a man dressed in camouflage crouching in aspen thirty yards below, glassing me through his binoculars. *DRATS!* Like a puff of smoke, he evaporated into the timber and vanished. Later, my informant tattled Dupe was extremely upset about losing the elk, and even more about how I knew to be there. Like a hawk missing a rabbit, I awaited another swipe, but Dupe endured as one who got away. I lost my chance of snagging him to cold bones and a full bladder, forever!

But the doggedly elusive do not always escape. One challenging, time-simmered incident slow cooked the demise of two proficiently evasive poachers, Ice Pettifogger and Ravin Killwild.

FOLLOWING THE YELLOW LEAFED ROAD

I first encountered Ice in January 1978 fishing on the South Delaney Butte Lake. At that time fishing with two poles was illegal but common. Not the wildlife crime of the century, it was rigorously enforced as a reminder there were wardens watching. After scoping Ice actively fish with two lines through several drilled holes, I drove into plain sight and chuckled as the wayward man immediately reeled in one of the poles. *HOKA HEY!* Checking his license, I informed Ice of his misdeeds, and listened as he arrogantly boasted he was a lawyer who would easily beat me in court. Long story short, he quickly learned a cocksure city attorney should not play childish lawyer games with a remote county judge. Conversations with my eastern comrades revealed Ice was well known as a cunning, case-hardened wildlife criminal using his legal expertise to defend those tangled in wildlife law.

Intriguingly, my second contact with Ice occurred while Wildlife Officer Kirk Snyder and I were investigating him for poaching a bull elk on private property. Aware of our investigation, Ice professionally represented two hunters I previously cited for allowing their harvested elk meat to spoil, wholly unfit for human consumption. The novice hunters, having no idea how to care for wild meat, were as innocent as they were guilty. Ice and I worked closely to reduce their costly, felony waste charges to pleading guilty to less stringent misdemeanors. Justice was served in a fully cooperative effort of warden, attorney, and clients.

Cutting to the chase, one late September evening in 1991, Officer Snyder received a complaint from a landowner regarding trespassing hunters on his property. His manager, a young Englishman, and his girlfriend, after hearing several rifle shots, tracked down two haughty men field dressing a large antlered bull elk on his employer's property. While the trespassers spoofed the time worn tale of wounding the bull on public land, tracking and killing it on this private land, the Englishman recorded the vehicle's license plate and left. Returning to the kill site, the Englishman found the thugs had removed the antlers and abandoned the carcass. Joining the Englishman and his girlfriend the following day, Officer Snyder and I were provided detailed physical descriptions of the poachers and their pickup. It was archery/muzzle-loader season and the Englishman specified the multiple shots they heard were not fired from a single shot, muzzle loading rifle. Collecting three .270 caliber shell casings and a beer can at the kill site, we transported the carcass to the Division of Wildlife lab in Fort Collins and verified the bull was killed by multiple shots from a high-powered rifle. Running the plate through Sheriff's Office, we learned the vehicle was registered to none other than Ice! Like hounds running a fox, Kirk and I contacted him at his city office and presented our evidence. Predictably, wearing his lawyer face, Ice argued having no idea what we were talking about and we had no authority accusing him of these wildlife crimes. We left his office challenged to spend the time necessary to prove our case. Pictures of Ice's vehicle provided by Wildlife Officer Courtney Crawford were positively identified by the Englishman. Wildlife Officer John Wagner provided key information from an informant regarding alleged but unsolved wildlife crimes committed by Ice.

Our case was weakened when our eyewitnesses, after studying our photo lineup, were unable to positively identify Ice as the one at the kill site. Also, since identifying his accomplice was equivalent to searching for fly crap in a pepper can, the District Attorney asserted we essentially had nothing until the poaching trespassers were positively identified. *NOTHING?* Viewing our case far differently than the D.A., Kirk and I , with the unwavering anticipation of a spider scrutinizing its web, spent countless hours evaluating our chain of evidence knowing, from experience, patience would provide the missing links necessary to shackle Ice and, hopefully, his comrade in crime

"Yeah, well, sometimes nothin' can be a real Cool Hand."
Cool Hand Luke

And, in January, out of the blue clear sky we were awarded gold-plated evidence beyond our wildest imagination, sealing the fate of not only Ice but also his ill-fated accomplice. Would you believe, Alaskan Federal Wildlife agents arrested a commercial poacher, Ravin Killwild, for killing protected, exotic waterfowl species and selling them to rogue taxidermists who mounted the rare, colorful specimens to wealthy clients for display in their homes and offices. Ravin, arrested in an Alaskan airport, vainly attempted to destroy a video tape that not only filmed his illegal Alaskan escapades, but also his criminal elk hunt with Ice west of Mexican Ridge! With persistent vigor, Kirk and I meticulously reviewed the tape scene by scene, had it professionally cropped, and stills printed of the most incriminating pictures. Words cannot express the pleasure of listening to Ice and Ravin hastily leave their vehicle in pursuit of the illegal bull and its harem. We could even hear the bull bugling! But wait, there is more! The tape also snitched the poaching of another elk, a cow, killed the same day on a section of Mexican Ridge private property where neither had permission to hunt. Continuing our cold pursuit, Kirk and I sporadically pestered Ice for additional information. The rogue attorney, knowing we had the tape, exercised his right to remain silent. Able to file charges anytime, we proffered Ice time to contemplate his inevitable fate, keeping our disreputable foe anxiously attentive.

Delaying the inevitable until June, we formally presented our rock-solid evidence to Ice in person and viewed his polar attitude thaw into heated arrogance. The infamous poacher haughtily testified an assortment of mistruths, declaring Ravin killed both elk, the cow with a bow and arrow and the bull with a rifle, and he (Ice) was simply along for the ride. Kirk clarified, as any attorney knows, being there was all we needed to file charges. Scratching tics with multiple charges for each elk, Ice melted into a puddle of illicit slime; shaken and stirred, Ice was ours!

Not satisfied, Kirk and I stubbornly trailed the exact location of the kill site of the cow elk, verifying the cow was illegally poached on private property. The still photos colorfully revealed a fall carpet of golden aspen leaves covering a timber tunneled corridor of privately owned road we annually traveled hunting deer and elk during the September muzzleloader seasons, we dubbed the YELLOW LEAF ROAD. And, a year later to the day the poaching crimes were committed, we tied our remaining loose ends into the proverbial hangman's noose. Sequentially tracking the still pictures backwards from the county road Ice and Ravin shot the bull, we conveniently crossed paths with the owners of the property, Carl and Ruth Ann Hanson, near the gate the stills revealed the poachers exited Mexican Ridge. Carl and Ruth Ann, living nearby in their original log ranch house, were solid Bull Pen pioneer stock. Carl, on oxygen from a lifetime of heavy smoking, routinely paused taking long breaths while speaking. Rolling down his vehicle's window, Carl asked, "What trouble are you headed for today, (long breath), Staïeve?" Carl's gasping pronunciation of my name became an acronym Kirk took great pleasure repeating in my presence. His son Keenan and my son Marc graciously maintain Kirk's legacy to this day. After Carl and Ruth reaffirmed Ice and Ravin had trespassed on their property, we continued piecing the stills until, THERE WE WERE, driving down the starkly illustrated, gilded YELLOW LEAF ROAD! Parking on the Hanson Ranch property where the stills showed the poachers had parked, we watched in disgusting awe as Kirks ailing black lab Sable, having consumed a bacon laden gob of greasy bear bait, attempted to expel the contents of its entire digestive tract from both ends. Leaving the dog in its convulsive state, we hiked up separate draws searching for evidence. Finding nothing, I watched Kirk return, his smirking face telling it all. He not only found the kill site but also a broken arrow lying with what remained of the cow's carcass. Incidentally, returning to the truck, we found the dog vivaciously alive, fully recuperated from its gastric anguish, now smearing the truck's bed.

Our chain of evidence securely linked, we presented our case file to the District Attorney who, in turn, provided it to Ice and Ravin's newly appointed attorney (working with two attorneys is like overhauling a two hole outhouse) sending our case into the nonsensical (our opinion) plea-bargaining stages. Kirk and I interviewed Ravin in December, incarcerated at the Denver Detention Center for not only the illegal waterfowl but also for, among other things, severely assaulting his wife in Oklahoma (he had changed his name to avoid arrest).

Ravin, a felonious wife beater and commercial poacher pled guilty to trespass and illegally killing the bull and arranged to have its antlers delivered to wildlife authorities. Ice pled guilty to trespass and illegally killing the cow elk. Ice was a poaching game hog. Put a shirt, tie, and

ING • 245

fancy suit on a pilfering pig, it is still a pig! Considering themselves invincible, they violated wildlife law as an avocation! In this case, however, the eluding con men were captured working their filching game by two relentless wildlife officers.

"So let it be written, so let it be done!"
Pharaoh Ramses II

AN ODE TO KIRK SNYDER

~

Many wardens have shared the Bull Pen's lairs,
Badged warriors safeguarding Nature's bounty.
But lucky were they sharing even a day
Riding herd with Kirk across Jackson County.
Great fortune had I sharing the North Park sky,
As his comrade in playing the grand warden games.
We worked and we played in forest and glade,
Timeless adventures now memories and dreams.

Scouring the land with law books in hand,
Through copse and sage we crawled.
Scratching tics to poaching pricks
We hounded til they bawled.
Playing good warden bad was a gift we had,
As we sharply honed our warden skills.
Such a good time, reminiscences sublime,
I shudder recalling our thrills.

In our days of yore waging wildlife wars,
Flushing out scumbags and scrotes.
Under Kirk's duress they would soon confess,
I swear he could make a mime talk.
Weaving silken verbal webs of miscreant fibs,
Trapping the wiliest of scheming spiders.
I can rightly tell no poacher from hell,
Would want to be in the sights of Kirk Snyder.

Hunting the 'Mexican' in our prime, a cherished time
To revitalize friendships while sharing our passion,
Stalking for tine, ghosting aspen and pine;
Hunting our mutual instinctive obsession.
Hunting with heart, as a team and apart,
Fulfilled and proud of our predatory feats.
Becoming quite clever in our endeavor
Of packing our freezers with wild game meat.

An aspen clone camp, cattle 'chipped' and tramped,
Our corralled home for a week in the fall.
Campfire feasts of roasted beasts,
Spirited by Makers Mark! Thank God bed a mere crawl!
Outdoor thrones, old elk bones,
A tent and hammock seized from a renegade guide.
So serene this 'Cabelas' scene,
Flinging spine quivering arrows through my hide.

Kirk met his fate on Augusts last date,
The year of twenty-eleven.
A blazing jolt, a life dousing bolt
Lasered downward from the heavens.
In the alpenglow of Sangre de Cristo,
Kirk was smitten without warn,
As he stood with a grande friend, a bewildering end
To be taken by a conscienceless storm.

As I try to console what I cannot control,
To mourn the first road to heart mending.
I must not slog through deaths dark fog,
For it is my time that I must be lending.
It is not Kirk's death, but his mortal breath,
That defines his reasons for being.
So I will focus on life to end my dark strife,
By sharing Kirk's purpose and meaning.

A man of means with principled themes,
Kirk was stubborn as a morning mule.
Brazen and brassy, with a dash of crazy
Stoked his blazing internal fuel.
Beaver tail tough, abrasively rough
He was soaked in vim, vigor and jest.
A one- of- a- kind chap who drew his own map,
A sourdough man of the mountain at his best.

A philosopher without banner, a doer not a planner,
Kirk's earthly wisdom exceeded current theory.
Land abuse rooted in overuse
And negligent land managers gave him great worry.
A habitat thinker eager to tinker
With new techniques of improving the health of the land.
Tractors and harrows making drunken sailor trails,
Kirk implemented his land management plans.

Direct and straight-forward, never he cowered,
Kirk was persistent, honest and shrewd.
His fluent English often extinguished
By words often rough and crude.
Fond of cheap brew and a cigar to chew,
A warden of the 'Eastwood' brand.
Pistol Pete "flys", reloading dies, Kirk-spell, raggedy plaid,
All aid in defining this greybeard family man.

There is so much more to scribing the lore
Of Kirk Snyder's life giving legacy.
You had to know him well to decipher his spell,
And break into the wisdom of his prophecy.
How lucky am I to have befriended this guy
Who so enriched my heart, soul and mind.
I will continue to share with those, whom I care,
What Kirk taught me during our prime times.

But no need to fret, I know where...you...are...at...!
Revealed in Iron Butterfly rants.
Metallic lyrics once weirdly perplexing,
I now clearly hear as bold love chants.
Kathy knew all along, this heavy metal song,
Was her thundering ballad from your heart true.
Having left your life garden, now in your Eden,
"In-A-Gadda-Da-Vida, honey. Don't You Know That I Love You?"

I will forever remember the tenth of September,
Your ashes spread upon revered high ground.
Now one with your mountain, Nature's recycling fountain
Returns you to life's endless bound.
Now a veiled treasure, your last full measure
Is a lifetime heritage big as the sky.
And deep in my soul burns a blazing coal,
A Kirk ember inspiring my soul til I die.

So I raise my glass high to this hell of a guy,
But higher to Kathy, Krista, Kelly, and Keenan.
Sharing their sorrows for all the tomorrows,
While living the joy of keeping Kirk's badge shinin'.
As I continue to grieve, I will always believe
That true friendships have no end.
And I shout out with pride, to be heard far and wide,
Kirk Snyder will always be my best friend!

Kurb,
Making tracks with you across the Bull Pen was a
Good job to take. Stan

PARTING SHOT

"Ordo ab chao."

Logically, Wildlife Officers are drawn into wide-ranging scenarios of outdoor misbehavior crafting noteworthy tales of people interacting with the wilds. My twenty plus years (1973-1993) as a Colorado District Wildlife Manager proffered a plethora of selectively chosen adventures included in my Chronicles. Written as memoirs, flavored throughout with the humor of human beings being human, I purposely emphasize the illicit activities of hunters and fishermen to underscore the problem and the essential forces working to resolve them.

Criminal behavior, found within all human activities, is in our DNA and will never be eliminated. Greed, jealousy, thrill killing, arrogance, aggression, notoriety, bragging rights, temptation, thievery, cheating, and money, are feral human attributes within our beast driving the behavior of troublemakers. Violations of wildlife law, indiscreetly taking place under cover of the wilds, are easily concealed, studies indicating less than 5% are even detected! Rest assured Wildlife Officers, your job is secure

During my law enforcement career, I was personally involved in well over 2,000 wildlife violations as the lead or backup officer; a number I modestly wear on my sleeve as a measure of the unjustifiable criminal behavior occurring in the outback. Over time, my colleagues and I became quite proficient rooting out and capturing individuals defiling the wild. Experience, knowing the landscape like no other, the haunts of game during different seasons, who to look for and where, and our innate knowledge of people, increased our enforcement success. Like owl on hare, our skills in preying on the outdoor bad soared, we took great sport outwitting violators in their own game. But understand, our law enforcement accomplishments were greatly augmented by a vigorous grapevine we cultivated during our many years living within the Bull Pen community. Relentlessly bearing fruit of illicit activity reported by the outdoor good, concerned citizens, scorned women, jealous associates, drunks, even local youth kept wildlife officers busy scratching tics, and those not apprehended looking over their shoulders. Undetected or unreported violations brought to our attention were catalogued for future reference, often raising interesting discussions during ensuing captures of the persistent outdoor bad.

Without debating the amount of outdoor misbehavior, my stories clarify there is simply too much! Ask any present-day hunter or fisherman if they know of recent wildlife violations committed by others. Although few will admit it, most have. My continuing conversations with wildlife officers, hunters, fishermen and the public attest the criminal activities of hunters and fishermen are at levels I encountered before my retirement (2003). Bull Pen wardens remain swamped tracking down outdoor culprits, the silent roar of the grapevine relentless whining, especially during the fall big game seasons. Some things will never change.

So, John Wagner, Kirk Snyder, Sir Don Gore, Sig Palm, Johnny Hobbs, Howard Spear, Jim Jackson, Drayton Harrison, Jay Wenum, Lauren Childers, Vicki Anthony Don Benson, Scott Hoover, John Bredehehoft, Larry Budde, Terry Grosz, Claude Wood, Donnie Rodriguez, Ken Kehmeier, Randy VanBuren, Steve Steinert, Andre Duvall, Arapaho National Wildlife Refuge Officers, and so many others, did we make a difference?

You bet we did!

Bonded as a corps of wildlife enforcement officers, we professionally maintained a semblance of order in the chaos instigated by illegal activities of individuals romping the outback. Our tenacity served as a communication pipeline for the majority good who understand the future of recreational harvest, especially hunting, demands a strict set of laws and regulations to ensure a fair, judicious, and humane system to manage sustainable game populations. Hunting and fishing is conservation; breaking wildlife law is not.

At the end of our watch, we passed our tenacious dedication to a new generation of wildlife officers, equally sharing our love for the wild and drive to weed out the bad. Our legacy is in good hands! Granted, times have changed and our time in the Bull Pen can never be duplicated. Exclusively ours, it was a very good to job to take!

But that was yesterday and yesterday's gone.

BOOK ENDS

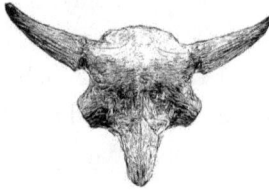

Some things never change...

My Chronicles, written as memoirs, embrace a portion of my early life, trails leading to North Park where my family and I thrived for over two decades, and tales emphasizing select human escapades encountered enforcing wildlife law. Understand, however, law enforcement consumed only 1/3 of my workload. The remaining 2/3 were invested in the closely linked tasks of public relations and wildlife management. The sum of these responsibilities made my avocation complete and, in my eyes, one of the most honorable occupations on earth.

Law enforcement the seasoning, the meat and potatoes of my obligations involved integrating people into the wide-ranging challenges of managing diverse wildlife populations. Boundless hours spent with landowners, hunters, fishermen, state and land federal land management agency personnel, educators, youth, county and state officials, was undoubtedly the most rewarding, productive measure of my achievements.

Contemplating the immeasurable hours spent on law enforcement, consider multiplying these by three to calculate a District Wildlife

Managers actual workload. During my watch, we were trained our duties required a 24/7 commitment. Loyal and driven, that is how we worked. I, a member of a family of dedicated field men and women tirelessly working to "protect, preserve, enhance, and manage the state's wildlife and their environment for the use, benefit, and enjoyment of people..." Living in a small, closely knit community where everyone knew my name, with people treasuring their wilds and voicing a variety of opinions, I not only worked my avocation, I lived it! Even off the clock, countless phone calls, visits to our home, calls sending me out day and night, answering questions wherever we were, was routine. Just ask my family, who dependably endured the challenges and played a significant role in the accomplishments of my job.

My undertakings, consistent with any Colorado District Wildlife Manager, includes but were not limited to;

- Game damage – diligently moving wintering elk from hay yards (late night chases on snowshoes, snowmobiles, or the Tucker Sno-Cat),fencing stackyards etc., eventually resolving hay damage by developing a system for constructing elk proof fencing for hundreds of hay yards. Processing claims for loss of forage, fence, and crops for landowners.
- Beaver control and management. Live trapping, moving them to other locations and/or setting leghold (kill) traps, blowing dams with explosives. Determining trapping permit numbers by drainage for sustainable harvest.
- Bear management. Live trapping and moving them to other locations.
- Lake and stream fish inventory, including remote, wilderness lakes.
- Wildlife inventory. Annual big game (deer, elk, antelope, moose) aerial census. coordinated bighorn sheep ground counts. Raptor, sandhill crane, waterfowl, eagle census.
- State Wildlife Area management plans.
- Review, comment, and recommend changes on current laws and regulations.

- The 1978/79 Moose Reintroduction and developing a management plan.
- Coordinated timber and wildlife management plans with USFS, BLM and State Forest.
- School and university classroom instruction and field trips.
- Testifying and writing reports on proposed activities impacting wildlife.
- Working with county officials on land use issues.
- Coordinate with local and statewide Stockgrowers Associations.
- Working with Boy and Girl Scouts and 4-H Wildlife and Shooting Sports.
- Instruct Hunter Education classes.
- Administering the Habitat Partnership Program.
- Coordinating the Owl Mountain Partnership.
- Vigorously enforce wildlife law.

The Habitat Partnership Program and the Owl Mountain Partnership provided me groundbreaking experience in resolving resource conflicts utilizing an empowered, funded coalition of landowners, government land managers, hunters, and the public. Managing these partnerships led to my career change and a move to Fort Collins in 1993 as the Statewide Coordinator of the Habitat Partnership and Game Damage Programs. This I know, there is no more powerful, more successful, more effective way to address resource issues than from the local level. For me, these Partnerships confirmed there no greater gift to mankind than investing time into something you believe in, something that outlasts you; conserving, preserving, managing that which sustains all life, the land.

After spending twenty plus years in North Park my tracks are all but erased. Dust in the wind. My traces have, however, been replaced by capable men and women upholding the legacy of managing the Bull Pen's wilds.

So, if the purpose of life is purpose, my family found ours in North Park, a sense of place where we, for a time, were meant to be. The honor of living in this remote mountain valley with great friends remains my life's anchor point – the place I know like no other. My legacy lies with family, as it should, and hopefully extends to those I may have influenced, and their ability to pass on any inspiration I may have nurtured. For all who touched my life, the mainstream good and the minority bad, I consider all friends, proffering valuable insights on the meaning of life most will never have.

"Do I not destroy my enemies when I make them my friends?"
Abraham Lincoln

Peculiarly, my writings have led some to say that I am living in the past. My respectful reply, "my past begins with yesterday and that, my friend, is my life!" Remembering yesterday, living for today, and focusing on the future proffers a very rewarding life, my past always reflecting the best days of my life!

One final note for all who cannot live without wild things,

Spend as much time enjoying the wild as possible. Nature is in our DNA, the eternal force sculpting human nature since time began. But do not stop there. Join, participate, mentor, vote, volunteer, fund, support, educate, learn, advocate, partner with anything and everyone, including landowners, associated with protecting the land's capability to preserve habitats. One does not have to be in the spotlight to achieve results, background noise accomplishes amazing consequences. Be an active crusader for protecting wild lands in whatever capacity you can; locally, nationally, internationally, and globally. Hunters and fishermen, continue your 150-year legacy as the long-standing economic foundation and workforce for wildlife conservation and management. But understand, the overwhelming tasks of sustaining our vanishing wilds have outreached your resources, requiring joining forces with a public majority sharing your same values but providing little money or manpower to meet these challenges. Partnering with and developing a funding source with the nonhunting public, will not only provide avenues to promote the economic, social, recreational, and nutritional values of your sports, but also deliver the resources necessary to successfully sustain all wildlife.

November 2021. Completing my Chronicles, geese are returning to the Front Range. I have hunted elk with Keenan and deer with grandson Conner Jack with duck, geese, and pheasant hunts in the works. Spending the Holidays with family and possibly a January waterfowl hunt in Idaho with grandson Lane, Life is Good!

I will not entice you with what I have not written. There are many stories reserved for family and friends around gatherings with good food, a glass of wine, iced whiskey, or a cold beer. You see, my stories are still being made!

And so they are written, and so they are done!

ABOUT THE AUTHOR

Throughout his boyhood, Ohio native Stephen H. Porter, was instinctively drawn to the rural woodlots and creek bottoms scattered throughout the farmlands. As a teenager, rifle or shotgun in hand, Steve invested his idle time hunting pheasants, quail, squirrels, raccoons, and woodchucks, further igniting his passion for everything wild. As a high school senior, discovering certain universities offered degrees in wildlife biology, Steve's restless spirit lured him west to Utah State University in Logan, Utah. Earning a Bachelor of Science degree in Wildlife Biology while working summer jobs with the U.S. Forest Service and the Utah Division of Wildlife doing rangeland inventory,

Steve realized the vast open space of the Rocky Mountains was where he belonged. Permanent employment in the western states scarce, Steve accepted a biologist position with the U.S. Fish and Wildlife Service in Raleigh, North Carolina. His overwhelming desire to return west intermixed with personal perseverance and the grace of God, Steve chased down and secured an incredibly competitive position as a Wildlife Conservation Officer trainee with the Colorado Division of Wildlife.

In 1973, following nearly a year of intensive classroom and field training based in Denver, Steve was awarded a permanent position in north central Colorado, North Park. Purposely selecting this remote, sparsely populated mountain park because of its diversity of wildlife resources, it was the people living in this unique, highly independent mountain culture that kept Steve and his family there for over two decades. Raising two children, Marc Alan and Anne Marie, Steve and his wife Betsy thrived in the massive, northern mountain park the Native Americans called the Bull Pen. Passionately working for Colorado's wildlife resources was an avocation defining Steve to this day.

In 1993, utilizing twenty plus years working with landowners, hunters and fishermen, government agencies and the public, Steve accepted Wildlife Biologist positions stationed in Denver and later Fort Collins, coordinating Colorado's Habitat Partnership and Game Damage Programs; a two-pronged approach for resolving statewide big game conflicts. Retiring from the Colorado Division of Wildlife in 2003, Steve and Betsy are enjoying their good life near the foothills of northern Colorado. Prioritizing time with family and friends, Steve nonetheless wanders the outback with a rifle, shotgun, flyrod, camera or binoculars in hand, marveling the natural world captivating his entire life. Frequently roaming the Bull Pen wilds, visiting old friends, roving haunts he knows like no others and, of course, sharing tales of past adventures, Steve and Betsy's lives are truly blessed.

"Good friends know all your stories.
A best friend helped you create them."

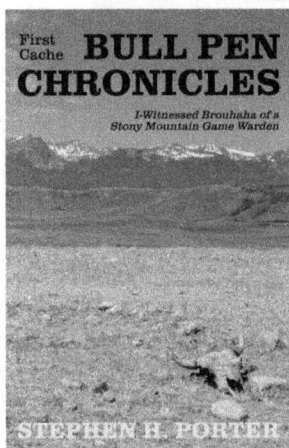

ACKNOWLEDGEMENTS

Once again, I extend a heartfelt thanks to my editor, Kerrie Flanagan. Kerrie patiently rode with me, a man packing a million notes, ideas, scribbles, and kept my wandering mind focused on the trail leading to legible, meaningful stories. It was a good ride, indeed!

THANK YOU, KERRIE FLANAGAN!

www.ingramcontent.com/pod-product-compliance
Lightning Source LLC
Chambersburg PA
CBHW031545260326
41914CB00002B/281